Death by Effigy

A Case from the Mexican Inquisition

Luis R. Corteguera

PENN

UNIVERSITY OF PENNSYLVANIA PRESS

PHILADELPHIA

Published by
University of Pennsylvania Press
Philadelphia, Pennsylvania 19104-4112
www.upenn.edu/pennpress

Printed in the United States of America on acid-free paper

10 9 8 7 6 5 4 3 2 1

Library of Congress Cataloging-in-Publication Data
Corteguera, Luis R.
   Death by effigy : a case from the Mexican Inquisition / Luis R.
Corteguera. — 1st ed.
      p. cm. — (The early modern Americas)
   Includes bibliographical references and index.
   ISBN 978-0-8122-4439-7 (hardcover : alk. paper)
   1. Inquisition—Mexico—Tecamachalco (Puebla)—History—
16th century. 2. Executions in effigy—Mexico—Tecamachalco
(Puebla)—History—16th century. 3. Trials (Libel)—Mexico—
Tecamachalco (Puebla)—History—16th century. I. Title. II.
Series: Early modern Americas.
BX1740.M6C67 2012
272'.2097248—dc23
                                                2012006131

Death by Effigy

Who done it

— asking some questions your

sources

THE EARLY MODERN AMERICAS

Peter C. Mancall, Series Editor

Volumes in the series explore neglected aspects of
early modern history in the western hemisphere.
Interdisciplinary in character, and with a special
emphasis on the Atlantic World from 1450 to 1850,
the series is published in partnership with the
USC–Huntington Early Modern Studies Institute.

Para Gil, Anita y Debbie, compañeros de viaje a Tecamachalco

CONTENTS

Contents

ABBREVIATIONS

AGI   Archivo General de Indias, Seville

AGN   Archivo General de la Nación, Mexico City

AHN   Archivo Histórico Nacional, Madrid

exp.   *expediente* (file)

f./fs.   *foja/fojas* (sheet/sheets of paper)

fol./fols.   folio/folios

HEH   Henry E. Huntington Library

HM   Huntington Library Manuscript

Inq.   Inquisición

PAF   Proceso de Ana de Figueroa (AGN, Inq. vol. 132, exp. 19, fs. 160–83)

PAMT   Proceso del Alcalde Mayor de Tepeaca (HEH HM 35097, fs. 12–37)

PAP   Proceso de Antonio de la Parada (AGN, Inq. vol. 132, exp. 19, fs. 184–98)

PBL   Proceso de Bartolomé Lozano (AGN, Inq. vol. 132, exp. 19, fs. 203–13)

PFS   Proceso de Francisco Solano (AGN, Inq. vol. 132, exp. 19, fs. 158–59, 200–202, 214–16)

PFY   Proceso de Francisco Yáñez (HEH HM 35097, bound with PAMT and PJLM)

PJL   Proceso de Juan López (AGN, Inq. vol. 1494, exp. 3, fs. 169–

203)

PJLM   Proceso de Juan López de Montalbán (HEH HM 35097, fs.
              38–61)

PJM   Proceso de Juan de Molina (excerpts transcribed mostly in
              PAF and PFY)

PJP   Proceso de Juan Pérez (AGN, Inq. vol. 132, exp. 9, pp. 48–61)

This book centers on a scandal that took place on 21 July 1578 in the Mexican town of Tecamachalco (in the present state of Puebla), the four-year investigation that followed, and nine trials conducted by the Inquisition. For more than two centuries, the documentation for these events belonged to the secret archive of the Mexican Inquisition, located inside the large building that served as the tribunal's headquarters, now a museum on the Plaza de Santo Domingo, near Mexico City's cathedral. After the abolition of the Mexican Inquisition in 1820, some of its papers became available for purchase. In 1909, an antiquarian bookseller based in Mexico City sold thirty-two volumes of inquisitorial papers to the Arizona mining engineer Walter Douglas, who, in 1944, bequeathed them to the Huntington Library in California.[1] One of these manuscripts (HM 35097), still in its original leather binding, contains the main group of documents dealing with the Tecamachalco scandal. The Huntington manuscript and other documents from the case that remained in Mexico total almost seven hundred pages of detailed information about what was little more than a minor, one-day incident in a provincial town. Still, the documentation is incomplete, since one of the nine trials is missing and presumed lost.[2]

My research on the Huntington manuscript began as part of a larger project on the power of images and symbols in the Spanish empire in the sixteenth and seventeenth centuries. The manuscript's description in the library's inventory was intriguing: a trial for "stealing" a "statue" and a number of *sambenitos*—garments that the Inquisition imposed on those found guilty of acting against God and the Catholic Church (see Figure 1).[3] The theft of the statue and the sambenitos recalled other Inquisition trials in Mexican and Spanish archives dealing with cases of sacrilege, blasphemy, and superstition involving sacred objects. Catholics who otherwise did not challenge Church dogma had nonetheless stolen consecrated hosts, attacked crucifixes, or destroyed religious paintings. Rather than deny useless

Figure 1. *Sambenitos*: garments worn by accused heretics.
Detail from Adrian Schoonebeck, *Procession to the Auto da Fé*,
in Van Limborch, *Historia Inquisitionis* (Amsterdam, 1692).
Kenneth Spencer Research Library, University of Kansas.

"idols," as Protestant iconoclasts did when they attacked sacred objects, sacrilege in those Inquisition cases reflected more "credulous forms of belligerence and delinquency."[4] In other words, a desire to appropriate the power believed to be in those objects inspired sacrilegious acts for aims as diverse as gaining protection from evil, making someone fall in love, or taking revenge for losing at cards.[5] Similar actions were not restricted to religious objects. Angry subjects took away royal symbols from officials, and rebels attacked royal paintings to denounce tyranny. Such acts and the response of authorities can reveal much about different forms of power and authority underpinning monarchies, religious persecution, and prejudice of all kinds.[6] Even though religious and secular authorities used images and symbols to exert their power and inculcate beliefs, those symbols and images were susceptible to falling into the wrong hands and being used in all sorts of ways not intended by the authorities.[7] With these issues and questions, I approached my reading of the Huntington manuscript.

It did not take long to see that the Tecamachalco case was unlike cases of credulous sacrilege. Whereas many of these cases typically ranged from five to twenty pages, the Huntington manuscript is almost 190 folios, or 380 pages. More important, the original cover page of the Huntington manuscript, which is damaged on the right side, does not mention that the trial involved a theft, as claimed in the inventory. Rather, the trial was "for the sambenitos put up in Tecamachalco"—or, more exactly, the sambenitos placed on the facade of the town's church. The "statue" mentioned in the inventory turned out to be no sacred image but a doll-like dummy, or effigy, with two faces and two mouths with different tongues and other symbols, accompanied by enigmatic signs slandering a town resident by labeling him a Jew. No sacrilege or other heresy had taken place, but the authors of the Tecamachalco scandal had insulted a neighbor by appropriating the power of symbols used by the Inquisition to dishonor heretics.

The scandal of Tecamachalco offers an eloquent example of the very real power of images to dishonor. The sixteenth-century French jurist Pierre Ayrault explained: "Of course, just as one may be honored with an image [*effigie*], by displaying, and by making an image, one may just the same suffer punishment and shame."[8] The loss of honor was therefore a serious matter. *Fama* and *reputación*—fame and reputation—influenced all aspects of people's lives, from the way men and women interacted with others, to the activities and work they engaged in, their prospects for marriage, and even access to credit. Not surprisingly, an attack against someone's honor through the spread of false rumor constituted a punishable crime.[9] The effects of the loss of honor were comparable to suffering bodily harm—or worse. According to the *Siete Partidas*, the thirteenth-century Castilian legal compilation and the basis for Spanish law in the Americas, "Two crimes are equal, to kill a man or to accuse him of wrong-doing; for a man once he is defamed, although he be innocent, is dead to the good and honor of the world; and besides, the slander may be such that death would be better for him than life."[10] As we will see, the authors of the Tecamachalco scandal chose to defame their victim with the effigy and the sambenitos precisely because they considered it worse punishment than a beating or even death.

The Tecamachalco case is therefore unlike most inquisitorial trials bent on rooting out heresy or disciplining behavior that did not conform with Catholic dogma. The Inquisition never investigated the charge that the victim of the scandal was a Jew. Serious as it was to dishonor a man, such concerns lay beyond the Inquisition's authority. The tribunal's decision to prosecute the authors of the scandal responded exclusively to the fact that the actions involved the misuse and misappropriation of the sambenitos and the effigy associated with the tribunal and its exclusive authority. As I will argue, the scandal took place at a time when the new tribunal of the Mexican Holy Office was intent on persecuting actions that it saw as a challenge to the respect owed to it. The Mexican inquisitors therefore deployed all their available resources to find out who was responsible for illegally using their symbols. It did not matter to the inquisitors that mundane passions, rather than a desire to challenge the tribunal or its officials, motivated the authors of the scandal. The culprits would still have to pay a heavy price for their unintended disrespect.

The strange "statue" and the sambenitos of Tecamachalco lay at the intersection of two very different stories, one about passions in a colonial Mexican town and the other about the authority of the Inquisition. On the one hand, the scandal revealed secrets and rumors that touched on the racial and sexual anxieties of Spanish society in colonial Mexico. On the other hand, the inquisitors had to immerse themselves in these rumors about friendships and love affairs, personal reputations, lies, and enmities to punish those guilty of challenging the tribunal's authority. As the historian Emmanuel Le Roy Ladurie showed nearly four decades ago in his magisterial *Montaillou: The Promised Land of Error*, the inquisitors' determination to find out the truth pried open a community to reveal the otherwise secret loves, hatreds, and prejudices of men and women.[11] However, the Tecamachalco case also reveals

the pitfalls of such information, which often proved unreliable and misleading. Rumor became central to resolve the mystery behind the scandal, but it
led inquisitors down a tortuous path that delayed that resolution. On several
occasions, the tactical spreading of rumors and lies nearly derailed the investigation and almost allowed the culprits to get away with their actions.

It would be misleading to assume that understanding this case only requires
summing up the documentation available. It is important to remember that the
Tecamachalco case consisted of several investigations carried out by different
officials, resulting in nine separate trials. Although all these trials were part of
the same case, they do not always add up to a single coherent whole.

The secretary Pedro de los Ríos was the Inquisition's notary who compiled and filed the documentation for the Tecamachalco case, including the
Huntington manuscript, which looks like a book with nearly four hundred
pages numbered successively, except for the last fourteen pages. Yet the secretary did not organize the documents in this manuscript with the aim of telling a story from beginning to end; rather, he organized them in the order in
which he received them. The Huntington manuscript is therefore not a single
document but many produced by multiple authors copied in several different hands. Most of the first eighty pages of documents consist of an initial
investigation conducted by royal officials, which ended abruptly in the last
days of July 1578, when the Inquisition took over the case. Next, we find the
papers from the Inquisition's first investigation and trial, which stops without
warning or explanation on 18 September 1578. Turning to the next page (f.
61, or p. 122), the investigation suddenly resumes more than three years later,
in October 1581. Pedro de los Ríos simply attached the new documents to the
old ones without bothering to note the long interruption between them. As
the case progressed in the course of the next two years and spawned new trials, the secretary copied and attached extracts of varying lengths from those
trials. Nearly 360 pages later, a final entry from 13 July 1582 indicates the sentencing in the case, which brings to an end the main story in the Huntington
manuscript. The last fourteen pages contain a final summation of the entire
case, but introducing new information, and even new names. The last document dates from 23 July 1582. The stories told by the rest of the trials, located
at the Archivo General de la Nación in Mexico City, are even more disjointed
than the story in the Huntington manuscript. They are part of different
volumes that add up to about three hundred pages—roughly a hundred pages
shorter than the Huntington document. Secretary de los Ríos did not find it
necessary to provide background or context for each of the trials. The less

important trials are virtually incomprehensible without taking into account the documentation from the other trials. Fortunately, Pedro de los Ríos had key passages from the now-missing trial transcribed in the trials in the Huntington manuscript and the other documents in Mexico.

Twice, the Inquisition summed up the story behind the Tecamachalco case. In both cases, the author of those summaries was almost certainly Secretary Pedro de los Ríos. In 1583, the Mexican Inquisition sent a brief report (*relación*) of the case to the royal council in Madrid that oversaw the work of the Inquisition across the Spanish empire, the Council of the Supreme and General Inquisition, known as the *Suprema*.[12] The report is little more than an abbreviated summary—about one paragraph long—of the final sentences in the case. In a couple of lines, it offered to the Suprema a cursory background to the case, the identity of the victim of the scandal, and the names of the principal culprits. This short summary underplays the difficulty and length of the case. A longer summary, and the only attempt at something close to a narrative of the case, appears in the last fourteen pages of the Huntington manuscript.[13] Secretary de los Ríos probably wrote it for the *pronunciación*, or the publication of the final sentences in the case, read at a ceremony on 22 July 1582 in Mexico City's cathedral. Unlike the short report sent to the Suprema, this longer summary more accurately reflects the complexity and length of the Tecamachalco case. It provides numerous excerpts, some quite long, from the trial depositions. Yet the sheer volume of information packed into these few pages makes it very difficult to follow by anyone not already familiar with the case.

Secretary de los Ríos had no interest in telling a story the way in which, say, the sixteenth-century French judge Jean de Coras used his knowledge of the strange case of Martin Guerre to create a gripping tale marked by surprising twists that would interest all kinds of readers.[14] In Secretary de los Ríos's summary of the Tecamachalco trials, the numerous unexpected twists read like a long line of non sequiturs. More important, Judge Coras described his reactions to his extraordinary story and thus shared the stage with his big cast of characters. In Pedro de los Ríos's accounts, the inquisitors remain off stage and virtually silent. The fault does not lie entirely with the Inquisition's secretary; even if he had wanted to write an account of the Tecamachalco case, the tribunal forbade publication of its secret documentation. De los Ríos therefore wrote for an audience of other officials of the Inquisition, more interested in an accurate summation of the case than in enjoying a good tale.

If understanding the Tecamachalco case cannot rely solely on summing up the documentation, its analysis in narrative form is the best way to resolve one of the greatest challenges of this case, namely, the unexpected twists that turned a seemingly mundane affair into a case hundreds of pages long. Following closely the evolution of the investigation reveals much about the inquisitors' approach to the investigation, as well as where they made mistakes or drew the wrong conclusions. The shifting directions in the investigation also reveal the inquisitors' confusion about the evidence and their false assumptions about the suspects. Without this information, one cannot understand the inquisitors' decision to begin each trial, whom to torture, and when. In addition, following the various turns in the investigation shows how remarkably skilled the authors of the execution in effigy were at hiding their tracks and creating false leads—something concealed in the Inquisition's summaries of the case. Narrative and analysis therefore intersect in my retelling of this fascinating case.

Virtually everything known about the Tecamachalco case comes from the Mexican Inquisition's documentation. Ordinary men and women were involved in the case and, in most cases, did not leave additional documents to supplement what we know from the inquisitorial trials.[15] Therefore, it is largely through the eyes of the Inquisition's officials that we must reconstruct the events of July 1578 and thereafter. Of course, suspects were well aware of the potential dangers of revealing the whole truth. It is not always possible to confirm the validity of testimony collected through torture or under its threat. This does not mean that an objective analysis of the evidence lies beyond our reach. The Inquisition encouraged suspects and witnesses to tell the truth and threatened them with severe punishment for lying. Moreover, despite their quest for the truth, the inquisitors were not neutral judges; they had a mission to stamp out what they considered to be threats to the Catholic Church and to the work of the Inquisition. Fortunately, the carefully collected records left by the specialized staff of the Inquisition make these documents extremely valuable, providing a window into the past not matched by most historical records.[16] The inquisitors were often highly professional bureaucrats rather than fanatics.[17]

Conveying the richness of inquisitorial documents poses important challenges. Although the depositions often have the feel of verbatim declarations, what we have are copies of the original statements taken down during the actual interrogations. Scribes, notaries, and secretaries made great efforts to be accurate, but they were not foolproof recording machines capable of total accuracy. In addition, these depositions are legal documents and, as such, are often repetitive and formulaic. Since the Tecamachalco case involved nine different trials, the Inquisition's officials treated each one as a separate unit requiring the transcription of relevant testimonies from the other trials. This practice further contributed to the repetitiveness of the documentation.

An English translation of the inquisitorial documents as they are in the original would prove frustratingly confusing for other reasons as well. Even something as simple as the identity of the men and women in the case poses problems for anyone not familiar with Spanish. The recurrence of popular first names—Juan, Juana, Francisco, and Catalina—and of common surnames might cause confusion. Though this was not generally a problem for those living in the community, they, too, occasionally got their names mixed up. Inquisitorial documents try to avoid the confusion by writing down the first and last names; they also included additional information, such as the individual's race, the name of a woman's husband, and which of two men with the same name was the father and which was the son (*el mozo*, "the younger"). I have compiled a list of names at the end of this book to help identify the numerous men and women who took part in this case. I have also followed the practice of other historians and changed the third-person singular, as recorded in the depositions, to the first-person singular, to re-create the sense of the original depositions.

The narrative moves mostly chronologically from July 1578 to July 1582. The preface describes the scene of the crime and provides background about the town of Tecamachalco, the Mexican Inquisition, and the practice of executions in effigy. The long history of the investigation has three parts. The first part examines the initial, failed, investigation of the scandal in 1578, begun by a royal official, and soon after taken over by the Inquisition, which lasted only weeks. The second part focuses on the resumption of the investigation in 1581, following an unexpected testimony made before the inquisitors. But a barrage of often contradictory and confusing testimonies soon threatened a similar outcome as in the first investigation. The third part focuses on the trials of the main suspects in 1582. By January of that year, the inquisitors thought that the investigation would soon end. Instead, the number of suspects and trials multiplied, until the final sentencing in July 1582, four years after the scandal. The epilogue presents the final analysis of the case and offers lessons drawn from it about the very real power of images in the sixteenth century.

PART I

1578

PROLOGUE

The Crime of Tecamachalco

Poor Tecamachalco, so unfortunate,
it never lacks some misfortune!
Diego de Trujillo, Spanish farmer, 1581

In the early hours of Monday, 21 July 1578, an effigy hung from an iron rod
nailed to the door of the church of the Franciscan monastery of Tecamachalco, located about eighty miles southeast of Mexico City (see Figure 2). The
effigy has not survived, but eyewitness testimonies provide detailed descriptions of its strange features. The "statue," or effigy, looked like a small man
or a doll. It was made of *tochomite*, an Indian wool cloth, sewn together and
stuffed with hay. The effigy's head had black chicken feathers instead of hair,
as well as two faces drawn with ink, one in front of the head and the other
"where the nape of the head should be."[1] Each mouth had a tongue sewn
onto it. One tongue looked like a snake's with a forked end; the other tongue
had a gag tied around it—or a needle piercing it, according to conflicting
descriptions.[2] The effigy's arms and feet were made of reeds. The effigy wore
a *sambenito*, the garment that the Inquisition imposed on those found guilty
of acting against God and the Catholic Church. The effigy's sambenito had a
red Saint Andrew's cross (like the letter *X*) painted over a yellow background.
Heretics condemned to death wore sambenitos on their way to the stake. Below the effigy lay a pile of firewood.

The effigy held in one hand a spindle and a distaff, common implements
for spinning thread. The other hand held a sign in large Gothic script that
read: "I, the great *Comendador* of Mount Calvary, Rubio Naranjo, as the lord
of this town, order all the neighbors to present me with all my forebears'
property, which are the coats of arms of the most blessed San Benito; no one is

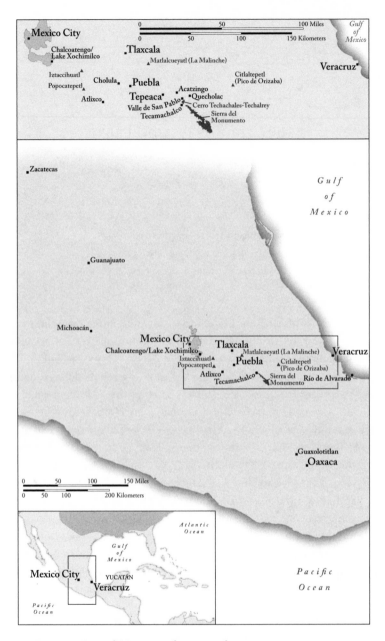

Figure 2. Central Mexico in the sixteenth century.

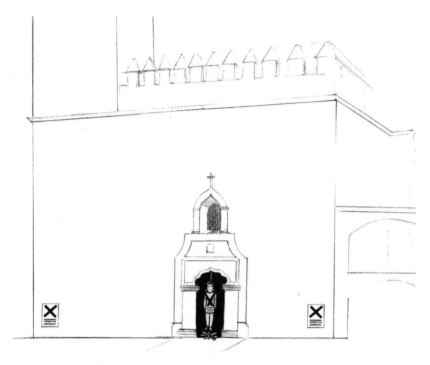

Figure 3. Rendition of the placement of effigy and *sambenitos* on the facade of Tecamachalco's church on the morning of 21 July 1578.

more worthy to have them than me, thanks to my great deeds, which are known to everyone. [Signed:] Hernando Rubio Naranjo."[3]

In addition to the effigy, two other sambenitos were nailed to the church's facade, on either side of the door of the temple (see Figure 3). These sambenitos were about one foot by eight and a half inches and did not have effigies. They were made of the same tochomite used for the effigy, glued onto deerskins. They had a big red Saint Andrew's cross painted over a yellow background. Below each sambenito was a sign, about half the size of the sambenito. One sign read: "No one take my coat of arms." The other sign warned: "Whoever removes me, let the same happen to you."[4] Both signs bore the signature of Rubio Naranjo, a trader (*tratante*).

Was the effigy's enigmatic message an inside joke "known to everyone" in town, like Hernando Rubio Naranjo's alleged "great deeds"? Its ominous message was certainly no laughing matter. The sign ordered the neighbors of Tecamachalco to recognize Rubio Naranjo with the coat of arms of Saint Benedict, or "San Benito," a play on the word *sambenito*. Such a coat of arms could bring only shame, or worse. Sambenitos branded their wearers with the infamy of heresy, which theologians defined as treason against God (*laesae majestatis divinae*). However, the infamy of the sambenito was closely associated with anti-Semitic prejudices because many heretics were "Judaizers" who secretly kept the "Law of Moses." Judaizers betrayed God by reneging on their avowed Catholic faith, just as Jews had supposedly betrayed Jesus Christ by calling for his death on Mount Calvary.[5] If Rubio Naranjo deserved a sambenito because it was his "forebears' property," it could only be because he descended from what was deemed the impure blood of Jews. Yet his unnamed "great deeds" meant that he was no ordinary Jew. This was the reason he had earned the title "Comendador of Mount Calvary." In late medieval Iberia, *comendadores* commanded religious-military orders of Christian knights in the wars against Muslim rulers for control of the Iberian Peninsula. No such order of Mount Calvary had ever existed. Instead, the title Comendador of Mount Calvary conferred on Rubio Naranjo the distinct dishonor of being a great Jew.

On the morning of 21 July 1578, the wind made the sambenitos flap against the facade of the church.[6] The menacing effigy of San Benito stood guard, waiting for everyone in Tecamachalco to heed its warnings. Meanwhile, across from the church, Hernando Rubio Naranjo slept inside his house, unaware of the scandal that would soon spread across the region.

Tecamachalco

Before this incident, Tecamachalco had witnessed considerable turmoil of a different kind. In the Nahuatl language of the Mexica, or Aztecs, the name means "the location of the jaw of stone."[7] The "jaw" referred to the dual-peaked Cerro Techachales-Techalrey, which was thought to resemble an open mouth. Atop this mountain, the original settlement overlooked the four distant volcanoes that preside over the landscape: to the northeast, the massive snowcapped Citlaltepetl (Pico de Orizaba, in Spanish; 18,406 feet), the highest peak in Mexico; to the west, the Popocatepetl (17,930 feet) and the Ixtaccihuatl (17,159 feet); and to the northwest, the Matlalcueyatl (La Malinche, in Spanish; 7,400 feet).[8] In 1451, Tecamachalco's rulers resettled its population a few miles east in the central part of a ridge now known as the Sierra del Monumento. From there, Tecamachalco exerted its lordship over a broad area of rich agricultural lands and strategic commercial routes used for transporting precious stones, prized feathers, cotton, and cacao from the Gulf of Mexico, Yucatán, and Oaxaca to the Aztec capital of Tenochtitlan. Because of its strategic importance, the Aztecs set out to conquer Tecamachalco and nearby lordships; in 1466, they made them into tributaries and military allies of their great empire.[9] The new Nahuatl-speaking lords of Tecamachalco ruled over a population of mostly Popoloca speakers, who still live in the region.[10]

In 1520, Tecamachalco fell to the Spanish conquistador Hernán Cortés, who enslaved two thousand prisoners and gave the town to one of his soldiers as an *encomienda*, or grant of land.[11] That year, Tecamachalco suffered the onslaught of the "divine rash," or smallpox, the first of several epidemics brought by the Spanish, which, over the course of sixty years, reduced its population by 90 percent.[12] In 1541, the first Spanish missionaries arrived in the town, which they renamed Tecamachalco de la Asunción, after the Virgin of the Assumption. Two years later, they resettled the town downhill from the Sierra del Monumento at the southern slope of the Cerro Techachales-Techalrey, nearer the route from the Spanish cities of Veracruz and Puebla to Mexico City. The Spanish divided the preconquest lordship and turned Tecamachalco into a smaller *cabecera*, a town with jurisdiction over a few nearby villages and an Indian governor with limited powers.[13] Real authority lay elsewhere. The principal law enforcer became the *alcalde mayor* (chief constable), who lived in the provincial capital of Tepeaca, eight miles west of Tecamachalco. Thirty miles northwest of Tecamachalco, Puebla was the seat of the bishopric of Tlaxcala, second only in importance to the archbishop of Mexico City. Eighty-two miles northwest of Tecamachalco, or three days' journey by road, was Mexico City, the seat of the viceroy, the archbishop, the Inquisition, and the Audiencia, or appellate court.

Geographical Relations, a document written in 1580 for the Spanish king Philip II to inform him about the region and its history, describes much of the province of Tepeaca as dry and cold land, good for growing wheat and raising sheep, the region's chief agricultural products.[14] However, Tecamachalco lay on "hot land," good for growing the traditional preconquest crops of corn, beans, and chili peppers. The region also exported the valuable cochineal for use as crimson dye.[15] According to the same document, Tecamachalco had well-designed, clean streets and a plaza sloping downhill to avoid flooding and diseases blamed on excessive humidity. A nearby stream powered a mill for grinding the wheat grown primarily north of town in the fertile valley of San Pablo, where

Figure 4. View of Tecamachalco's Church of the Assumption, with the ruins of the Franciscan monastery to the right. The bell tower dates from around 1591. Photo by Gilles Mermet.

there were seventy Spanish farmers. A second stream supplied water to Tecamachalco's residents, who lacked the convenience of a fountain in the plaza. On that busy plaza, farmers brought their vegetable and fruit produce, Indian women sold blankets and other wares, and neighbors came to discuss business and collect tribute at the "pretty and well-built" *casas reales*, or town hall.

Uphill from the plaza was the Church of the Assumption—where the scandal of July 1578 took place. The church still stands today, adjacent to the ruins of the former Franciscan monastery (see Figure 4). Construction of the monastery may have begun as early as 1543. Some of its first friars were famous for their knowledge of native languages, such as Francisco del Toral, the future bishop of Yucatán, who composed the first Popoloca grammar. The consecration of the church took place in 1551. A fire in 1557 required its reconstruction, which was completed in 1561.[16] The church's architecture is typical of early Franciscan fortress-churches, which look like medieval castles with a flat facade, massive walls, and crenellated roofs.[17] The bell tower, built around 1591, rises above the roof on the right side of the facade. The main church door's Gothic arch frames the doorway. Directly above, a smaller arch topped by a cross frames a window.

Inside the church, painted on the vaulted ceiling just past the entrance, is one of most celebrated works of early colonial Mexican art, by the native painter Juan Gersón. Named after the medieval French theologian Jean Gerson, Juan Gersón probably descended from the preconquest lords of Tecamachalco, since he received the privilege to dress in Spanish clothes, carry a sword, and ride a horse.[18] He may have studied at the monastery, where he later became lay overseer of the upkeep of the church's single chapel. Beginning in May 1562, Gersón painted twenty-eight scenes from the Old Testament and the Book of Revelation, inspired by prints from artists such as Albrecht Dürer and Hans Holbein the Younger. Gersón painted the scenes on paper made from the bark of fig trees, which were then affixed to the vaulted ceiling below the choir loft.[19] Noah's ark, full of animals, is one of the few peaceful images among scenes of violence and divine retribution. Whereas the Four Horsemen of the Apocalypse recalled the wars, plagues, hunger, and death brought on by the Spanish conquest (see Figure 5), the scene of Cain about to strike a helpless Abel was a reminder that death need not come from the hand of a stranger (see Figure 6).[20] On 21 July 1578, only the church's door separated these paintings from Hernando Rubio Naranjo's double-headed effigy and its own ominous warning.

Tensions occasionally disrupted Tecamachalco's mostly uneventful existence. Across Mexico, the Spanish conquest had sought to establish an order based on the segregation of the "Republic of Spaniards," residing in cities and towns, from the "Republic of Indians" in the countryside. In Tecamachalco, the hundred or so "Spanish" residents lived in town near the plaza or near the church.[21] They were mostly farmers, but there were also scribes, artisans, and traders—such as Hernando Rubio Naranjo. The seven thousand "Indians" lived in nearby villages.[22] Under Spanish rule, the Indian governors continued to descend from the preconquest lords who spoke Nahuatl and, like the painter Juan Gersón, could wear Spanish clothes, ride horses, and carry swords. Spanish farmers from the region gladly socialized at the home of the Indian governor, Don—the title reserved for Spanish nobles—Joaquín de Peralta, who lived in the nearby town of Quecholac.[23] In sharp contrast, Spaniards often looked down on

Figure 5. Juan Gersón's painting of the Four Horsemen of the Apocalypse, Tecamachalco's church (begun in 1562). Photo by Gilles Mermet.

Figure 6. Juan Gersón's painting of Cain slaying Abel, Tecamachalco's church (begun in 1562). Photo by Gilles Mermet.

the Popolocas, whom they treated as servants and subjected to all kinds of abuse.[24]

The *república de los españoles* was even more heterogeneous than that of the Indians.[25] Spaniards in town came from different regions of the Peninsula, including Andalusia, the Basque country, Castile, and Extremadura. Among them, a Portuguese migrant could settle, marry a local mestiza, and have a *castizo* son (strictly speaking, the offspring of Spanish and mestizo parents); that son would eventually marry a mestiza and expect his share of the Indian service to which Spanish landowners were entitled.[26] By the 1570s, the *casta* system developed by Spanish authorities to establish a clear racial hierarchy was only beginning to take shape. Yet life in a small community like that of Tecamachalco could breed a familiarity that often wrested importance from those racial differences. This was especially true for the poorer residents not competing for the coveted privileges and offices that authorities sought to restrict to Spaniards. Excluding Indian servants and black slaves, friendships and family ties were common among Spaniards—whether born in the Peninsula or in the Americas—mestizos, castizos, and mulattos. In fact, outside authorities might view poor Spaniards with the same disdain that they expressed toward the mixed-race rabble.[27]

The slander against Hernando Rubio Naranjo points to another source of friction not predicated upon the divide that pitted Spaniard against mixed-race or Indian. Spanish origin did not soften the prejudice against impure Jewish blood dating back well before the conquest that led to legal restrictions against those who descended from Jewish converts to Christianity, the *conversos*, on both sides of the Atlantic. The allegation that Rubio Naranjo had inherited from his "forebears" the shameful coat of arms of "San Benito" left no doubt that his anonymous accuser, or accusers, considered his blood tainted. Yet other aspects of the insults against Rubio Naranjo pointed to what David Nirenberg has described as the "strategic adaptation and adoption of vocabularies of hatred."[28] Within the republic of Spaniards in New Spain, personal rivalries often invoked this protean image of the evil Jew to attack enemies.[29] In particular, the deeds allegedly committed by the trader, hinted at by the various symbols on the effigy, referred to the Jew as a double-crosser and a "bad Christian," which meant anything from seeming a shameless sinner to being suspected of not fulfilling prescribed acts, such as abstaining from meat during Lent or confessing, or worse.

Calling someone a *judío*, or a *perro judío* (Jewish dog), was an everyday insult intended to sting, but it did not always rise to the level of a formal accusation of being a Judaizer, a matter over which the Inquisition claimed exclusive authority.[30] Inquisitors knew well the distinction between the Jew that was merely an insult, with or without merit, and the Jew in the sense of the Judaizer. The former did not always concern the Inquisition; the latter certainly did. Questions of honor could therefore cause internal rifts whose ripples might threaten the political order of New Spain. Authorities could not allow the desire to vent anger against a neighbor to challenge the normal channels for resolving disputes. Any unauthorized abrogation of power, even for a good end, required punishment lest it undermine trust in legitimate authority. The effigy with its sambenitos hanging over a pile of wood, the additional sambenitos affixed to the church's wall, and the signs denouncing Rubio Naranjo as a Jew left no doubt that someone in Tecamachalco had staged a mock execution in effigy.

Execution in Effigy

Executions in effigy bring to mind popular forms of justice and protest used to intimidate or to vent anger by burning, hanging, or attacking a crude dummy of whoever is the target of anger, whether a public figure or an unfortunate neighbor.[31] However, across the early modern world, lay and religious authorities reserved formal executions in effigy for dead and absent criminals guilty of "very grave and enormous crimes," such as heresy, treason, parricide, suicide, and other heinous crimes worthy of this ignominy.[32]

Executions in effigy elicited strong emotions. In 1462, Pope Pius II ordered an execution in effigy made memorable by the solemnity and attention to detail lavished on it. A court in Rome found Sigismondo Malatesta, lord of Rimini, guilty of rapine, arson, murder, adultery, incest, parricide, sacrilege, treason, and heresy. Since Malatesta was away in his territories in northern Italy, the pope ordered the execution of the sentence in effigy to take place at three different locations in Rome. At the steps of Saint Peter's basilica, a clothed effigy resembling the accused lay atop the pyre. Like Hernando Rubio Naranjo's effigy in Tecamachalco, Malatesta's effigy had a sign in the shape of a scroll coming out of its mouth with the following words: "I am Sigismondo Malatesta . . . king of traitors, the enemy of God and man, by sentence of the Sacred College condemned to the flames."[33] Upon hearing the news, the angry Malatesta promised to take revenge for the insult, although instead he eventually recanted his heresies and received a papal pardon. The public watching those events could react even more strongly, sometimes attacking images with stones, daggers, and pikes.[34] Such executions continued to take place across Europe well into the eighteenth century.

Spain had its own tradition of shaming and punishing individuals by the use of effigies. In 1471, four horses dragged the effigies of four men declared traitors across the streets of Barcelona. Until authorities could carry out the executions in person, the effigies hung in the house of the royal official in charge of keeping order in the city. In addition, images of the four traitors painted in three public locations reminded Barcelona residents of the ransom for turning in the men, alive or dead.[35] Rebels also resorted to similar acts of defamation. In 1465, a group of nobles in Ávila deposed in effigy the king of Castile Henry IV, brother of the future Queen Isabella. A wooden statue of the king bearing royal insignia sat on a throne placed on a large platform beyond the city's walls. The conspirators walked up to the stage and read the king's crimes, which included an accusation of sodomy. One by one, each of the leading conspirators removed the crown, the sword, the scepter, and finally threw the statue from the stage, "uttering furious and dishonest words," such as "To the ground, sodomite!" The crowd watching the ceremony cried for "the wretched death of the dethroned" king.[36] Henry IV, who remained in power, compared the disrespect shown toward his image to Israel's betrayal of God—that is, an act of heresy.[37]

By the sixteenth century, the Inquisition had appropriated, perhaps exclusively, formal executions in effigy for the punishment of heretics across the early modern Spanish world.[38] The Inquisition's term for the sentence was *relajación en estatua*, or "relaxation" (that is, surrender to civil authorities) in effigy, in contrast to the *relajación en persona*, when civil authorities carried out the death sentence on the actual person. The author of the first history of the Inquisition and a former official of the tribunal, Juan Antonio Llorente (1756–1823), asserted that from its foundation in 1478 to 1808, the Inquisition burned more than seventeen thousand effigies, a number that the great American historian of the Inquisition Henry Charles Lea dismissed as "extravagant guesses."[39] Nonetheless, the Inquisition burned a very large number of effigies in its effort to demonstrate that flight and death would not stop the tribunal from prosecuting heretics.[40]

Figure 7. Iberian Peninsula in the sixteenth century.

According to one estimate, between 1540 and 1700 the Inquisition burned 778 effigies, representing 1.7 percent of the Holy Office's cases in the Iberian Peninsula and the Americas.[41] In the Mexican tribunal alone, as many as 107 individuals, or 3.4 percent of sentences, were executions in effigy.[42]

These numbers do not reflect an important fact relevant to the Tecamachalco crime: the Inquisition disproportionately punished accused Judaizers with executions in effigies. Between 1540 and 1700, half of the effigies burned in the Peninsula and America were for individuals accused of Judaizing.[43] Yet this proportion would certainly rise if these estimates went back seventy years, to the early days of the Spanish Inquisition, when the vast majority of cases dealt with Judaizers. No effigies burned at the first Spanish auto de fe, which took place in Seville on 6 February 1481; but within a few years, burning the effigies of deceased or

Figure 8. Effigies of accused heretics wearing *sambenitos* and
corozas; bones of the deceased were carried inside the boxes.
Detail from Francisco Rizi, *Auto de Fe in the Plaza Mayor of
Madrid* (1683), Prado Museum. Photo © Fundació Institut
Amatller d'Art Hispànic. Arxiu Mas.

escaped Judaizers had become widespread. The historian Henry Charles
Lea described an execution that took place in Toledo on 8 May 1487, during which four hundred effigies burned: "A great monument, covered
with black, was erected in front of the staging occupied by the inquisitors. The sentence of each culprit was read, and his name was called. The
monument was opened and an effigy, arrayed in Jewish grave-clothes, was
brought out and condemned as a heretic. Then a great fire was built in the
center of the plaza, and all the effigies were consumed, together with the

Figure 9. Effigies carried on poles at the auto de fe in Valladolid in 1559; the effigy on the left is followed by a casket with the disinterred bones of the accused "Judaizer" Leonor de Vivero. Detail from *Hispanissche Inquisition* (1560?), Bibliothèque Nationale, Paris.

disinterred bones. Afterward, the names were read in the cathedral with summons to the heirs to render account of the inheritances that belonged to the king."[44]

In these early autos, the number of dead and absent was sometimes so large that the Inquisition resorted to what Lea called the "economical though somewhat grotesque device" of Janus-faced effigies—like the effigy in Tecamachalco. Unlike Hernando Rubio Naranjo's effigy, these double-faced effigies represented two different individuals or a husband and wife.[45]

In 1578, the year of the Tecamachalco scandal, the Spanish jurist Francisco Peña discussed the legal basis for executions in effigy in his commentaries on the most influential work on inquisitorial practice, the *Inquisitors' Manual*, written in 1376 by Nicolau Eimeric. According to Peña, "civil law declares that in general the death of a guilty person annuls the possibility of prosecuting a crime."[46] However, citing the opinion of

councils and doctors of the church, he explained that this general prin-
ciple was not valid in the case of treason and heresy. A postmortem sentence of heresy was not enough to condemn the memory of the deceased,
Peña declared; it also required burning his or her remains—along with
an effigy of the convicted. An execution in effigy for persons accused
in absentia required a different explanation. Failure to appear before
the Inquisition to address charges of heresy put the accused in a state of
excommunication. Papal decrees determined that after a year of excommunication, a person became an "impenitent heretic," carrying a death
sentence, which authorities could execute in effigy.[47] This did not nec-
essarily mean that the Inquisition had forever finished with the accused
or that the latter did not have to fear further prosecution. According to
an apocryphal story, a man in Amsterdam approached the Spanish playwright Antonio Enríquez Gómez in 1660 and said, "Oh, Señor Enríquez!
I saw your effigy burn in Seville," to which Enríquez replied, laughing,
"Let them do to me whatever they will over there."[48] In reality, he was living in Seville disguised under several pseudonyms and watched his own
execution in effigy at the auto de fe of 3 April 1660.[49] A year and a half
later, the Inquisition arrested Enríquez Gómez in Seville and retried him
for Judaizing. He repented but died in prison in March 1663 while awaiting sentencing and was buried at the church of Santa Ana. The Inquisition would commission a second effigy of the playwright for a different
purpose from the first one. In 1665, at another auto de fe in Seville, the
Inquisition had Enríquez posthumously "reconciled"—received back into
the Church—in effigy.[50]

Despite the widespread use of effigies, inquisitorial manuals and
instructions do not offer descriptions of what these dummies looked
like, which burned at the stake and therefore did not survive.[51] Written
accounts of autos de fe and contemporary illustrations and paintings provide the only details available. The brief life of the effigy usually began
eight to ten days before the staging of an auto de fe. City authorities com-
missioned local painters to make the inexpensive effigies, masks, and
corozas, or cone-like miters. Tailors made the sambenitos.[52] Effigies were
made of plaster or paperboard and ranged from life-size to half-size. Hair,
beards, and other details on the effigy's painted mask, as well as the clothes
worn, indicated the person's sex. A sign in the front and back of the effigy
indicated the person's name, place of origin, and whether he or she was a
fugitive or deceased.

By far the most impressive visual representation of these effigies appears in Francisco Rizi's large (more than nine feet by fourteen feet) *Auto de Fe in the Plaza Mayor of Madrid* (1683), painted for King Charles II and now at the Prado Museum (Figure 8).[53] For the occasion in 1680, Madrid's authorities built a raised stage on the Plaza Mayor. Above the center of the painting, Charles II and the royal family watched the ceremony from a balcony in one of the buildings surrounding the square. To the right, one sees two dozen very tall men and women, which are, in fact, effigies hanging from poles carried by individuals. The effigies' faces have hair, beards, and other details, and wear the required corozas and sambenitos with writing and other symbols on them. They also have dangling arms and legs. Some of the effigies carried in their hands a small chest containing the remains of the deceased person.[54] As a court painter living at the royal palace in Madrid, Rizi probably witnessed the auto de fe and could have asked other witnesses for accurate information about details. In addition, he followed a detailed account of the auto, which included an engraving.[55] This is not always true of earlier and later illustrations, which nonetheless managed to capture the essence of what these effigies must have looked like.[56]

On the day of the auto de fe, paid beggars carried the effigies on poles in the procession of the sentenced, during the auto proper, and afterward to the stake. If the condemned were dead, a coffin or chest with the disinterred bones accompanied the effigy. At the Toledo auto de fe of 1487 mentioned above, effigies of accused Judaizers wore Jewish graveclothes. At the great 1559 Valladolid auto de fe (Figure 9), attended by King Philip II, the effigy of the deceased Leonor de Vivero led the procession. The effigy had a widow's dress and a miter painted with flames. Behind it was a coffin with her remains.[57] As was the case with individuals accused of heresy, authorities removed the sambenitos before burning the effigy in order to hang them in the church where the condemned had resided, "for the eternal memory of the infamy of those heretics and their descendants."[58]

Whatever the reason for insulting Hernando Rubio Naranjo in this unusual way, the execution in effigy at Tecamachalco had usurped the symbols of the Holy Office of the Inquisition for the purpose of injuring someone's reputation. In the course of four years, the tribunal conducted multiple trials, during which inquisitors interrogated dozens of suspects, accomplices, accessories to the scandal, and witnesses. The time and effort made it clear that the inquisitors did not treat this act of disrespect lightly;

they insisted that it interfered with the Inquisition's work in Mexico and therefore threatened their duty to defend the Catholic Church against its enemies in the New World. The inquisitors' response had much to do with the timing of the scandal in the history of the Mexican tribunal.

The Inquisition in Mexico

In 1578, the Mexican Inquisition was a newly established institution still trying to assert its authority in the viceroyalty. Although the establishment of the Spanish Inquisition dates back to 1478, it was only in 1571 when the monarchy established a tribunal like the ones that had been active for nearly a century in the Iberian Peninsula. During the half-century between the conquest of Mexico in 1520 and the establishment of the Mexican tribunal, religious orders—particularly the Franciscans and the Dominicans—and bishops carried out most of the limited inquisitorial activity in New Spain. Some periods, such as 1528–36, saw little activity; but even the 243 cases conducted during the busy periods of 1536–41 and 1555–71 pale in comparison with the caseloads in the sixteen Spanish tribunals, which had tiny jurisdictions compared with the size of the viceroyalty of New Spain.[59] Despite their limited activity, the Mexican inquisitors faced challenges from settlers and local authorities who refused to comply, from critics who denounced abuses, and even from members of the clergy claiming their own inquisitorial authority.

In 1524, the Franciscan Martín de Valencia arrived in Mexico as the first commissioner of the Inquisition, a title that did not prevent opposition to his authority. Within a year, Hernán Cortés's deputy and Mexico City authorities denounced the friar as trying to usurp civil and criminal cases that lay beyond his inquisitorial jurisdiction.[60] Even without these challenges, the lack of staff and funds prevented Martín de Valencia from doing much inquisitorial work, which ended in 1526. His Dominican successors faced similar conditions. That situation improved in 1535, with the appointment as apostolic inquisitor of the Franciscan Juan de Zumárraga, the first bishop (and later the first archbishop) of Mexico City. Counting on a larger staff than his predecessors, he conducted more than a hundred trials.[61] Nonetheless, his aims did not always coincide with the monarchy's interests. In 1543, Zumárraga was stripped of his inquisitorial powers, allegedly for exceeding his authority during the trial of the indigenous leader Don Carlos of Texcoco, burned at the stake four years earlier for "dogmatizing heresy."[62] Beginning in 1556, Alonso de Montúfar, Zumárraga's successor as archbishop of Mexico City, resumed a relatively vigorous inquisitorial activity, which ended in 1571 with the establishment of the inquisitorial tribunal.[63]

The archbishops in Mexico City were not the only ones who claimed inquisitorial authority.[64] In the 1560s, the Yucatán Peninsula witnessed a heated dispute between Franciscan missionaries and the bishop Francisco del Toral, who had previously served as guardian of the Tecamachalco Franciscan monastery. In 1562, Franciscans in the Yucatán investigated claims of idolatry and human crucifixion that culminated in an auto de fe on 12 July. Within three months, 4,500 Indians suffered torture. This resulted in 158 deaths during interrogations and at least thirteen suicides of natives trying to avoid torture. Such high numbers of deaths during torture were unheard of in Spanish inquisitorial tribunals, prompting Bishop Toral to assert his episcopal authority over the friars by barring them from all inquisitorial activity.[65]

By the 1560s, religious strife between Catholic Spain and its Protestant enemies across the world had convinced the Spanish monarch to exert greater control over inquisitorial activity in the New World. In 1562, French Huguenots attempted to establish a colony in Florida, until their massacre three years later by Spanish forces put an end to their venture. In 1568, the Spanish attacked an English flotilla in the Mexican port of San Juan de Ulúa and imprisoned what they considered to be pirates under the command of John Hawkins, who escaped with great difficulty.[66] Moreover, the papacy threatened to end its sanction of the Spanish monarchy's claims in the New World for supposedly failing to carry out its duty to Christianize the indigenous population.[67]

On 25 January 1569, Philip II issued a decree establishing two inquisitorial tribunals, one in each of the two American viceregal capitals of Lima and Mexico City.[68] The decree wrested away the inquisitorial authority from bishops and made it the exclusive domain of the two new tribunals, which would answer directly to the Suprema—the Council of the Supreme and General Inquisition—in Madrid. The jurisdiction of the Mexican tribunal would extend over all the viceroyalty of New Spain, which included Mexico and Central America, the Caribbean, and the Philippines. Two inquisitors and a small staff would coordinate from their headquarters in Mexico City all inquisitorial activity in this vast area. In August 1571, the first inquisitor, Pedro Moya de Contreras, arrived in Mexico, along with the Inquisition's secretary, Pedro de los Ríos, and the prosecuting attorney (*fiscal*), Alonso Fernández de Bonilla. The second inquisitor, Juan de Cervantes, fell ill during the voyage and died in Cuba a month before he was to assume office.[69]

On 4 November 1571, the tribunal officially began its work, with a procession to Mexico City's cathedral, where Inquisitor Moya de Contreras took an oath from everyone present to aid the Inquisition in its persecution of heresy.[70] The viceroy of New Spain, Martín Enríquez de Almansa, also took the oath, followed by the judges of the Audiencia and Mexico City's councilmen (*regidores*). The ceremony concluded with the proclamation of the first edict of grace, which listed the heresies that men and women should confess to the tribunal.

The viceroy had assisted the inquisitor in finding a house for the tribunal in the central Plaza de Santo Domingo, where the Inquisition remained until its abolition nearly 250 years later. By late November 1571, construction of the prison cells was under way; a year later, these cells would accommodate nearly forty prisoners.[71] By mid-1572, Inquisitor Moya de Contreras had appointed the rest of the tribunal's staff of sixteen, which included the defense lawyer for prisoners (*abogado de los presos*), notaries, a chaplain, a constable, a jailer, a physician, and a barber. The Inquisition of Mexico was ready to undertake its mission.

Yet from the start of their activities, the new tribunal and its officials confronted challenges to their respect and authority. Inquisitor Moya de Contreras complained to Madrid that neither Viceroy Enríquez de Almansa nor the Audiencia had welcomed him in person upon his arrival in Mexico City. At their first meeting, the viceroy used an abrupt tone and showed insufficient respect by keeping the inquisitor standing and without asking him to cover his head. Initially, the viceroy did not want to take the oath to assist the Inquisition; he did, however, relent. The two men clashed again over the inquisitor's determination to prosecute the French corsair Pierre Sanfoy. The viceroy insisted that the Inquisition did not have jurisdiction in this case, but he finally surrendered the Frenchman after Philip II intervened on behalf of the inquisitor. Rather than oppose the Inquisition's mission, the viceroy, who was a Catholic of strong convictions, sought to assert his authority, threatened by the inquisitor's actions. After all, the endless sparring between the viceroy and Moya de Contreras continued after the latter became archbishop of Mexico City.[72] Likewise, Archbishop Moya de Contreras and his successors as inquisitors had their own differences. In 1577, the archbishop refused to attend the auto de fe, saying that he did not like the seating arrangement. In truth, he was unhappy that the Inquisition had claimed jurisdiction over one of his cases. Rather than a change of heart about the tribunal he had helped to found, the archbishop felt a sense of duty to defend the prerogatives of his new office.[73] In this sense, viceroys, archbishops, and inquisitors were men of their times, concerned about the minutest details that recognized precedence and honor, not because they were especially vain but because such matters were of utmost significance in early modern societies.[74] The personal and institutional disputes that made up much of the history of the Inquisition in Mexico from its beginning to its abolition remind us that the inquisitors saw it as their duty to remain on guard about asserting the prerogatives of the Holy Office and its officials, whether in Mexico City, Tecamachalco, or anywhere else.

Although Mexico had already seen several small autos de fe, the first one under the new inquisitorial regime took place on 28 February 1574 outside Mexico City's cathedral.[75] Most of the prisoners were French Huguenots and English Anglicans, along with a few local bigamists; twenty received sentences as galley slaves; two foreigners burned at the stake. At a ceremony in August of that year, the inquisitors placed on either side of the main altar in the cathedral the sambenitos of those who were not present in the city with the name of the accused and the heresy committed.[76] Present at this auto de fe were the viceroy, the Audiencia judges, bishops, members of the university and religious orders, and other prominent city residents. A huge crowd of Spaniards and Indians watched the ceremony from the cathedral's plaza and from the attics and roofs of nearby buildings. Accompanying Inquisitor Pedro Moya de Contreras was Inquisitor Alonso Fernández de Bonilla, who had taken up his post the previous year. In October 1574, Alonso Granero Dávalos became the new inquisitor, filling the vacancy created by Moya de Contreras's appointment as archbishop. Bonilla and Dávalos were *licenciados*, or university licentiates, in canon law.[77] Licenciados Bonilla and Dávalos were the first inquisitors to investigate the Tecamachalco scandal.

Inquisitors Bonilla and Dávalos were no less vigilant about asserting the tribunal's authority against seemingly mundane acts of disrespect, as demonstrated by several trials that took place before the 1578 scandal in Tecamachalco.[78] The tribunal could obviously not tolerate it when the canon from the cathedral of Michoacán (now Morelia), Diego de Orduña, slapped and kicked the Inquisition's commissioner in that diocese. In 1575, Licenciados Bonilla and Dávalos fined and banished Orduña from Michoacán for one year. Inquisitor Bonilla insisted that the crime deserved "greater and harsher penalties," but the final sentence was milder because Orduña was a priest and had voluntarily appeared before the Inquisition.[79] Less blatant acts of disrespect resulted in even harsher punishments. At their third auto de fe, on 19 February 1576, Bonilla and Dávalos banished eighteen-year-old Pedro Cabeza de Vaca from the New World for six years for falsely pretending to be an official of the Inquisition, allegedly in order to rape a woman and extract alms in Zacatecas. Initially, the inquisitors also sentenced Cabeza de Vaca to a hundred lashes, but his appointed lawyer asked for mercy because the accused was not an adult and came from a noble family. However, the *fiscal* insisted on maintaining the full sentence, claiming that, had Cabeza de Vaca been an adult, he would have spent the rest of his life as a galley slave.[80] That same year, the inquisitors banished the cleric Antonio de Andrada from Mexico City and Michoacán for four years for falsifying two letters with arrest warrants from the Inquisition.[81] In March 1578, Bonilla and Dávalos sentenced another eighteen-year-old, Francisco de Peralta, to a fine of a hundred pesos and five years of banishment from Mexico City and Michoacán for impersonating an Inquisition constable.[82]

Lying, forgery, defamation, rape, theft, and physical aggression did not concern the Inquisition as much as the misuse of the Holy Office's name in committing these crimes. Licenciados Bonilla and Dávalos said as much regarding the case of Diego Arias de Rivera, a Spanish resident of the city of Guanajuato. In 1576, the accused ordered that city's alcalde mayor to comply with a supposed warrant from the Inquisition to arrest and shackle two men. Three days later, a contrite Arias de Rivera appeared before Bonilla and Dávalos in Mexico City to confess that he had lied about the warrants. The inquisitors launched an investigation, which revealed that Arias de Rivera had acted "with little fear of God and in great disregard for this holy tribunal," causing "great harm and prejudice" to the two men he had wanted arrested by saying that their parents and forebears had worn the shameful sambenito in Spain. Yet, as in Tecamachalco's case, defamation alone did not warrant the Inquisition's attention. Arias de Rivera's affront against the Inquisition lay in the fact that, out of sheer anger and the desire for revenge, he had used the Inquisition's "title and name." His crime deserved a severe punishment, but the inquisitors showed mercy because the accused had voluntarily turned himself in. They condemned Arias de Rivera to attend a public mass in Guanajuato as a penitent (without a hat or sword, carrying a candle) and to four years' banishment from the city.[83]

Bonilla and Dávalos acknowledged that personal hatreds, not heresy or an attack against the Catholic Church, lay behind the actions of Diego Arias de Rivera, as well as those of the authors of Tecamachalco's scandal. Regardless of the banality of the motivations—whether anger, lust, or greed—the inquisitors could not allow the misuse of the name and symbols of the Holy Office to go unpunished in Mexico City or Guanajuato, in Tecamachalco or Zacatecas. Failure to punish would earn the Inquisition disrespect and threaten its vital mission against heresy in the New World. Irene Silverblatt sums up the logic at work in the Peruvian Inquisition, which the Mexican tribunal fully shared: "The Inquisition represented itself as it was perceived by many: as the defender of the colony's religious and civic order. Its job was to protect the viceroyalty from enemies within, from the heretics—fraudulent *beatas* [holy women], witches, blasphemers, bigamists, adulterers, and hidden Jews—who would undermine the Spanish empire and civilization, one and the same. Its purview was religious crime; but as the Inquisition explained to everyone—to the Supreme Council, to the viceroy, to the king, and to the people—its mission was unmistakably political."[84] The reaction to the scandal in Tecamachalco alerts us to the extent to which this political mission required defending the Inquisition's symbols.

The strict protocol and the presence of the most important dignitaries in the viceroyalty during its ceremonies underscored the solemnity of the Inquisition's business and the respect that everyone was required to demonstrate toward the tribunal and its symbols.[85] Take, for instance, the "standard of faith," a banner made of crimson damask with a cross of gilded silver (Figure 10). On 4 November 1571, the then-fiscal of the Inquisition, Licenciado Bonilla, carried the standard of faith during the Mexican tribunal's first public ceremony, during which Inquisitor Moya de Contreras took the oath from everyone present to support the work of the Inquisition.[86]

Without any authority other than their own, the conspirators used the sambenitos to defame Hernando Rubio Naranjo at the little auto de fe outside the church of Tecamachalco. What were the deeds of this "Comendador of Mount Calvary" that deserved a punishment reserved for heinous

Figure 10. Standard of faith (showing cross with sword and olive branch on either side). Notice the effigies carried on poles wearing *sambenitos* and *corozas*. Detail from Adrian Schoonebeck, *Procession to the Auto da Fé*, in Van Limborch, *Historia Inquisitionis* (Amsterdam, 1692). Kenneth Spencer Research Library, University of Kansas.

crimes? What was the meaning of the strange symbols on the effigy—the double face, the different tongues, and so on? Who could have organized his execution in effigy, and why? Before they could answer these questions and punish all those involved in the conspiracy against Rubio Naranjo, the inquisitors had to learn the most intimate details of a relatively small community.

CHAPTER ONE

False Start

On 27 July 1578, the *alcalde mayor* of Tepeaca, Jorge Cerón Carvajal, requested the prompt intervention of Fray Rodrigo de Seguera, the Inquisition's commissioner for the Franciscan Order in Mexico, to resolve a crime in Tecamachalco.[1] The alcalde mayor told Fray Rodrigo that on 21 July, Fray Jaime Navarro, a Franciscan, found two sambenitos, two signs, and a "statue" (*estatua de bulto*) with insults against a town resident, Hernando Rubio Naranjo, outside Tecamachalco's church. The friar immediately removed them and gave them to Fray Cristóbal del Barrio, the prior in charge of the Franciscan monastery. (In his rush, Fray Jaime missed one sambenito nailed to the church's facade, which Pedro Beristain, "the younger," later removed upon his mother's orders.)[2] The alcalde mayor immediately launched an investigation into this "grave offense" against Rubio Naranjo. It would serve God and the king, the alcalde mayor told the Franciscan commissioner, if "such a great evil deed" were punished; "the just" should not suffer at the hands of "evildoers." In order to complete his investigation into this "affair among laymen" and punish the culprits, the alcalde mayor needed the offending objects as a key piece of evidence. However, Tecamachalco's Franciscan prior refused to hand over the effigy and the sambenitos to the alcalde mayor, claiming that he did not have them. In a letter to Commissioner Fray Rodrigo, the alcalde mayor asked him to order the prior to turn in the sambenitos and the statue.

Rather than comply with the alcalde mayor's request, Fray Rodrigo personally brought the letter to the Inquisition in Mexico City and, on 30 July, explained to Inquisitor Licenciado Alonso Fernández de Bonilla that he knew nothing more about the matter in the letter.[3] Realizing the gravity of the incident, Licenciado Bonilla and the other inquisitor, Licenciado Alonso Granero Dávalos, immediately issued a decree ordering the alcalde mayor of Tepeaca to surrender to the Inquisition all information and the suspects related to his case.[4] The strategy of Tepeaca's alcalde mayor had backfired: the Holy Office of the Inquisition would now take over the investigation of the scandal in Tecamachalco.

What was the name of the crime that took place in Tecamachalco over which the inquisitors claimed sole jurisdiction? It defied the usual categories of heresy, such as blasphemy and desecration, and sexually immoral acts—including bigamy and sexual solicitation by clergymen. This case was different. The alcalde mayor of Tepeaca launched an investigation into the *delito*, or crime, of injuring a person's reputation. In his letter to Fray Rodrigo de Seguera, the alcalde mayor stated that the effigy and the sambenitos in Tecamachalco had gravely injured a "third party." Hernando Rubio Naranjo had woken up on 21 July 1578 to the news that someone had publicly besmirched his name. Someone had branded him a Jew, which constituted a serious insult in early modern Spanish society, whether in the Iberian Peninsula or in its territories across the world. Starting in the mid-sixteenth century, an increasing number of laws banned those unable to demonstrate "purity of blood" from offices, professions, and most honors (those with purity of blood had no Jewish or Muslim ancestors). In the eyes of their neighbors and of the Inquisition, the New Christians remained suspect of secretly keeping their old faith. Authorities widely accepted that calling someone a Jew constituted a punishable offense that might even excuse the defamed victim for taking revenge on the defamer. To defend one's name and honor was to defend one's life. Dishonor turned a person into a social outcast and, in some cases, made life unbearable.

Yet the inquisitors did not take the accusations that Hernando Rubio Naranjo was a Jew seriously. Calling someone a Jew had become a common insult, and the Inquisition tried to stamp out this practice.[5] The inquisitors learned that Rubio Naranjo was a thirty-five-year-old unmarried man who traded between Tecamachalco and Oaxaca, whose wealth was estimated at between three and four thousand pesos.[6] (Rubio Naranjo would later describe a neighbor with four thousand pesos as a rich man.) In addition, Rubio Naranjo had family ties to the wife of a judge (*oidor*) of the Audiencia of Mexico.[7] Neither his wealth nor his family connections would be of much interest to the inquisitors; the inquisitors considered the scandal a grave offense, but their concern had little to do with Rubio Naranjo's tarnished reputation.

When it came time to identify the investigation and subsequent trial, the alcalde mayor of Tepeaca labeled it vaguely as a "criminal trial about certain crimes committed in the town of Tecamachalco against Rubio Naranjo."[8]

Those crimes (plural) included the attempt to defame him. Yet the defamation of a layman itself did not fall under the Inquisition's purview. The scandal involved another type of crime: the appropriation of symbols that belonged to the Inquisition, "in great contempt and disrespect of this Tribunal."[9] Since such disrespect ultimately obstructed the tribunal's work, the inquisitors claimed exclusive jurisdiction to investigate and punish those who put up the sambenitos.

An early seventeenth-century definition of "sambenito" was "the device [*insignia*] of the Holy Inquisition, which it places on the chest and the back of a reconciled penitent." The name derives from the Latin *saco benedicto*, or blessed sackcloth:

> As is known, in the primitive Church those who made public penance wore certain sackcloth or hair shirts, blessed by a bishop or a priest; with them [the penitents] stood by the doors of churches until they had served their penance, were absolved of their sins, and were admitted with the rest of the faithful into the fold of the Church. From this [practice], it was decided that the Holy Inquisition would put the same sackcloth on penitents. Thus, even though the world may see them as an ignominy and an affront, if those who wear them patiently bear what the rabble says, it will be of great merit to God.[10]

The last sentence indicates the double meaning of the sambenito: to the Inquisition, it was a sign of reconciliation; but to the "the world," it was a great dishonor. It was in the latter sense that everyone seemed to understand the sambenitos of Tecamachalco.

Whatever the specific motives, whether heretical or not, it seemed obvious that the culprit, or culprits, misused the sambenitos for an evil purpose without the Inquisition's consent. Whoever planned, carried out, knew about, or encouraged these actions shared responsibility for illegally usurping the Inquisition's symbols for reasons that the tribunal would thoroughly, and ruthlessly, investigate.

CHAPTER TWO

Trial and Failure

A Town Full of Suspects

On 28 August 1578, the inquisitors began to review the information collected as part of the investigation launched by the alcalde mayor of Tepeaca into the effigy and the sambenitos discovered on 21 July. The documentation amounted to twenty-one folios, or forty-two pages, of testimony from eleven witnesses and suspects interrogated after the incident.

The alcalde mayor arrested several suspects, based largely on information provided by the victim of the libel, Hernando Rubio Naranjo. The greatest suspicions fell upon three men: Francisco Miguel, Pedro Hernández, and Juan López de Montalbán. The first two had been involved in suspicious activities on Sunday evening, 20 July. Francisco Miguel had arrived in Tecamachalco only five days earlier. A thirty-two-year-old mestizo shoemaker, he was the son of a glassmaker from Mexico City, where he was born. He now lived in Chalcoatengo, on Lake Xochimilco, about sixty-five miles northwest of Tecamachalco. When asked the reason for his visit, Miguel explained that he had come to collect a debt owed to him by a local trader. After collecting his payment, another shoemaker in town invited him to help with his work.

On 20 July at sunset, three young men arrived on horses at the place where Miguel was lodging. Pedro Hernández, a twenty-one-year-old mestizo from Tecamachalco, tended his father's goats "in God's fields." For Hernández, who had lived his entire life in town and had left only twice to travel to Mexico City, the older Francisco Miguel must have seemed a man of the world. Hernández's two other companions were even younger: Juan Morillo, a nineteen- or twenty-year-old Spaniard from Córdoba, who was beardless, had a swollen cheek and jaw, and worked for his uncle; and Lope Jaramillo, *el mozo* ("the younger"), aged nineteen, who worked for his cattle rancher father.[1] The three young men asked Miguel to bring his little dog and come with them to hunt wild turkeys (*gallinas monteses*) while there was still daylight. Off they went into the countryside.

After killing two wild turkeys, Hernández invited his companions for supper at his house. After dinner, they played guitar and listened to Francisco Miguel speak in *guineo*, the broken Spanish of recently arrived African slaves. He was so good at it that one of his new friends exclaimed: "This lad's a devil the way he speaks in black!" (*¡Diabólico es este mozo como habla en negro!*).[2] The four friends set out to serenade the town with their guitar and to show off Miguel's black routine. "Here we bring the best black in all of New Spain!"—Hernández told two passersby, who dismounted their horses to join the group. One of them replied: "In that case, we won't sleep all night!"

By ten that night, the band of revelers had grown to seven. One of them proposed visiting the trader Hernando Rubio Naranjo, who lived across from the church. After several weeks in Oaxaca, Rubio Naranjo had returned to Tecamachalco only a week earlier. When they reached the trader's house, the revelers asked Francisco Miguel to call out to Rubio Naranjo "in black language." Miguel asked his companions, "Who is this man?" Lope Jaramillo replied: "He's a man with an evil tongue. No man in this town is on good terms with him."[3] Miguel later remembered the name from the northern mining city of Zacatecas, where Rubio Naranjo had had some trouble with the authorities. Miguel walked up to the small front door and called out, "Rubio, come out here!"

Hernando Rubio Naranjo came out, accompanied by an Indian servant. It was dark, so he could not recognize the man calling to him in the black accent:

Hernando Rubio Naranjo: Is it Cotlastes?
Francisco Miguel: There's no Cotlastes here!
Rubio Naranjo: Is it Cristóbal?
Miguel: No!
Rubio Naranjo: Brother, what do you want? Who are you?
Miguel (still in black language): You don't know me now, but you'll know me tomorrow.[4]

The group then left Rubio Naranjo's house. He saw seven men out in the street but could not determine who they were because it was dark and the men's hats hid their faces. Rubio Naranjo went back inside his house.

The seven men continued their stroll around town, waking up neighbors with their guitar music, and stopping now and then to show off Francisco Miguel speaking in his black language. Everyone particularly enjoyed it when two African slave women came out to a window to talk to Miguel in his funny talk. It was getting late, so despite earlier vows to stay up all night, the group began to disperse and go home to sleep. Around eleven, the party ended where it had begun, at Pedro Hernández's house. Since it was already late, Hernández asked Miguel and another of the friends to sleep over. When later interrogated by the alcalde mayor, the three friends swore that they had slept until the next morning.

In addition to suspecting Francisco Miguel and Pedro Hernández, Rubio Naranjo informed the alcalde mayor that he had even greater suspicions about Juan López de Montalbán, a twenty-one-year-old collector of cochineal (cactus-eating insects used for making brilliant red dye). Born in the town of Menasalbas, in Toledo's archpriesthood of Montalbán, Juan López de Montalbán had resided in Tecamachalco for the last ten months. Rubio Naranjo declared that, on 22 July, the day after the sambenitos appeared in Tecamachalco, López de Montalbán allegedly said "ugly and injurious words" about him at a gathering on the Feast of Mary Magdalene in the neighboring town of Quecholac. There, the cochineal collector supposedly declared that the sambenitos were "little," compared with what Rubio Naranjo deserved.[5] The alcalde mayor of Tepeaca arrested López de Montalbán, who admitted having said that Rubio Naranjo had defamed many married women from Tecamachalco, but he otherwise denied insulting his neighbor.

Under orders from the inquisitors, the alcalde mayor sent two prisoners, Juan López de Montalbán and Pedro Hernández, to Mexico City. The inquisitors also wanted to interrogate the black-speaking Francisco Miguel. However, because of lack of evidence, the alcalde mayor did not arrest Miguel, who had since left the region.

On 30 August, a little over six weeks after the scandal, the cochineal collector Juan López de Montalbán made his first appearance before Inquisitor Bonilla.[6] When asked about the "ugly words" that he had allegedly spoken in Quecholac on the Feast of Mary Magdalene, López de Montalbán repeated his previous denials. However, he now revealed that, when Rubio Naranjo returned from Oaxaca, López de Montalbán had asked him, "Why did you come back?" He had also warned Rubio Naranjo that many in Tecamachalco wished him ill for defaming their women. On 2 September, during a second interrogation, López de Montalbán insisted that he had no specific knowledge of the actual incident with the sambenitos. He did not know the materials used to make the effigy. He could not write the "Gothic" letters on the signs accompanying the sambenitos. When the inquisitor finally presented López de Montalbán with the effigy and the sambenitos taken from the scene of the crime, the startled man could only exclaim, "May God reveal the truth out of His holy mercy!"

That same day, Pedro Hernández, the second man arrested by the alcalde mayor of Tepeaca and transferred to Mexico City, had even less to say to the inquisitors; he did not even know what a sambenito was. After the interrogation, Licenciado Bonilla allowed Hernández to return home. A week later, he also set López de Montalbán free on bail.

On 4 September, the inquisitors received a letter from the defamed Hernando Rubio Naranjo containing a long list of potential witnesses and individuals he suspected of involvement with the sambenitos of Tecamachalco.[7] Rubio Naranjo was unaware of the inquisitors' decision to free Juan López de Montalbán and Pedro Hernández, both of whom he continued to suspect, along with the following people:

1. Alonso Rodríguez, from Puebla: after defaulting on a loan for fifty pesos made by Rubio Naranjo, he called Rubio Naranjo a criminal (*facineroso*), a usurer, and a rabble-rouser (*rebolbedor de pueblos*) of "bad life and reputation," no conscience, and a "Jewish scoundrel" (*vellaco judío*). He also claimed that Rubio Naranjo ignored the Church's injunction to Catholics to avoid meat for Lent.

2. Francisco Miguel (whose name Rubio Naranjo did not recall), a mestizo: around ten on the evening before the sambenitos appeared, he came to Rubio Naranjo's house, calling to him in "black language." When Rubio Naranjo asked what he wanted, the mestizo responded in black language: "You don't know me now, but tomorrow you'll know me." Accompanying the mestizo were six men covered up (presumably with hats and cloaks), and for that reason Rubio Naranjo did not recognize them. The next day, when Rubio Naranjo came for his arrest after the discovery of the effigy and the sambenitos, the mestizo supposedly said, "Señor Rubio . . . I know why you have come to arrest me. I swear to God that all of those who came with me [to Rubio Naranjo's house] will go to jail, because I won't pay for the others."

3. Juana de Montoya, wife of Benito Galiano, from Tecamachalco: four or five months earlier, she came to Rubio Naranjo's door and said that she would make someone "tie a gag to the tip of your tongue." On a different occasion, she said the same thing, this time while he was in her house. Rumor in town had it that she was responsible for putting up the sambenitos, making Balmaceda, a male servant who tended her sheep, do it.

4. Luis de Cepeda, a mulatto saddle maker from Tecamachalco: he had warned Rubio Naranjo to await a letter of excommunication (which did not arrive).

5. Juan Pérez, a mestizo from Oaxaca: two days before Rubio Naranjo arrived from Oaxaca, Pérez came to Tecamachalco and hid inside his sister's house; he then left Tecamachalco the day after the discovery of the sambenitos.

6. Juan López, a mestizo from Tecamachalco (a cousin of the cochineal collector Juan López de Montalbán): he should declare whether on the night before the sambenitos appeared, the royal scribe Juan de Molina and the castizo *labrador* (farmer) Francisco Yáñez slept in López's house, which made Rubio Naranjo suspect them.

7. Martín López, a slave trader from Tecamachalco: One or two days after the 21 July incident, he asked Rubio Naranjo: "How much will you give me to shut up? . . . If you don't [pay], I'll say what I know." Although Rubio Naranjo was willing to pay, López did not tell him anything.

This list of suspects and potential witnesses represented a cross-section of Tecamachalco's society. Although most of them were poor, the wealth of the Spanish slave trader Martín López, the last man on the list, was valued at the considerable sum of four thousand pesos. The sole woman named on the list, Juana de Montoya, wife of the Spaniard Benito Galiano, who raised sheep and collected taxes in the meat markets of Tecamachalco and Tepeaca, was "a prosperous woman."[8]

On the morning of 11 September, a week after the inquisitors received Rubio Naranjo's letter with a long list of suspects, Juan López de Montalbán reappeared before Inquisitor Bonilla, this time voluntarily.[9] The former suspect had been "searching his memory and thinking about this business" and had pieced together hearsay from several sources to come up with a con-

voluted hypothesis about those responsible for the incident in Tecamachalco. His theory complemented some of Rubio Naranjo's vague suspicions.
The Gothic letters on the signs accompanying the effigy and the sambenitos, which López de Montalbán had first seen at his last inquisitorial audience, reminded him of the handwriting of a young, unmarried scribe named
Alonso García. A thin man in his twenties, with a "sickly" aspect and only a
few hairs on his beard, García looked like a eunuch (*capón*). He was in charge
of the accounting books for the meat markets because Juana de Montoya's
husband, who farmed the meat taxes, did not know how to write. López de
Montalbán had seen García write the title of one of those accounting books in
black letter and suggested comparing some of García's handwriting with that
on the signs accompanying the sambenitos.

Besides Alonso García and Juana de Montoya, López de Montalbán now
implicated a third suspect, the farmer Francisco Yáñez. Shortly after the discovery of the statue and the sambenitos, the alcalde mayor of Tepeaca rounded
up several young men and ordered them to stay in the city's inn until further
notice. López de Montalbán was among them. One day, he saw the eunuch-
looking scribe Alonso García bring roasted mutton "sent by another person" for
two other men held in Tepeaca, one of whom was Francisco Yáñez. Yáñez told
López de Montalbán, "I swear that many women in Tecamachalco have wept
over my imprisonment." López de Montalbán asked who these women were.
Yáñez replied, "I know that Juana de Montoya has wept much." López de Montalbán now wondered whether Montoya had asked Yáñez to put up the sambenitos, for which the scribe García could have written the signs. Further hearsay
supported this hypothesis. While in Tepeaca, López de Montalbán heard that,
several months previously, someone had drawn horns on the door of Montoya's
house. Rumor had it that Rubio Naranjo had done it. Moreover, Rubio Naranjo
had bragged to Yáñez that Montoya "had a big *natura*," or female genitalia.

López de Montalbán added a fourth suspect to his hypothetical plot.
Someone besides the scribe Alonso García could have written the signs for
the sambenitos. Juan de Molina, "a very good scribe" from Tepeaca, also knew
black letter, as could be seen in the books of his father, the scribe Francisco de
Molina. Moreover, everyone who visited the imprisoned López de Montalbán
accused Juan de Molina and Francisco Yáñez, who were "great friends," of
involvement in the scandal. As Rubio Naranjo reported in his list of suspects,
Molina and Yáñez had slept in the same house the night before the discovery of the sambenitos. Shortly after the incident, Molina left town. López de
Montalbán had nothing more to tell the Inquisitor; he had said plenty.

The testimonies of Juan López de Montalbán and Hernando Rubio Naranjo appeared to agree on the rough outlines of a plot that involved four or more persons. Both suspected Montoya, who was on bad terms with Rubio Naranjo, of ordering "a servant," perhaps along with Yáñez, to put up the effigy and the sambenitos in Tecamachalco. This was as far as the two testimonies coincided. López de Montalbán suspected that Montoya's "servant" may have been Alonso García; Rubio Naranjo thought that it was a certain Balmaceda. Everyone seemed to know that the two friends Yáñez and Molina had spent the night before the incident together, although it remained unclear what role Molina may have played. López de Montalbán suspected that the scribe Molina may have written the signs *if* García had not done it; Rubio Naranjo said nothing of the sort. Moreover, Rubio Naranjo continued to suspect López de Montalbán, in addition to several other men.

To add to this jumble of speculation and gossip, on 18 September, one week after López de Montalbán's voluntary declaration, Licenciado Bonilla received a second letter from Rubio Naranjo that only further confused the matter. It began: "Most Illustrious and Reverend Señor: I have to inform your lordship that, ten or twelve days ago, in this town of Tecamachalco, a young man named Juan Gómez, recently married, put a certain libel on a physician named Espinosa, and hung from his door a bundle of wood, branding him a burned man. I understand that [Juan Gómez] habitually does these things; and I am told that he knows about my affair. Your lordship, for the love of God, look into this matter."[10]

That was just the beginning. Rubio Naranjo added yet another suspect not mentioned in the long list he had previously submitted to the Inquisition. Pedro Ruiz, a rich man with a wealth estimated at five thousand pesos, had been away from Tecamachalco on 21 July, the day of the incident with the sambenitos. Previously, Rubio Naranjo had had a tiff (*enoxuelo*) with Ruiz and his wife. More important, Ruiz used to feed and let sleep in his home none other than Juan López de Montalbán. The alcalde mayor of Tepeaca told Rubio Naranjo that Ruiz and López de Montalbán had carried out the crime in Tecamachalco. Two additional rumors reaffirmed the suspicions about Ruiz. First, Ruiz allegedly inquired whether López de Montalbán had been freed from the Inquisition's prison; and second, a Spanish-speaking Indian woman (*india ladina*) overheard Ruiz uttering certain unspecified, and presumably ill, "words" about Rubio Naranjo before the latter's return from Oaxaca (where Rubio Naranjo had defamed the women of Tecamachalco). "For the love of God," Rubio Naranjo implored Licenciado Bonilla, "I beg your lordship to look into it for my justice, as a Christian; and this is the present situation to report to your lordship." Yet this was not the end of the letter.

Rubio Naranjo's rambling letter offered more suggestions. The inquisitor should command the guardian friar of Tecamachalco's Franciscan monastery to read in church an edict requiring anyone with information on the case to declare it or face excommunication. Rubio Naranjo also included a confusing reminder of the threats made by Juan López de Montalbán, whom he now described as "a very good scribe" who had twice been a friar. Rubio Naranjo emphatically added one final comment. He could not comprehend why the alcalde mayor had freed "the mestizo" (Francisco Miguel), who had fled Tecamachalco. He offered to apprehend the mestizo if the inquisitor sent him a warrant for his arrest. Rubio Naranjo had nothing more to add.

Licenciado Bonilla added no marginal comments or underlining to Rubio Naranjo's second letter. Had the "Most Illustrious and Reverend Señor" not found the latest information as urgent and helpful as Rubio Naranjo considered it to be? More likely, Rubio Naranjo's desperate missive only confirmed that the investigation had stalled.

Dead End

Less than two months after the incident of 21 July, the Inquisition's investigation had reached an impasse. The alcalde mayor of Tepeaca's investigation, lasting about ten days, had resulted in the arrest of several men, with most of them freed and no conclusive evidence. The inquisitors had devoted nearly six weeks to the investigation but still could not identify the culprit or culprits. It was clear from the testimonies collected thus far that Tecamachalco suffered from an excess of gossip and speculation about who put up the effigy and the sambenitos.

The inquisitors failed to identify a single credible suspect, but they now had an unflattering portrait of the victim of the defamation, thus shedding light on the meaning of the effigy. Hernando Rubio Naranjo had a reputation as a "Jewish scoundrel" not because of any real suspicion about his heritage but because of what the sign on the effigy described as his "great deeds, which are known to everyone." Had he been a Christian of good reputation, would someone have accused him of eating meat during Lent, or told him to expect a letter of excommunication? A mere tiff with his neighbors would not have garnered him a reputation as a "criminal," a "usurer," and a "rabble-rouser." Like his effigy, the two-faced Rubio Naranjo had a loose and sharp tongue, which he unleashed to defame neighbors who considered him a friend. He had allegedly bragged about Montoya's large genitalia and supposedly insulted her husband by drawing horns on the door of their house. The gag on one of the effigy's tongues must have reminded Rubio Naranjo of her threat to have someone "gag the tip of your tongue." The second tongue on the effigy was forked, "like a viper's," according to one testimony.[11] Likewise, Rubio Naranjo's tongue had spread poisonous rumors in the city of Oaxaca about several women from Tecamachalco. It is no wonder that López de Montalbán asked Rubio Naranjo why he had returned home after what he had done in Oaxaca.

Referring to Rubio Naranjo's reputation in Tecamachalco, one witness summed up the motivation for the use of the sambenitos, as well as the meaning of the signs and of some of the effigy's attributes. She explained that "all in town, men and women were on bad terms with him," calling Rubio Naranjo "a loose-tongued scoundrel" (vellaco deslenguado).[12] Whoever defamed Rubio Naranjo most likely did it in revenge for his insults.

Since the discovery of the effigy and the sambenitos, everyone presumed that such an elaborate plot required the participation of more than one person. Rubio Naranjo was in the habit of insulting women. According to witnesses, the effigy's careful stitches betrayed the work of a woman.[13] It therefore seemed likely that a woman had been the intellectual author of the crime, or at least its instigator. She would have needed the assistance of one or more men, one of them capable of writing the careful Gothic letters of the signs.

Such insights into the meaning and motivations behind Rubio Naranjo's execution in effigy provided important clues about the identity of the culprits. There was one obvious problem: too many people in Tecamachalco and its surroundings fit that identity. Rubio Naranjo's bad reputation in town made it virtually impossible to narrow down the list of suspects. By his own count, Rubio Naranjo suspected more than a dozen individuals he could name:

1. Juan López de Montalbán, the cochineal collector
2. Juan López (mestizo, cousin of Juan López de Montalbán)
3. Martín López (not related to Juan López), a rich Spanish slave trader
4. Luis de Cepeda, a mulatto saddle maker
5. Juan Gómez, the man who hung a bundle of wood from the physician Espinosa's door
6. Juan de Molina, the Spanish royal scribe
7. Juan Pérez, a mestizo horseshoe maker

8.   Alonso Rodríguez, who called Rubio Naranjo a usurer
9.   Pedro Ruiz, who had had a tiff with Rubio Naranjo
10. Francisco Yáñez, a castizo farmer
11. Juana de Montoya, the woman with the "big nature"
12. Juana de Montoya's husband's servant Balmaceda
13. Francisco Miguel, the mestizo shoemaker who spoke "in black"
14–19. The six unidentified men who accompanied Francisco Miguel on the night of 20 July.

One would have to add Juana de Montoya's cuckolded husband, the sheep- and tax-farmer Benito Galiano, not to mention the husbands and male relatives of the women Rubio Naranjo had insulted in Oaxaca.

Not surprisingly, following the receipt of Rubio Naranjo's second letter—on 18 September, containing the names of additional suspects—the investigation came to a halt. After that date, there were no more arrests, no more depositions, and no more serious leads to pursue. One might surmise that the inquisitors simply lost interest in the case of defamation against a man whose reputation everyone in town seemed to have a reason for injuring. However, the Inquisition's real interest in the case lay elsewhere: in the misuse of its symbols. The inquisitors could not willingly have given up the opportunity to defend the tribunal's authority, even in provincial Tecamachalco. The investigation had simply reached a dead end. In the meantime, the ugly San Benito continued to stick out its tongues at the inquisitors as an annoying reminder that the Holy Tribunal had failed to crack its mystery.

PART II

1581

CHAPTER THREE

Surprise Witness

In Mexico City, before the Señores Inquisitors Licenciados Bonilla and Santos García, during the morning audience on 27 October 1581, a man came without being called, and swore to tell the truth. His testimony read:

> DIEGO DE TRUJILLO, a farmer from San Pablo, near Tecamachalco, originally from Ciudad Real, in Spain; age: forty-two years old, more or less;
>
> SAID that he came to say and to declare before this Office that, while on his farm, two leagues [about six miles] from Tecamachalco, about two and a half or three years ago, more or less, he heard that several sambenitos had been put up in Tecamachalco against a certain Rubio Naranjo. In this matter, he did not know how many had been arrested, and it was never known who had done it. [Then] about two months ago, he was walking from San Pablo to Quecholac (one league [about three miles] from Tecamachalco) alongside Francisco Yáñez, a castizo farmer from Quecholac; Francisco Hernández, a servant; and several Indians who worked the fields . . . [As they were walking, Trujillo overheard] the said Francisco Yáñez and Francisco Hernández talking about certain signs recently discovered in Tepeaca.[1]

Diego de Trujillo went on to recount the conversation between Yáñez and Hernández, which led to an unexpected revelation:

> *Francisco Hernández*: They haven't found out who did it
>   [in Tepeaca] . . . just like with the sambenitos put up in
>   Tecamachalco against Hernando Rubio Naranjo. . . .

Francisco Yáñez: Don't you know who put up those [in
  Tecamachalco]?
Hernández: No.
Yáñez: Well, I know.
Hernández: Then why don't you go to the Inquisition? You'll be
  excommunicated.
Yáñez: They never threatened excommunication; if they had, I would
  have already gone.
Hernández: Then who put them up?
Yáñez: I think Juan Pérez brought them from Oaxaca in small
  pieces, and his stepmother Juana Muñoz put them together and
  finished them;[2] and Juan Pérez and his half-brother Francisco
  Pérez . . . put them up [in Tecamachalco].
Hernández: How do you know this?
Yáñez: Someone told me. . . . That person had asked [Juan Pérez's
  stepmother] Juana Muñoz how she had dared to do that, and she
  had replied, "What do I know about what that was or wasn't for,
  or that it was such a big deal?"

After a few additional details about the woman and her two sons, Diego
de Trujillo had nothing more to declare. Yet the inquisitors had questions
about this unexpected new information on an old unresolved case:

Inquisitors: Who else might know about this business?
Diego de Trujillo: I suspect Francisco Yáñez's mother-in-law, who
  lives in Quecholac, may have been the person who told her
  son-in-law.
Inquisitors: Have you made this declaration out of hatred or enmity
  toward anyone?
Trujillo: No. I've come because the friars in Quecholac I talked to
  told me to inform the Holy Office, which would give me two
  hundred lashes if I didn't declare what I'd heard. . . . I understand
  that Francisco Yáñez and Francisco Hernández will also come,
  because they were also told to do so.

As was customary with all Inquisition witnesses, the inquisitors ordered
Trujillo to keep secret everything he had said or risk excommunication.
Inquisitor Bonilla did not record his reaction to this unexpected declara-

tion about a case that remained unresolved after more than three years. He had been one of the inquisitors in 1578. The other inquisitor, Alonso Granero Dávalos, had become bishop of Charcas (now Sucre, Bolivia), in the viceroyalty of Peru.[3] Licenciado Bonilla must have welcomed Dávalos's departure, since the two men had strong differences, which Dávalos ascribed to Bonilla's jealousy.[4] The new inquisitor, Licenciado Santos García, had risen from his post as prosecuting attorney (*fiscal*) in the Mexican Inquisition. The two inquisitors now had a second opportunity to investigate the scandal that had defied the Inquisition's authority.

However, a quick solution to the case was unlikely. Diego de Trujillo's statements were vague. The witness recounted one conversation overheard (between Yáñez and Hernández) about a second conversation (between Yáñez and an unnamed person, possibly his mother-in-law) based on yet another conversation thrice removed (between the unnamed person and Juana Muñoz). This new evidence did not differ much from the endless gossip and suspicions that ultimately frustrated the investigation back in 1578. Three years later, the new evidence provided a variation on the initial assumption that the scandal was probably the work of more than one individual instigated by one or more women, who had been the victims of Rubio Naranjo's sharp tongue. In the latest version, the alleged plot involved two men (the half-brothers Juan and Francisco Pérez) and one woman (their mother and stepmother Juana Muñoz). Yet the story did not indicate a motive for the incident. Juana Muñoz had not been the victim of Rubio Naranjo's insults, and the relationship between Rubio Naranjo and the two Pérez brothers remained unknown. Allegedly, Muñoz had simply helped her stepson, Juan, who carried out the deed along with his half-brother, Francisco. If the hearsay was true, she did not care to know her stepson's motives for an action that she did not think was very serious.

Although it was vague, the inquisitors decided to look into Diego de Trujillo's denunciation. On 30 October, three days after his unexpected testimony, they issued an arrest warrant for the horseshoe maker Juan Pérez for putting up the effigy and the sambenitos in July 1578. They would also order the interrogation of the other individuals whom Trujillo mentioned. With these actions, the inquisitors officially reopened the Tecamachalco case.

* * *

Diego de Trujillo's revelations would prove crucial to the investigation in ways that neither he nor the inquisitors could have imagined. It would become clear that his motivations for denunciation were not as simple as he had stated, and the inquisitors and their subordinates would make a number of assumptions that would lead them to dead ends. This was not entirely their fault. Given the absence of any hard evidence, the officials of the Inquisition had no choice but to step into the labyrinth of gossip, rumors, and secrets at the very heart of the scandal in Tecamachalco. Separating truth from lie was very difficult even for those who knew the ins and outs of the love affairs and animosities that made up much of everyday life in this region of Mexico. As a result, the dizzying amount of gossip and rumor that derailed the first investigation would almost do so again. Unbeknownst to nearly everyone, many of the dead ends and apparently irrelevant information were part of a strategy to avoid capture—a strategy that would become evident only at the very end of the case.

CHAPTER FOUR

The Mother, the Son, and the Stepson

Puebla, 2–4 November 1581

On the evening of Thursday, 2 November 1581, the Inquisition's notary (*notario del juzgado*), the Valencia native Jerónimo de Euguí, arrived in the city of Puebla carrying the inquisitors' order to the Inquisition's commissioner general of Puebla, whose jurisdiction included the town of Tecamachalco. The trip from Mexico City to Puebla took the notary the usual three days, and was otherwise uneventful.[1] After a night's rest, on Friday morning Notary Euguí delivered the inquisitors' letter to the commissioner Alonso Hernández de Santiago, canon of the cathedral chapter of Puebla.

Canon Santiago had a difficult challenge ahead of him. As the Inquisition's commissioner, he would have to carry out two different, though interrelated, investigations. The first consisted of looking into the convoluted series of assertions that the farmer Diego de Trujillo had made in the previous month about the authors of the effigy and the sambenitos of Tecamachalco in 1578. The second consisted of revisiting the testimonies collected during the first, and failed, investigation, which had taken place between July and September 1578. The commissioner's double investigation required reviewing dozens of pages of old testimony, which Notary Euguí must have brought with him from Mexico City, along with the effigy and the sambenitos. In addition, interviewing dozens of men and women would take several weeks of travel to several towns in the region. Two things made Canon Santiago's mission especially difficult. First, a number of key witnesses had left the region or, in some cases, were no longer alive. Second, all available witnesses remembered the scandal in Tecamachalco, but after nearly three and a half years, memories were fading about many of the details needed to resolve the case.

Canon Santiago therefore needed to conduct a speedy interrogation of the surviving witnesses. Fortunately for him, Puebla was only thirty miles from Tecamachalco. Whereas it had taken Notary Euguí three days to travel from Mexico City to Puebla, it would take only hours to travel from Puebla to the towns and cities where most of the witnesses lived.

Perhaps the most important witness whom Canon Santiago would need to examine was the farmer Francisco Yáñez, who allegedly knew the authors of the scandal in Tecamachalco. He lived in the town of Quecholac, about thirty miles east of Puebla. Yáñez's mother-in-law, Catalina Gómez, the supposed source of Yáñez's information, lived in Quecholac as well. A few miles south, the village of San Pablo was home to the servant Francisco Hernández, to whom Yáñez had revealed the names of the Tecamachalco conspirators in the conversation overheard by Diego de Trujillo. However, Canon Santiago would not be able to interrogate the most important witness, horseshoe maker Juan Pérez, the supposed mastermind of the conspiracy, who lived in Oaxaca, beyond Canon Santiago's jurisdiction. Neither could he interrogate Juan Pérez's half-brother and alleged coconspirator, Francisco Pérez, who was dead. In the absence of the two brothers, Canon Santiago could at least interrogate Juana Muñoz, Juan and Francisco Pérez's stepmother and mother, respectively. She lived in Tepeaca, where the Inquisition's commissioner and notary would make their first stop.

Tepeaca, 4–7 November 1581

On Saturday, 4 November, Canon Santiago and Notary Euguí arrived in Tepeaca and lodged at the Franciscan monastery, across from the town hall and the jail on the city's plaza. From there, they issued orders for the first witnesses to appear before them. On the following Tuesday, Francisco Hernández came and confirmed the general outlines of the conversation that Diego de Trujillo had reported to the inquisitors, in which Yáñez had told Hernández the names of the supposed conspirators behind the scandal in Tecamachalco.[2] The servant Hernández remembered hearing from Yáñez that the alleged mastermind was from Oaxaca, but he could not recall his name. Pressed to provide further details, Hernández explained that Trujillo and Yáñez argued over the matter two or three times, but he did not hear what the two farmers said to each other because they were riding ahead of him on their horses. Hernández told the Inquisition's commissioner that Trujillo urged him to report to the inquisitors what Yáñez had said, but the servant replied, "Let him who knows this better do it, because I don't know anything." Asked about Yáñez's whereabouts, Hernández said that the farmer had been absent from Quecholac for the last eight or nine days and may have gone to Puebla or to Mexico City.[3]

Quecholac, 7–9 November 1581

In search of Francisco Yáñez, Canon Santiago and Notary Euguí arrived in Quecholac the same day, but no one knew where Yáñez was. Before the end of the day, they did have time to interrogate Catalina Gómez, Yáñez's mother-in-law and his supposed source of information about the authors of the delinquent acts in Tecamachalco. She was a forty-year-old Spaniard—a native of Badajoz, in Extremadura. She was married, although her husband "was absent." Her daughter was married to Yáñez. Gómez remembered the 1578 incidents because at the time, she was living in Tecamachalco. In October of that year, she moved to Puebla, and now lived in Quecholac, where her daughter and son-in-law lived. Everywhere she went, the scandal had become a topic of conversation. She recalled having had one especially revealing exchange in Puebla on the subject with María de Vargas (now dead), the former lover of the wronged trader Hernando Rubio Naranjo, who was the father of Vargas's daughter. Not long after the incident in Tecamachalco, Gómez visited Vargas and asked her about Rubio Naranjo. Vargas replied that, if she and Rubio Naranjo had not "fallen out with each other . . . she would have avenged him for the sambenitos that had been put up against him."[4] Gómez then corrected herself and said that actually, Vargas did not mention any sambenitos, but rather, that she would avenge Rubio Naranjo for something she had heard from another Puebla neighbor, Juana Muñoz. Vargas and Muñoz had been talking, when Vargas relayed the news about the scandalous incident in Tecamachalco. On hearing what happened, Muñoz exclaimed, "Oh, poor old me if my son is traveling around there!"[5] Naturally, this outburst made Vargas suspect that Muñoz knew something about the affair. This was all Gómez had to tell the Inquisition's commissioner.

Canon Santiago was not satisfied with the testimony and threatened Catalina Gómez with "grave punishment" if she did not tell the truth. She now related a more recent conversation that had taken place a few months earlier at the home of her son-in-law, Francisco Yáñez. After dinner, she, Yáñez, the farmer Diego de Trujillo, and others sat around the table talking. The subject of defamatory "papers" recently put up in Tepeaca came up, which made

everyone recall the similar incident three years earlier in Tecamachalco. Trujillo remarked: "Poor Tecamachalco, so unfortunate, it never lacks some misfortune!" "You're right," Yáñez replied. This prompted Gómez to tell them
about her conversation with the late María de Vargas.

Asked about the whereabouts of her son-in-law, Gómez explained to
Canon Santiago that, twelve days earlier, Yáñez had gone to Tlaxcala to collect an inheritance left by his mother, who had recently died. Canon Santiago
urged her to come back the following day, in case she remembered anything
else. If she had anything else to add to her deposition, Gómez told the commissioner, "I would have said so rather than wait for later."[6] Since she had
nothing more to declare, the interrogation ended.

The next day, 8 November, Catalina Gómez did have something to add to
her previous testimony.[7] A little over a month earlier, on 24 September 1581,
the Feast of Our Lady of September, she saw Diego de Trujillo at the home
of a neighbor. She had heard that he was going to Mexico City, and said to
him, "For your life, tell me the reason you're going away." Trujillo said that
he was going to report what her son-in-law had told Francisco Hernández
on the road from San Pablo to Quecholac, where Yáñez had accused Juan
Pérez, Francisco Pérez, and Juana Muñoz of being behind the 1578 scandal
in Tecamachalco. Trujillo's words "saddened" her, since the matter involved
her son-in-law. When she saw Yáñez later that evening, she warned him that
it would be better to tell the inquisitors what he knew about the affair before
Trujillo did. Yáñez swore to God that he did not say what Trujillo accused
him of saying: Trujillo was a lying drunk, and Yáñez would deny the accusation to his face. That was the first and last time that Gómez raised the matter
with her son-in-law. Canon Santiago was not pleased. He accused Gómez
of not declaring this in her first testimony in order to protect Yáñez, but she
insisted that she did not know anything more.

Canon Santiago: Then what was the purpose of asking Trujillo so
   insistently to tell you his reason for going to Mexico City?
Catalina Gómez: Because it involved my son-in-law, and I was sad
   and worried that he might have done something. A friar in
   Quecholac . . . had also warned me after confession to tell my
   son-in-law to think about what had happened in Tecamachalco
   three or four years ago and to discharge his conscience as the
   Christian that he was, because a man had denounced my son-in-
   law. I wasn't told the man's name or the matter.

That was all Gómez had come to report. But Canon Santiago was not finished; he wanted to review the previous day's testimony:

> *Canon Santiago*: Who else was present when María de Vargas told you that Juana Muñoz had said, "Oh poor old me if my son is traveling around there"? Where did she tell you this?
> *Catalina Gómez*: María de Vargas said this in her house in Puebla. I had gone to visit her because she had a sick son. No one else was present—just the two of them alone.

Gómez went on to explain that four or five days after that conversation, Vargas came to her house after her confessor had ordered her to take back the "unwarranted and baseless" suspicions about Juana Muñoz. Gómez did not know if Vargas had ever asked Muñoz for pardon. Nonetheless, Gómez had not believed Vargas's belated recantation, and told her son-in-law that "it could only be that . . . Juana Muñoz and her sons were guilty in this affair." Gómez now admitted that her suspicions were baseless. The interrogation continued:

> *Canon Santiago*: Then why did you tell your son-in-law that you were suspicious of Juana Muñoz?
> *Catalina Gómez*: Deep down, I always had this suspicion and couldn't get it out of my heart.

After Gómez revealed her suspicions to her confessor, he ordered her to ask for Muñoz's pardon. Gómez agreed to do so if she were to see Muñoz. With that, the interrogation ended.

On 9 November, Francisco Yáñez appeared before Canon Santiago to clear the record and establish what he knew about the Tecamachalco affair. As the son of a mestiza and a Portuguese man, Yáñez was a castizo, but those who did not know his parents sometimes guessed that he was Spanish or mestizo.[8] The thirty-year-old farmer, a native of Tecamachalco, had recently married a sixteen-year-old mestiza from Quecholac, where they resided. His name had come up several times in 1578 during the initial investigation by the alcalde mayor of Tepeaca, who imprisoned Yáñez but later released him for lack of evidence. Three years later, Yáñez came before Canon Santiago not as a suspect in the crime but as a witness who allegedly knew its authors.

Asked if he knew the reason that they had called him to testify, Yáñez imagined that it was about what the farmer Diego de Trujillo had gone to declare in Mexico City before the inquisitors regarding an after-dinner conversation at his house a few months earlier.[9] Yáñez had invited Trujillo for dinner. The conversation revolved around the incidents in 1578 involving the sambenitos put up against Rubio Naranjo. They were talking about the possible reason for some of the arrests, when Yáñez's mother-in-law, Catalina Gómez, related a conversation that she had had with a woman, now deceased, named Vargas— perhaps her full name was Isabel de Vargas, but Yáñez could not remember. Yáñez admitted that Trujillo had warned him to declare what he knew to the inquisitors, but Yáñez replied, "Then for your life, take matters into your own hands." Yáñez, in turn, warned his mother-in-law that she might need to report her own suspicions about Juana Muñoz to the inquisitors.

Thus far, Yáñez's testimony was consistent with what his mother-in-law had declared. Then he added new information based on other conversations. According to Yáñez, Rubio Naranjo once told him that the late Vargas, who everyone knew had been Rubio Naranjo's "friend," had accused the horseshoe maker Juan Pérez and his half-brother Francisco of carrying the sambenitos from Puebla to Tecamachalco. Next, Yáñez related various conversations he had had about the subject with Diego de Trujillo, his mother-in-law, and his mother-in-law's sister (Leonor Gómez). All of them discussed their suspicions about Juan and Francisco Pérez and their stepmother and mother, Juana Muñoz. Yáñez suggested that Alonso Pérez, brother-in-law of Juan and Francisco Pérez, who lived in Tepeaca, might know more about this matter.

Canon Santiago read Yáñez the long testimony that Trujillo had given to the inquisitors the previous month. Was there anything else Yáñez wished to declare? He did have one more thing to add to the declaration. It was rumored that in 1578, someone had brought the sambenitos from Oaxaca, where Rubio Naranjo had spoken ill of the honor of certain persons. At the time when the sambenitos and the effigy appeared, Juan Pérez traveled from Oaxaca to Tecamachalco; so it seemed possible that Pérez brought the sambenitos. Since on his travels to Tecamachalco, Pérez usually stayed in Puebla with his stepmother, Juana Muñoz may have known about this as well. Yáñez did not know any of this "for a fact," but this was the rumor.

Canon Santiago concluded the interrogation with a stern warning to Francisco Yáñez: it was evident that he had not declared everything he knew about this matter. Yáñez should therefore "search his memory tonight" and return tomorrow to make another statement under threat of a heavy fine of five hundred pesos, in addition to excommunication.

Tepeaca, 10–12 November 1581

On 10 November, Yáñez traveled from Quecholac to Tepeaca, where Canon Santiago had gone. The farmer recounted to the commissioner yet other conversations about the events in Tecamachalco in 1578. Only four months earlier, Yáñez had been at the house of his mother-in-law, Catalina Gómez, with his mother-in-law's sister, Leonor Gómez, and Yáñez's wife, Catalina Núñez. Once again, the conversation turned to the sambenitos of Tecamachalco, which they had talked about "a thousand times, every time they had the opportunity to do so." On this occasion, Leonor Gómez recalled that she and her sister (Yáñez's mother-in-law) had heard María de Vargas tell them that Muñoz admitted that "those who put up the sambenitos left from her house."[10] Yáñez therefore guessed that Muñoz "assembled" the sambenitos at her house in Puebla with the materials that her stepson, Juan Pérez, brought from Oaxaca.[11]

Next, Yáñez explained his whereabouts in the previous thirteen or fourteen days: he had been on business in Puebla and Tlaxcala. When he arrived in Quecholac the day before yesterday, he learned that the Inquisition's commissioner was looking for him. After first going to his fields, Yáñez arrived at home that evening. His wife told him that the commissioner had come again looking for him. Yáñez said that he would go to see him the next morning. Concerned, his wife asked, "What's the matter?" "Nothing," he replied. Still worried, she guessed what the matter might be: "I don't know why my mother and my aunt told you and [Diego] Trujillo what that woman Vargas said, since she denied it after confessing to the priest."

Canon Santiago: Who else was present when María de Vargas talked to your mother-in-law and her sister in Puebla?
Francisco Yáñez: . . . My wife—I think, since at the time we weren't married yet.
Canon Santiago: It's evident that you aren't telling the whole truth about what you know. . . .
Yáñez: I have told the truth and don't know anything else about this matter.
Canon Santiago: Were you ever imprisoned for this matter? Where were you the night the sambenitos were put up?
Yáñez: . . . I was in Tecamachalco. A few days later, I was notified to appear before the alcalde mayor of Tepeaca, which I did. . . . I don't remember if I made a declaration. I was never imprisoned,

and I didn't go to jail. The alcalde mayor gave me permission to return home.[12]

Still not satisfied with the answers, Canon Santiago ordered Yáñez's imprisonment in Tepeaca's city jail. The jailer took Yáñez away in shackles.

Yáñez's nonchalance before Canon Santiago raised suspicions. After returning from his trip to Puebla and Tlaxcala, why did he wait a day to appear before the Inquisition's commissioner? Why had Yáñez refused to heed Diego de Trujillo's warning to report what he knew about the Tecamachalco scandal to the Inquisition? Yáñez did not bother to explain. In addition, his statements consisted of little more than hearsay, leaving out any mention of his brief imprisonment in Tepeaca in 1578 as a suspect in the Tecamachalco scandal. Still, the commissioner had no hard evidence against him. If Yáñez was hiding something or trying to protect someone, Canon Santiago would leave it to the inquisitors to investigate. On 11 November, Canon Santiago set Yáñez free on bail and ordered him to appear before the inquisitors in Mexico City within twelve days or pay a fine of a thousand pesos.[13]

It was now time to interrogate Juana Muñoz, one of the three alleged accomplices in the Tecamachalco scandal. According to the testimonies made thus far, she had sheltered at her house in Puebla her stepson, Juan Pérez, when he arrived from Oaxaca carrying the materials for making the sambenitos and the effigy against Rubio Naranjo. She had allegedly helped to finish the defaming objects, which Juan and his half-brother Francisco Pérez put up in Tecamachalco. Her testimony was especially important to Canon Santiago, since he could not interrogate her son Francisco, who had recently died, or her stepson, who was in Oaxaca.

Even though Muñoz was only thirty-six years old, she was already twice a widow. Born in Puebla, she grew up in her father's house there and in Mexico City. At the age of eight, she moved to Tecamachalco to marry her first husband, the miner Francisco Pérez (senior), who died ten years later.[14] They had a son, Francisco Pérez, the younger, who died in February 1580 at the age of twenty-one, and a daughter, also deceased. Her stepson, the mestizo horse-shoe maker Juan Pérez, who lived in Oaxaca, was the out-of-wedlock son of her first husband and an Indian woman.[15] At the age of twenty-two, Muñoz married her second husband, Pedro González, a sheep farmer, who died in Puebla in 1576. A few years later, she moved from Puebla. She presently lived in Tepeaca.

Canon Santiago placed Juana Muñoz under arrest in Tepeaca, suspected of involvement in the Tecamachalco scandal. On 11 November, the jailer brought her to the Franciscan monastery to answer the questions of the Inquisition's commissioner.

Canon Santiago: Do you know, or presume to know, why you're
    being interrogated?
Juana Muñoz: No, I don't.

The Inquisition's commissioner warned her that the Holy Office did not arrest anyone without just cause. Muñoz protested that, as a "Good Christian" who was fearful of God, she had "done or said nothing against the faith or the Holy Office, and don't know anyone guilty of doing so."

Canon Santiago: Do you know of anyone who may have put
    up . . . sambenitos with signs to injure a person's honor . . . ?
Juana Muñoz: About three years ago, when I was living in Puebla, I
    used to see a friend and acquaintance, María de Vargas, who died
    two years ago. She was a friend of a certain [Rubio] Naranjo, who
    lived in Tecamachalco.

She went on to recount a conversation she had had in 1578 with the late María de Vargas. One day, Vargas came with her young daughter to Muñoz's house to deliver some embroidery that Vargas had made. Muñoz noticed that the little girl was practically naked and, knowing that her father was the trader Hernando Rubio Naranjo, asked Vargas:

Juana Muñoz: Doesn't that pretty boy buy clothes for the girl?
María de Vargas: To the devil with him! I don't have anything
    more to do with him. He left me for Catalina Rodríguez [de
    San José], the widow of Benavides, from Tecamachalco. . . . Do
    you know what happened? Someone in Tecamachalco insulted
    [Rubio Naranjo] by putting up sambenitos and an effigy with
    two faces and two tongues. Naranjo came to my house and told
    me himself; he was on his way to the Holy Office in Mexico
    City.[16] . . .
Muñoz: Who did it?
Vargas: That pretty girl Catalina Rodríguez [de San José] and another
    woman from Tecamachalco, married to a sheep farmer.

María de Vargas did not tell Juana Muñoz the name of that second woman. However, Muñoz told Canon Santiago that the scandal had been so public that everyone knew about it. She added that her son-in-law, Alonso Pérez, as well as her sister, Isabel Suárez, might know more about it, since both had been in Tecamachalco when the events happened.

> *Canon Santiago*: We have information to the effect that you know
>   who brought the sambenitos and who made them. . . .
> *Juana Muñoz*: By the oath I've made, I don't know anything more
>   than what I've said about this matter or about this accusation
>   against me! Since it deals with the Holy Office, for no reason
>   would I leave out the truth, as María de Vargas said it to me. . . .
> *Canon Santiago*: Do you know if María de Vargas told anyone else
>   what she told you? . . .
> *Muñoz*: I don't know.

After restating that conversation, Muñoz's interrogation ended. The jailer took her back to her prison cell.

Following her suggestion, Canon Santiago and Notary Euguí decided to interrogate Muñoz's son-in-law, the Spanish attorney (*procurador*) Alonso Pérez, who lived in Tepeaca. Since he lay ill in bed with a severe case of gout, the Inquisition's commissioner and notary went to his house. After stating that he did not know the reason for his interrogation, Pérez suddenly cried out, "Holy Mary, an attack is coming!" His family rushed to the sick man's side to hold him while his "eyes turned white." Once he recovered, the interrogation began in earnest. Yet the man had little to say. Yes, he knew about the events in Tecamachalco because he had acted as Hernando Rubio Naranjo's attorney. Pérez therefore knew about the failed investigation that took place in 1578, and remembered telling his defamed client, "By God, it will never be resolved!"[17]

Back at the Franciscan monastery, Canon Santiago began the second part of his investigation: re-interrogating the witnesses from the failed investigation of 1578. In a sign of what lay ahead for the Inquisition's commissioner, the first of those witnesses offered little information. Luis de Manzanedo, a Spanish tailor who resided in Tepeaca, had an accurate memory of the defaming effigy and of the text on its accompanying sign. This was not because he had ever seen them but because the scandal had been so public that "boys big and small went around town saying it." Manzanedo added, "May God not save my soul!" if he had ever again said anything or discussed the subject with anyone, or remembered anything more about it. Since this was a matter involving the Inquisition, the tailor insisted, even if he had to denounce the father "who gave me life," he would not refrain from telling the truth as if he were kneeling before his confessor. The interrogation ended.[18]

* * *

It had been a long day for Canon Santiago and Notary Euguí, but they had little to show for their efforts. Thus far, witnesses had failed to provide concrete evidence to confirm Yáñez's accusations against Muñoz, her stepson, and her son. Her testimony shed no light on their role in the 1578 incident. Instead, the number of possible suspects, both men and women, continued to grow, fueled by rumors of Rubio Naranjo's suspicions. Given his universal antipathy, it was impossible to pinpoint a potential culprit. The only concrete action that Canon Santiago had taken was to order Yáñez to appear before the inquisitors in Mexico City so that they could decide what to do with him. Muñoz remained imprisoned in Tepeaca, although it was unclear how that would help the investigation. Meanwhile, the Inquisition's commissioner and notary continued to pursue every lead despite their lack of progress.

* * *

On 12 November, Canon Santiago interrogated Isabel Suárez, the younger sister of Juana Muñoz, who might know more about the case because she had been in Tecamachalco in 1578. She was the thirty-year-old widow of a cattle rancher, originally from Puebla, but for years she had been a resident of Tepeaca. She was unaware of the reason for her interrogation until Canon Santiago finally asked if she recalled some sambenitos discovered in Tecamachalco in the past. Although she could not remember the exact year, Suárez remembered an incident related to the scandal. Three weeks after the discovery of the sambenitos and the effigy, she had traveled with many people from Tepeaca to Tecamachalco to celebrate the eve of Our Lady of August— the Feast of the Assumption (15 August), the town's patron saint. There she visited Catalina Rodríguez de San José, widow of Benavides, and found in her house none other than Rodríguez's former lover, Hernando Rubio Naranjo. While Catalina Rodríguez did chores around the house, Isabel Suárez talked to the defamed man:

Isabel Suárez: How are you?

Hernando Rubio Naranjo: Do you know that someone put up some sambenitos against me?[19] . . . I suspect that those who did it were the mestizos Alonso Rodríguez . . . and Juan Pérez, the mestizo horseshoe maker and brother-in-law of the attorney Alonso Pérez.[20] . . . If the sambenitos had been made of cloth, I could have at least gotten something out of them, but they were made of tochomite [Indian cloth]. Now I will have to go to Mexico City and spend all my money there.

As she related her story to Canon Santiago, Suárez did not remark on the fact that the same Juan Pérez whom Rubio Naranjo had accused of the crime was her sister's stepson. Suárez did not know any details about the sambenitos or about who may have made them. Instead, she provided additional comments about Rubio Naranjo, "who had a bad tongue and was disliked by everyone."

Canon Santiago: Who in Tecamachalco was an enemy of Hernando Rubio Naranjo and for what cause?

Isabel Suárez: In general, the whole town was on bad terms with him, men and women, calling him a loose-tongued scoundrel [and] defamer of women, but I don't remember anyone in particular.

Canon Santiago then warned her that he had information to the effect that she knew more than she cared to say, in order to protect someone. Suárez swore that this was not true, and on that note, the commissioner let her go.

Tecamachalco, 13–17 November 1581

Unable to make any progress in Tepeaca and Quecholac, Canon Santiago and Notary Euguí headed for Tecamachalco. They installed themselves at the Franciscan monastery adjacent to the scene of the crime, which had dormitories, upper and lower cloisters, and a fruit garden with a fountain.[21] There the two men spent several days interrogating many of the witnesses who had testified during the failed 1578 investigation. The list of witnesses and the questions posed to them suggest that Canon Santiago pursued a double strategy: to confirm Yáñez's accusations against the Pérez brothers and Muñoz; and to implicate Yáñez in the 1578 scandal. Unfortunately for the Inquisition's commissioner, his success depended on witnesses with increasingly unreliable memories about events that had taken place years earlier.

On 13 November, Canon Santiago first interrogated Catalina Núñez, wife of Yáñez and daughter of Catalina Gómez. Núñez was sixteen years old and lived with her husband in her hometown of Quecholac. For the interrogation, she had to travel to Tecamachalco, her husband's birthplace, while he was preparing to travel to Mexico City to appear before the inquisitors. If her testimony revealed inconsistencies in the statements made by her husband and her mother, the investigation might take a new turn.

Canon Santiago: Do you know why you have been called to declare?
Catalina Núñez: I imagined that it is because of some words that my
    mother, Catalina Gómez, heard. . . . María de Vargas had told
    her, regarding some sambenitos put up in Tecamachalco against
    Hernando Rubio Naranjo, that the widow Juana Muñoz . . . had
    said: "Oh my sorrow, if they take my son, they will detain him!"[22]
    On this matter, my mother suspected that Francisco Pérez, son
    of Juana Muñoz, and Juan Pérez, her stepson, were guilty in that
    affair. My mother had told María Vargas: "If that were true, you
    should report it, and if not, then you should confess." . . . A few
    days later, María de Vargas told my mother, "I misspoke and lied
    about what I said against Juana Muñoz." My mother was telling
    this to her sister and my aunt, Leonor Gómez, and did not say
    anything more. . . . Then a few months ago, at an after-dinner
    conversation at my house with Diego de Trujillo and my husband, my mother recounted the story about María de Vargas.[23]

She did not know anything more. The statement confirmed what her mother had declared, which was the basis for what her husband had testified. However, Canon Santiago must not have thought that this witness could reveal anything else of substance, especially since she was only thirteen at the time of the 1578 events. He therefore dismissed her without further questions.

The next witness was Juana de Montoya, wife of a Spanish sheep-farmer and tax-collector from Tecamachalco. Back in 1578, her name had repeatedly come up as a suspect. The ill-spoken Hernando Rubio Naranjo had treated her with special contempt, saying that she had a "big nature," or large genitals. Aside from implying that he may have had carnal knowledge of this married woman, the vulgar remark portrayed Montoya as a highly sexual woman, whose husband could not satisfy her voracious lust; hence the allegation that Rubio Naranjo had drawn horns outside her house. There were rumors that her lovers included a scribe who worked for her husband, as well as Francisco Yáñez, who, back in 1578, was still a bachelor. Some thought that during a group beating in Quecholac against Rubio Naranjo—which prompted him to flee to Oaxaca several weeks before the scandal—Yáñez had slashed Rubio Naranjo's face with a knife to avenge Juana de Montoya. Later, when the alcalde mayor of Tepeaca briefly imprisoned Yáñez as a suspect in the Tecamachalco scandal, Yáñez reportedly named Montoya as one of the "many women" who had wept about his arrest. This contributed to speculation that Montoya may have told Yáñez to put up the effigy and the sambenitos in revenge for Rubio Naranjo's offense. However, as happened with many of the accusations made in 1578, nothing came out of the allegations against her.

Juana de Montoya told Canon Santiago that she did not know the reasons for her interrogation. The Inquisition's commissioner therefore turned to the scandal: "Do you know about a person, or persons, who had . . . put up sambenitos in the past to insult someone?" After summing up the scandal of 1578 and the failed investigation that followed, she speculated on the possible causes of the insult against Hernando Rubio Naranjo:

> *Juana de Montoya*: As I said, it took place eight days after his return
> from Oaxaca; and it was publicly said that [the sambenitos]
> might have been brought from there, where Rubio Naranjo had
> had a woman over which he had been in some kind of trouble I
> don't know about. Everyone in town had an opinion about who
> could have dared to do such a thing.
> *Canon Santiago*: Who said so . . . ?
> *Montoya*: The entire town said it. I wouldn't know of anyone in
> particular.
> *Canon Santiago*: What were the sambenitos like? Did you see them
> or the effigy?

Montoya described the sambenitos and the effigy but insisted that everything she knew she had heard from a Spanish neighbor in town, who helped the friar who took them down from the church's door and facade.

> *Canon Santiago*: At the time, who were Rubio Naranjo's enemies in
> town . . . ?

Juana de Montoya: It was said that before he went to Oaxaca, he had
been beaten up in Quecholac and wounded in the face; but it
was never known who did it. In this town, he was widely held as
an ill-humored man for his evil tongue and for boasting about
things that he hadn't done, which offended the honor of certain
persons.

Canon Santiago: Have you heard of any woman in particular who
had been defamed, whether married or single . . . ?

Montoya: By my life, I don't know this. He was ill-tempered and evil-
tongued, and, for that reason, there were a thousand opinions
about him. . . .

Canon Santiago: We have information to the effect that you know
more than what you have said. . . .

Montoya: May I not rise from this place and go back to my house if
I know anything else! I don't know, or suspect, who did it, or else
may God not save me!

Canon Santiago: Do you know of anyone who at that time had come
to town from Oaxaca?

Montoya: I never heard that anyone came from there at that time.

Canon Santiago: Do you know of anyone in town at the time known
for being a good scribe?

Montoya: . . . At the time, a Spanish young man called Francisco—I
mean, Alonso—García lived in my house. He was a good scribe;
he wrote anything my husband ordered him to, whether letters or
accounting books.

Canon Santiago: Where is Alonso García now?

Montoya: He went to San Pablo to the allotment of Indian servants
and should be back in the afternoon.[24]

This ended the interrogation. On 14 November, the Inquisition's commissioner interrogated two more Tecamachalco neighbors. None provided
any new information. Later that day, Canon Santiago expressed his growing
frustration with the pace of his mission in a letter to the inquisitors. Some of
the problems were simply bad luck. Six days earlier, he had sent a letter for
the inquisitors with a Basque muleteer, who was headed to Mexico City with
a small shipment of salt. In that letter, the Inquisition's commissioner had
complained that the witnesses examined to date were leading him nowhere.
Evidently, that letter did not reach its destination. In that presumably lost let-

ter, Canon Santiago had requested that the inquisitors issue an "edict of faith" calling for anyone with information about the 1578 incident to come forward or face the possibility of excommunication.[25] The edict seemed necessary because Yáñez's testimony did not agree with that of Diego de Trujillo. In addition, Muñoz "says nothing; in fact, there's evidence in her favor." Overall, the commissioner's inquiries had achieved nothing "because everything has already been forgotten"; and the answers he receives are such that, without the edict, "nothing will come to light." He had hoped to have the edict before he arrived in Tecamachalco. Now it was too late. Canon Santiago wanted the Basque muleteer, when found, to be punished.

Canon Santiago intended to wrap up his work in Tecamachalco and return to Puebla, where he would await the inquisitors' reply to his missive. As he concluded the letter, the Inquisition's commissioner underscored the need for the edict in order to end "all the secrecy" and encourage others to "discharge their conscience."[26]

* * *

Although Canon Santiago had little hope that he would achieve much in Tecamachalco, he still had business to conduct before returning to Puebla. On 15 November, he interrogated Alonso García, the "good scribe" mentioned two days earlier by Montoya during her interrogation. He was a thirty-year-old unmarried Spaniard who had settled in Tecamachalco, where he worked for Montoya's husband. His name had come up several times during the 1578 investigation as the scribe who may have written the signs on the sambenitos under orders from Montoya, whose hatred of Rubio Naranjo was common knowledge in town. As with so many of the rumors surrounding the case, nothing had come out of these suspicions.

After some prompting by Canon Santiago, the scribe remembered the 1578 scandal from hearsay but otherwise had little new information to help with the investigation:

> *Canon Santiago*: At that time, did Rubio Naranjo have a feud with anyone in town . . . ?
> *Alonso García*: I don't know any. On the contrary, he's such a peaceful man that I have never seen him have any hatred [*pasión*] with anyone.

Canon Santiago: Have you heard whether he had defamed any
    women in particular, married or single, or any other person . . . ?
García: No, and I wouldn't have wanted to hear it.

The Inquisition's commissioner now turned to the possible author, or
authors, of the signs on the offending sambenitos and the effigy, which García
said that he never saw:

Canon Santiago: Do you know of anyone still in town who, at the
    time that the sambenitos were put up, was a good scribe and
    knew black letter?
Alonso García: . . . Juan Baptista, the son of Francisco Sán-
    chez, . . . Pedro Beristain, and Juan López de Montalbán know
    how to write, but I don't know if they know black letter.

Next, Canon Santiago asked García to write the first seven letters of the
alphabet, followed by this list of words and phrases:

In the town of Tecamachalco in New Spain
On the second day of July of the year of the Birth of Our Savior Jesus
    Christ
Plátanos (sycamore or banana trees)
Mirtos (myrtles)
Naranjos (orange trees)
Asañas (García misspelled the word and was asked to write it again.)
Hazañas (deeds)
He. (abbreviation for the name Hernando)
Hernando
World
Better
Neighbors
Property
Rubio
Remove[27]

Having completed the task, the interrogation resumed:

Canon Santiago: Do you know how to write black letter?

Alonso García: By God, I don't know how to make any other letter than this plain letter [*letra llana*]. They never taught me any
other.[28]

This was the end of the interrogation. One of the three good scribes in
Tecamachalco whom García had mentioned was Pedro de Beristain, who
came next for questioning. He was a Spaniard from Guipúzcoa (in the Basque
country) and a longtime resident of Tecamachalco. He was forty years old,
married, and had at least one son. Beristain first described his role in 1578 as
a scribe for the alcalde mayor of Tepeaca during the initial investigation into
the scandal. The scribe's testimony to Canon Santiago also offered ample evidence about the speed of gossip in the region and the disregard for the Inquisition's secrecy about its investigations. Beristain had already heard from
two farmers from the nearby village of San Pablo about the commissioner's
arrival. These farmers had also told him what the late María de Vargas had
said to Yáñez's mother-in-law regarding Muñoz's alleged outburst: "If they
have taken my son there, then they have detained me."[29] After adding no new
information, the Inquisition's commissioner continued:

> *Canon Santiago*: At that time . . . who was Rubio Naranjo's enemy in
>   town . . . ?
> *Pedro de Beristain*: By the oath I've given, I only know that he was
>   held as a man who could be a little loose with his tongue. . . .
> *Canon Santiago*: Who in town or in Oaxaca may have defamed
>   Rubio Naranjo . . . ?
> *Beristain*: At the time, Rubio Naranjo's concubine was Catalina
>   Rodríguez [de San José], who was married. I heard this from
>   her relatives and from many people. Two years ago, Dr. Alzor-
>   riz, dean [of the cathedral chapter] of Oaxaca, told me that,
>   after news arrived there about the sambenitos against Hernando
>   Rubio Naranjo, it was said that in Oaxaca, too, Rubio Naranjo
>   had been a man with an evil tongue and that he had been beaten
>   up in the nearby town of Guaxolotitlan.

However, Beristain did not know of anyone at the time who had arrived
in Tecamachalco from Oaxaca. With nothing else to add, Canon Santiago
showed him the original signs on the sambenitos and the effigy. Beristain
recognized them but did not know who might have written them:

Canon Santiago: Do you know anyone at that time, whether Spaniards or Indians, who would have known how to write black
letter?

Pedro de Beristain: Juan López de Montalbán [the cochineal col-
lector] was here at the time; he's a good scribe, and had been
appointed scribe to judges and officials, but I never saw him
write black letter.

Following Beristain's testimony, a pair of Franciscan friars who knew
"the language of the Indians" assisted Canon Santiago in questioning three
unnamed individuals said to have been the only Indians in town who knew
how to write.[30] Through the interpreters, Canon Santiago asked each of them
to write the first seven or so letters of the alphabet. The commissioner then
showed them the libelous sambenitos posted against Rubio Naranjo. The
three witnesses did not recognize the handwriting.

On 16 November, the sole witness questioned proved similarly unhelpful.
The shoemaker Francisco Rodríguez did not even recall whether the hand-
writing on the effigy and the sambenitos was in Greek or in Latin characters.
The rest of his statements were similarly vague.

Canon Santiago: Have you heard whether, before or after Hernando
Rubio Naranjo was in Oaxaca, he had defamed any women, married or not, in this town . . . ?

Francisco Rodríguez: I asked Rubio Naranjo, who responded that he
suspected Juana de Montoya for telling him, "I'll make you pay
for it." I don't know the reason Montoya said this.[31]

On 17 November, Canon Santiago interrogated one scribe not mentioned
in any of the previous testimonies: Francisco de Molina, a forty-year-old
public scribe from Tepeaca.[32] He was a Spaniard from Guadalupe (now in
Extremadura), the site of a famous old shrine and pilgrimage destination. In
1569, he left Spain with his wife and three sons, including the future royal
scribe Juan de Molina, a close friend of Yáñez.[33] After working at the Audiencia in Mexico City, Francisco de Molina moved to Tepeaca, where he assisted
the alcalde mayor during the 1578 investigation.[34]

In his deposition before Canon Santiago, Francisco de Molina reviewed
what he remembered from that investigation. Back in 1578, the scribe witnessed the Inquisition's notary comparing the handwriting on the sambenitos

with that on a petition written by the cochineal collector Juan López de Montalbán—mentioned as a good scribe by two previous witnesses—and found a few similarities.[35] Molina also told the commissioner about rumors that the authors of the scandal had come from Oaxaca, as well as suspicions about Francisco Yáñez and Francisco de Molina's son Juan. Canon Santiago pressed the scribe to say more:

> *Canon Santiago*: What was the reason that it was said that Francisco
>   Yáñez . . . and Juan de Molina . . . might be guilty in this case . . . ?
> *Francisco de Molina*: . . . People [*el vulgo*] only blamed them because
>   they were young bachelors who were in the streets at all times of
>   the day. But in my heart, I never gave credit to Juan de Molina's
>   guilt because I remember that fifteen or twenty days before [the
>   scandal in Tecamachalco], Juan de Molina had come to Tepeaca
>   to bid me farewell, announcing that he was moving to Río de
>   Alvarado [in Veracruz] to work as the scribe of the alcalde
>   mayor. . . . It's a well-known fact and the truth that Juan de
>   Molina lived there for two years and wasn't present in this prov-
>   ince at the time of the incident.

Francisco de Molina added that he was not aware of any ill will between, on the one hand, the friends Juan de Molina and Yáñez, and, on the other, Rubio Naranjo, whom the entire town hated and accused of having a harmful tongue (*lengua perjudicial*) with which he had defamed some women in Tecamachalco as well as in Oaxaca.

> *Canon Santiago*: Who were the persons Rubio Naranjo defamed with
>   his tongue?
> *Francisco de Molina*: I recall that, at the time, I heard some people in
>   town suspected a certain Montoya, wife of Benito Galiano, whom
>   Rubio Naranjo had defamed with his tongue. . . . It was said
>   that she had someone do it. . . . At the time, I heard that Rubio
>   Naranjo had said heinous words to Montoya . . . calling her a
>   whore, that she had ruffians, and other words to that effect [*tenía
>   gayones y otras al pelo*].[36]
> *Canon Santiago*: At the time . . . had anyone you might suspect in
>   this matter come from Oaxaca?
> *Molina*: I heard it said publicly that, at the time, a train of pack ani-

mals had arrived in Tecamachalco from Oaxaca, and a man was
seen who had had certain differences with Rubio Naranjo. It was
suspected that this man might have put up the defaming signs.

Canon Santiago concluded the interrogation by showing the scribe the
infamous sambenitos and the effigy. Francisco de Molina recognized them
as the ones he had seen in 1578, but he did not identify the handwriting on
them.[37]

That evening, Canon Santiago and Notary Euguí left Tecamachalco to
return to Puebla. That same day, the Inquisition's commissioner ordered the
release of Muñoz from prison in Tepeaca.[38] The documents do not indicate
the reason for the commissioner's decision.

As predicted by Canon Santiago in his earlier letter to the inquisitors, the
interrogations in Tecamachalco revealed little specific information. Nonetheless, Notary Euguí may have begun to harbor new suspicious as he took
depositions from witnesses. Those suspicions would grow as the investigation
moved into its final days.

Puebla, 18–20 November 1581

On their first full day of work back in Puebla, the Inquisition's commissioner
and notary watched the investigation take an unexpected turn. The interrogations on 18 November 1581 began with a witness whose name had first
come up during the 1578 investigation. Luis de Cepeda was a mulatto, originally from San Salvador, "in the province of Guatemala," who now lived and
worked as a saddle and harness maker in Puebla. During the 1578 investigation, Hernando Rubio Naranjo listed Cepeda as one of many suspects
because, before the scandal broke, the saddle maker had allegedly warned
him to await a letter of excommunication. That letter never arrived. Neither
the alcalde mayor of Tepeaca nor the inquisitors in Mexico City ever interrogated Cepeda. Canon Santiago decided to interrogate him anyway.

As so many of the preceding witnesses had done, Luis de Cepeda began
his testimony recalling various rumors about the suspects whose names had
come up in 1578 in the days following the discovery of the sambenitos and
the effigy. Perhaps because he did not think that he was the target of suspicions, the saddle maker spoke freely about events on the night before the
scandal broke, as well as about the arrests that followed the discovery of the
defaming objects. None of these statements held much promise for Canon

Santiago, since in 1578 the Inquisition had already cleared the names that Cepeda mentioned.

Then Cepeda recounted a recent incident that at first seemed irrelevant but that ultimately produced one of the most important revelations that Canon Santiago would discover from his otherwise frustrating investigation. About eight months earlier, the saddle maker said, his wife received a visit at their house in Puebla from a woman from Tepeaca called Catalina Rodríguez (not to be confused with Catalina Rodríguez de San José, Rubio Naranjo's former lover). While the two friends talked, Catalina Rodríguez's nephew, the Cuban tailor Tomás Peña, called out for his aunt. The nephew complained loudly that Juan de Molina—"said to be the son of Francisco de Molina, the scribe from Tepeaca"—refused to pay for clothes that Peña had made for him. Juan de Molina had also defamed Catalina Rodríguez, saying that he would "give her a beating." An enraged Catalina Rodríguez shouted "not once but a hundred times" the following words: "Don't do this to me, Molina, or you'll make me take you to the Holy Office for the sambenitos that you put up in Tecamachalco!"[39] Cepeda did not know what happened afterward.

> *Canon Santiago*: Who else heard this conversation?
> *Luis de Cepeda*: . . . My wife, whose name is Madalena Rodríguez, also heard it.
> *Canon Santiago*: Did Catalina Rodríguez and her nephew Peña affirm that [Juan de] Molina put up the sambenitos against Rubio Naranjo?
> *Cepeda*: They didn't say that they knew this; but both of them said aloud that [Juan de Molina] shouldn't make them take him to the Holy Office because of the sambenitos that he had put up in Tecamachalco. [Rodríguez and Peña] asked me to ask Molina to pay in peace. I did so without saying anything about the sambenitos, but he did nothing because he didn't feel like paying. . . .
> *Canon Santiago*: Where are Catalina Rodríguez and her nephew?
> *Cepeda*: I heard that they now live in Puebla, next to the Franciscan monastery, because they were banished from Tepeaca for reasons I don't know. . . .
> *Canon Santiago*: Where is Juan de Molina?
> *Cepeda*: Fifteen or sixteen days ago, I talked to him in Mexico City, on Saint Augustine Street. I asked him if he would come this

way. Molina replied that he would return soon. I don't know why Molina went to Mexico City.

Cepeda never talked to Juan de Molina about the 1578 events. Canon Santiago wanted to know more about who might have carried out the insult against Rubio Naranjo:

Canon Santiago: Do you know, or have you heard, about anyone defamed by Rubio Naranjo in Tecamachalco, Oaxaca, or other parts, whether married, single women, or other persons, who were suspected of ordering such an insult as a revenge?

Luis de Cepeda: In Tecamachalco, everyone complained that Rubio Naranjo had said in Oaxaca that there were few women in Tecamachalco he didn't command. Rubio Naranjo was a loudmouth with an evil tongue [*un baladronazo de mala lengua*].[40]

Canon Santiago: Did you tell Rubio Naranjo that he would receive a letter of excommunication?[41]

Cepeda: I don't know what you're referring to and don't remember having said anything of the kind to anyone.[42]

The questioning ended. Canon Santiago quickly followed up on Cepeda's information about Catalina Rodríguez's whereabouts, calling her to appear before him on 19 November. She was a twenty-seven-year-old native of Tepeaca. In 1578, she was recently married to the shepherd Antón Martín and resided in Tecamachalco. He later joined an expedition led by the governor of Florida, and in 1581 was living in Havana. Catalina Rodríguez had another Cuban connection through her nephew, the Cuban tailor Tomás Peña. Recently, Rodríguez and her nephew had moved from Tepeaca to Puebla. As Luis de Cepeda had indicated the previous day, the authorities banished her and her nephew from Tepeaca in 1581 for reasons unknown to him. Catalina Rodríguez's name never came up in any of the investigations until Cepeda mentioned her.

After the usual prompting by Canon Santiago, the witness Catalina Rodríguez offered a torrent of sometimes confusing and contradictory information about the events of 1578: "At the time, I lived in Tecamachalco and had recently married my husband. One day, I heard it said in public from persons I don't remember that a sambenito with Rubio Naranjo's name and a gag had been put up in church.[43] . . . I don't remember if there was one sambenito, two, or more."

Rodríguez did not know what a sambenito was—and she was not the only one who did not know.[44] However, she knew that putting up sambenitos against someone was bad. She then reviewed some of the names of those arrested and eventually set free. None of this information was new except for one statement regarding a conversation she had had at the time of the "hurly-burly" (*baraúnda*) over these arrests with her neighbor Domingo López de Montalbán, brother of the cochineal collector Juan López de Montalbán: "One day, at my house after we had finished dinner, Domingo López de Montalbán told me: 'Señora Catalina Rodríguez, it seems to me that they're going after your son Juan de Molina because they say he knows about [the sambenitos, and he is] suspected like the others because he had disappeared at the time they were making arrests.'"[45]

Canon Santiago did not have to stop Rodríguez to ask why her neighbor had referred to Juan de Molina as "her son." She offered a confusing explanation: They called Juan de Molina "her son" because he was the son of the scribe Francisco de Molina, "who took the place of my father, and for this reason I treated Juan de Molina as my son." She did not elaborate, and without pausing, recounted another incident that occurred the night before the effigy and the sambenitos appeared. Catalina Rodríguez remembered that on that night, "Juan de Molina called at the door of my house. It was midnight. He arrived on a horse. My husband let him in, and they talked for more than an hour. I don't know what they discussed. . . . When my husband came to bed, I asked him, 'What are these long conversations with Juan de Molina? What did you talk about with him?' My husband replied, 'There's no reason why women should know men's business. Get up and make him a bed.' I did so."

The next morning, between six and seven, when the "tumult began to be heard," Juan de Molina saddled his horse and left, "saying he was going to Río de Alvarado," in Veracruz. He didn't return "to these parts until six or eight months later," when she saw him sick in bed at Francisco de Molina's house. She heard that ten or twelve days ago, "father and son" were together in the town of Acatzingo. Canon Santiago continued:

> *Canon Santiago*: Why did Domingo López de Montalbán tell you
>   that they were going to arrest . . . Juan de Molina, and did he tell
>   you . . . what [Molina] was guilty of?
> *Catalina Rodríguez*: I don't know, and he didn't tell me what [Juan de
>   Molina] may have been guilty of but only that they were going
>   after [Molina], which he told me not just once but a hundred

times. . . . Maybe it was because of the arrest of his brother Juan
López [de Montalbán], who was a comrade and was always
together with Juan de Molina and Francisco Yáñez. [Molina] may
have been thought guilty because of their friendship. Domingo
López suspected something, because he asked me many times
about the night that [Molina] was home.[46]

Canon Santiago finally turned to the declaration made the previous day by
Cepeda to the effect that Rodríguez had threatened to take Juan de Molina to
the Inquisition for putting up the sambenitos after Molina had refused to pay
for the work done by her nephew the tailor. The Inquisition's commissioner
impressed upon her the dangers of not telling the truth and the grave consequences of giving false testimony. She vehemently denied threatening Juan de
Molina with denouncing him to the Inquisition: "May God never have allowed
me . . . to have talked about sambenitos and the Holy Office!" She did not deny
her anger at her purported son but confused the incident referred to by Canon
Santiago with a different confrontation with Juan de Molina:

> *Catalina Rodríguez*: I remember that I was so enraged with Juan de
> Molina that I said in front of Francisco de Molina, his father—
> complaining about [Juan] for having insulted me: "What do
> you think, Señor Francisco de Molina, that in return for all that
> I've done for him, covering up [Juan's] dishonesties (. . . I had a
> woman friend of his in my house) and looking after his things,
> he should be so mean to defame me?!" But I never said anything
> to [Juan] about any sambenitos.
> *Canon Santiago*: Who else could be interrogated about this matter?
> *Rodríguez*: Domingo López de Montalbán and my husband, as I've
> been saying now for more than an hour.[47]

Canon Santiago found in Catalina Rodríguez a person eager to talk who
also provided extremely important revelations for the stalled investigation.
Notary Euguí did not provide any explicit description of the speed or the tone
of her speech. He could not always keep up with her words and had to sum
them up quickly. Instead of presenting events in a chronological order, she
jumbled them and strung one statement after the other; as a result, her story
was not always coherent. Why would her neighbor Domingo López de Montalbán call Juan de Molina "her son"? The explanation that she provided—

that because Francisco de Molina was like a father to her, she treated Juan like a son—made little sense without further explanation. More important was her suspicion about Juan de Molina's guilt in the 1578 scandal, because he had been at her house in Tecamachalco the night before the discovery of the effigy and the sambenitos. However, Canon Santiago could not question her husband, who was in Cuba. Likewise, Juan de Molina was in Río de Alvarado, Veracruz. Finally, when questioned by Canon Santiago about her threat to denounce Molina to the Inquisition, Rodríguez mentioned a different incident.

Rather than call Catalina Rodríguez back to clarify her statements, Canon Santiago summoned Madalena Rodríguez, the twenty-year-old wife of Cepeda, on 20 November. Despite their same surname, Madalena and Catalina were not related. The Inquisition's commissioner seemed exclusively interested in corroborating the account of Madalena Rodríguez's husband of the loud conversation between Catalina Rodríguez and her nephew that had taken place at her house several months earlier. Madalena Rodríguez explained to Canon Santiago that she and Catalina Rodríguez had been talking alone when Peña arrived. Catalina Rodríguez went out to meet him in the courtyard and said "with anger and loudly": "Juan de Molina better not make me reveal that he put up sambenitos in Tecamachalco!" When her friend came back inside the house, Madalena did not ask her about the conversation with her nephew—Madalena did not even know what a sambenito was. Nor did she know about the 1578 incident because at the time, she was just "a lass" (*una mochachuela*: she would have been sixteen or seventeen), and she did not pay any attention or know anything else about the matter.[48] The commissioner asked no more questions.

* * *

Later on 20 November, Notary Eguí drafted an extraordinary letter to the inquisitors describing how his mission for the past three weeks had left him bewildered. He and Canon Santiago were groping in the dark (*a ciegas*), unable to find something to hold on to (*sin tener de qué assir*).[49] The notary regretted that the Basque muleteer had failed to deliver the letter of 8 November requesting that the inquisitors issue an edict of faith to publicize the investigation. As a result, Canon Santiago and Eguí had learned little more than "generalities" instead of the much-needed details that could resolve the case. But they had at least taken care of a few important matters. Yáñez had orders to appear before the inquisitors. In addition, the statements made in the previous two days by Luis de Cepeda and by Catalina Rodríguez now underscored the need for the royal scribe Juan de Molina to appear before the inquisitors. However, the testimony collected was not enough to establish the guilt of these two suspects, not even to allow for their torture. Notary Euguí warned that this posed an enormous problem, since "it will never be possible to shed any light" on the case without resorting to *rigor*—the harsh methods without which suspects would never tell the truth. The Inquisition's commissioner and notary would also have learned much if they had only been able to put to torture Juana de Montoya, the woman defamed by Rubio Naranjo and suspected of being Yáñez's lover. The notary assured the inquisitors that if the "screws were turned on" Francisco Yáñez and Juan de Molina, they would confess.

No less important was the fact that the scribe Francisco de Molina had tried to protect Juan de Molina by giving him an alibi that was an "evident lie": that Juan had moved to Río de Alvarado fifteen days before the scandalous incident. It had now been "very well demonstrated" that Juan de Molina was in Tecamachalco the night before the effigy and the sambenitos appeared, and may even have slept in Catalina Rodríguez's house. It was also not true, as Francisco de Molina had declared, that Juan had not come back from Río de Alvarado in two years. Catalina Rodríguez had since seen Juan in Francisco de Molina's house in Tepeaca and in Acatzingo. Luis de Cepeda had seen him recently in Mexico City. (In fact, in February 1581, Juan de Molina had come to Tepeaca and Quecholac in his capacity as royal scribe as part of an investigation led by the judge of the Audiencia of Mexico, Dr. Pedro Farfán.)[50] For the Inquisition's notary, it was therefore important to arrest Juan de Molina because Molina and Yáñez were *los gallos de la tierra*, or the "cocks of the walk." These "fast friends"—*como uña y carne* (literally, "as inseparable as nail and flesh in a finger")—had both been in Tecamachalco on "that night" of 20 July 1578, the eve of the scandal. Moreover, Euguí now reinterpreted Francisco de Molina's assertion about the widespread suspicions that the defamed wife Juana de Montoya had "ruffians" (*gayones*) she could command to take revenge on Hernando Rubio Naranjo for insulting her. It now seemed clear that the cocks of the walk Juan de Molina and Francisco Yáñez were those very same ruffians capable of avenging Montoya and the other defamed women from Tecamachalco.

For now, Notary Euguí had concluded his mission in Puebla. There, he received orders from the inquisitors to travel about fifty miles east to Veracruz to deliver letters on a different case.[51] It might therefore take him at least eight days to complete his new mission and return to Mexico City. Only then could he bring the effigy and the sambenitos from Tecamachalco to the inquisitors. In the meantime, he was forwarding the depositions taken during the past three weeks.

Notary Eugui may have intended his letter as a guide to the inquisitors while they reviewed the statements of the eighteen witnesses. He seemed convinced that by following this blueprint for the next steps in the investigation, the inquisitors would soon end a case that had taken too long to resolve. However, this would not happen.

On the same day (20 November) that Notary Eugui finished his letter, Dr. Sancho Alzorriz, dean of the Cathedral of Antequera (Oaxaca) and the Inquisition's commissioner in the province of Oaxaca, wrote a letter to the inquisitors.[52] Dr. Alzorriz had carried out the inquisitors' order issued a month earlier to arrest Juan Pérez, the mestizo horseshoe maker accused of putting up the effigy and the sambenitos in Tecamachalco with the aid of his now-deceased half-brother Francisco Pérez and his stepmother, Juana Muñoz. A constable would accompany Pérez all the way to Mexico City. The constable shackled the accused man to prevent his escape. Upon Pérez's arrival in Mexico City, the inquisitors would begin his trial as the author of the scandal in Tecamachalco.

CHAPTER FIVE

Mistrial

Mexico City, 9–22 December 1581

On Thursday morning, 7 December 1581, Juan Pérez entered the Inquisition's prison. Licenciados Bonilla and Santos García wanted to question him regarding the accusation that Pérez had put up the effigy and the sambenitos in Tecamachalco. His name had come up before the inquisitors only six weeks earlier, on 27 October, when the farmer Diego de Trujillo offered his surprise testimony. Trujillo reported that Francisco Yáñez told the servant Francisco Hernández how Pérez put up the effigy and the sambenitos: "I think that Juan Pérez brought them in little pieces from Oaxaca, and his stepmother, Juana Muñoz, put them together and finished them; and Juan Pérez put them up with the help of [his half-brother] Francisco Pérez." On 30 October, three days after Trujillo's testimony, the inquisitors issued a warrant for Juan Pérez's arrest. That same day, the inquisitors also ordered the Inquisition's commissioner in Puebla, Canon Santiago, to investigate Trujillo's allegations and interrogate other witnesses. Pérez's arrest coincided with the end of Canon Santiago's investigation.

Juan Pérez, a thirty-five-year-old unmarried horseshoe maker, was born in Puebla, the mestizo son of Francisco Pérez, senior, a miner from Puebla, and María Ramírez, an Indian. Apparently, Juan's parents never married. They also had a daughter, Juana Ramírez (same surname as their mother), who lived in Tecamachalco. Juan's father later married Juana Muñoz. The son from this marriage, Francisco Pérez, junior, was fourteen years younger than his half-brother. Juan Pérez was only a year younger than his stepmother, and the two remained in contact after Juan's father died and Juana Muñoz remarried. At some point, Juan moved to Tecamachalco, where he lived until 1576.

That year, he moved south to Oaxaca, where he lived with his mother, who was now married. At the time of his arrest, Pérez declared that his only possessions were a horse and the clothes he was wearing—though not his cloak, which belonged to someone else.[1]

On 16 November, Dr. Alzorriz, the Inquisition's commissioner in Oaxaca, arrested Juan Pérez and turned him in to Oaxaca's city jailer. The prisoner would remain shackled until further notice. Four days later, a shackled Pérez left Oaxaca with a muleteer hired to act as constable in charge of transporting the prisoner to the Inquisition's headquarters in Mexico City. The long trip took eight days. On 7 December, Pérez arrived, unshackled, at the Inquisition.[2] It appears that the constable had either become impatient with their slow pace or unconcerned that his prisoner might flee—or both.

By the time Juan Pérez arrived in Mexico City, the inquisitors had had an opportunity to review the interrogations conducted by Canon Santiago in Puebla, Tepeaca, Quecholac, and Tecamachalco. The evidence against Pérez consisted of the following:

1. Francisco Yáñez's mother-in-law and her sister (Catalina and Leonor Gómez) testified that in 1578, the late María de Vargas heard Pérez's stepmother, Juana Muñoz, express great worry about her "son" (no name was given) upon hearing about the discovery of the effigy and the sambenitos in Tecamachalco. María de Vargas later retracted her accusation against Juana Muñoz. It was impossible to confirm María de Vargas's statements because she died around 1580.

2. Also in 1578, the defamed Hernando Rubio Naranjo declared on a number of occasions—such as in a letter to the inquisitors and in person to Francisco Yáñez and to Juana Muñoz's sister (Isabel Suárez)—that he suspected Juan Pérez of coming from Oaxaca to carry out the public defamation. Rubio Naranjo provided no motive or any evidence for his accusation. Pérez was only one of more than twenty individuals whom Rubio Naranjo suspected.

3. Several witnesses declared that in 1578, they heard rumors that those responsible for putting up the effigy and the sambenitos came from Oaxaca, where Rubio Naranjo's infamous sharp tongue and philandering had won him the kind of hatred he had already brought on himself in Tecamachalco. The Tecamachalco scribe Pedro de Beristain stated that Dr. Alzorriz, the Inquisi-

tion's commissioner in Oaxaca who arrested Juan Pérez, told Beristain that Rubio Naranjo had suffered a beating in an Oaxacan town for an affair with a married woman. However, none of these testimonies affirmed that the perpetrator from Oaxaca was Juan Pérez.

4. Yáñez declared that at the time of the scandal, Juan Pérez traveled to Tecamachalco[3] and stayed with his stepmother, then residing in Puebla. In contrast, the defamed ("big nature") Juana de Montoya never heard that anyone from Oaxaca had been in Tecamachalco when the scandal occurred.

The accusation against Juan Pérez partly fulfilled an assumption that lay behind the original investigation into the scandal. Such an elaborate plot required several individuals, and the principal motive for the crime was likely to be revenge against Rubio Naranjo for defaming one or more women. The case against Pérez rested on the following plot:

1. Juan Pérez: as plot leader, he would have taken the sambenitos and the effigy "in little pieces" from Oaxaca to Juana Muñoz's house in Puebla a few days before 20 July 1578.
2. Francisco Pérez: on the night of 20 July, he would have helped his half-brother Juan to transport and put up the sambenitos and the effigy in Tecamachalco.
3. Juana Muñoz: she would have helped to assemble the effigy and the sambenitos brought by her stepson, and later provided cover for the brothers after they carried out their action in Tecamachalco.
4. Alonso Pérez, attorney from Tepeaca and Juan Pérez's brother-in-law: the farmer Diego de Trujillo described him as "a man from Castile who could cause trouble, was a good scribe, and was as skillful as a demon."[4]
5. Alonso Rodríguez, a mestizo from Puebla: according to Rubio Naranjo, he and Juan Pérez carried out the crime against his reputation.[5]

As was the case with all the suspects in the investigations until now, the evidence against this group of conspirators remained slim, even after the numerous interrogations recently conducted by Canon Santiago. Reviewing that evidence for the inquisitors, Notary Eugui recommended that the investigation focus instead on Francisco Yáñez and his friend the royal scribe Juan de Molina. He also suggested investigating Juana de Montoya, the woman Rubio Naranjo said had a "big nature." Yet the inquisitors were not ready to release Juan Pérez, based on Notary Euguí's suggestions, which were, after all, little more than a hunch.

The greatest challenge to the inquisitors was that, after three and a half years, they still had no hard evidence against anyone for the incident in Tecamachalco. Notary Euguí was not even sure whether there was enough information to torture anyone in order to arrive at the detailed answers needed to make a formal accusation. As in 1578, the mystery of who put up the sambenitos and the effigy against Hernando Rubio Naranjo remained tangled in the endless gossip buzzing across the region from Tecamachalco to Puebla and from Tepeaca to Oaxaca. Popular opinion pointed to no one in particular. Nearly every witness had taken part in a conversation about other conversations that referred to previous conversations, and in each instance, the information changed slightly. Now, in late 1581, the problem had worsened because some of the sources of these stories, along with potential witnesses and suspects, had either moved away from the region or died. These frustrations were expressed by Canon Santiago and Notary Euguí in their letters to the inquisitors.

* * *

By late November 1581, the inquisitors were ready to "turn the screws" on Juan Pérez. Before his arrival on 7 December, the farmers Francisco Yáñez and Diego de Trujillo, along with the servant Francisco Hernández appeared for the first time before the inquisitors, in compliance with Canon Santiago's order. The inquisitors took the opportunity to interrogate firsthand the principal witnesses who had led to Pérez's arrest.

The first to appear before the inquisitors was Yáñez, who arrived at the Inquisition on Thursday, 23 November. The inquisitors ordered his immediate imprisonment. The following Tuesday afternoon, Licenciados Bonilla and Santos García summoned Yáñez to ratify his statements made to Canon Santiago. The jailer brought Yáñez to the solemn audience chamber of the Inquisition, which doubled as the tribunal's chapel (Fig. 11).[6] On a raised platform covered with a green wool carpet, the inquisitors sat on mahogany chairs behind a large table covered in black velvet adorned with a band of gold and

Figure 11. Audience chamber. J. F. Bernard, *Historie générale des cérémonies, moeurs, et coutumes religieuses de tous les peuples du monde* (Paris, 1741). Kenneth Spencer Research Library, University of Kansas.

silk. Above them was a canopy of black velvet with a band of gold and silk. Embroidered tapestries adorned the walls of the chamber. On the table was an iron cross for taking oaths from witnesses and suspects.

The confident Francisco Yáñez, who had testified before Canon Santiago only a few weeks earlier, now appeared before the inquisitors as a shaken man. Before, he had taken his time to appear before the Inquisition's commissioner and answered questions without expressing remorse for not having come forward earlier with the information he had about the authors of the Tecamachalco case. Since then, the farmer had become a prisoner of the Inquisition and now feared what would happen to him. Now in the presence of the inquisitors at the audience chamber, a contrite Yáñez got down on his knees and sought "penance with mercy."

After reading to Yáñez the statements he had made earlier that month to Canon Santiago, the inquisitors began:

> *Inquisitors*: In addition to this information, we warn you that the Holy Office has detained you based on more inculpating information than you have declared. . . . Tell the truth so that your case may be dispatched with the usual timeliness and with the mercy of the Holy Office to those who confess.
>
> *Francisco Yáñez*: May God let me know it! If it is found that I had any part or knowledge of the sambenitos, let them burn me as a treacherous heretic. I don't know more than what my mother-in-law and her sister Leonor have said. If I knew more, let me die a painful death [*a malas lançadas muera*].[7]

The inquisitors ordered Yáñez returned to his prison cell. He would now have eight days to "search his memory" inside his prison cell. During this time, he must have reviewed the reasons that led to his arrest and how to prove his innocence. He blamed Diego de Trujillo for his predicament. The problem for Yáñez was not that Trujillo revealed to the inquisitors the suspicions about Juan Pérez, his half-brother, and his stepmother. Clearly, Yáñez had no intention of keeping this information secret, since he had told it to the servant Francisco Hernández in the presence of Trujillo. Rather, Yáñez's troubles resulted from the fact that Trujillo told the inquisitors that he first learned about those suspicions from Yáñez, instead of admitting that both of them had heard the information at the same time from Yáñez's mother-in-law as they conversed after dinner—as three witnesses had testified before Canon Santiago. Why had it not been sufficient for Trujillo to denounce those suspicions? Instead, Trujillo told the inquisitors that Yáñez and Hernández had also been told to report voluntarily to the Inquisition what they knew about this affair. Why was Trujillo so intent on Yáñez denouncing Juan Pérez to the Inquisition? The two men were not just friends; they were *compadres* who ate together like family. Yáñez was now angry at what Trujillo had done to him. Therefore, in order to save himself, Yáñez would have to reveal to the inquisitors a painful secret about Trujillo.

On the morning of 6 December, Yáñez decided to clarify his previous accusation against Juan Pérez. Nearly a month earlier, Yáñez had recounted to Canon Santiago the after-dinner conversation at his house, during which his wife, his mother-in-law, his mother-in-law's sister, and Diego de Trujillo discussed the Tecamachalco crime. Yáñez now explained to the inquisitors that his mother-in-law purposely left out the names of Juan Pérez and of his half-brother Francisco because she did not want to upset Trujillo (*para no alborotarle la sangre*). Trujillo had once caught Juan Pérez with Trujillo's wife and responded to the affair by attacking him with a knife. The inquisitors were not pleased with Yáñez's latest revelation: "Tell the truth! It's evident from your inconsistencies that you're not doing so."[8] They ordered that he return to his prison cell.

On the morning of 7 December, the farmer Diego de Trujillo and the servant Francisco Hernández appeared before the inquisitors. Hernández did little more than reaffirm what he had declared a month earlier to Canon Santiago: in the conversation with Yáñez on the way from San Pablo to Quecholac, Yáñez had indeed stated that he knew who had put up the sambenitos. For his part, Trujillo insisted that he had only heard the rumors about Juan Pérez from Yáñez on the road from San Pablo to Quecholac. Trujillo denied Yáñez's claim that he first heard the rumors from Yáñez's mother-in-law during an after-dinner conversation at Yáñez's house. "If she ever said it," Trujillo declared, "I didn't hear it."[9] He was willing to tell this to Yáñez face-to-face.

This disagreement over whether Trujillo had listened to an after-dinner conversation may have seemed insignificant, but it was not. Its importance lay not with Trujillo's memory but rather with the source of Yáñez's information about the authors of the crime. Back in early November, Yáñez had insisted to Canon Santiago that his suspicions about Juan and Francisco Pérez and Juana Muñoz came from his mother-in-law, who had learned this information from the late María de Vargas. Yáñez later told Canon Santiago that he had also heard Rubio Naranjo's suspicions about Juan Pérez. The inquisitors suspected that Yáñez was trying to protect someone, perhaps the source of his information about Juan Pérez.

The inquisitors brought in Yáñez to confront Trujillo face-to-face. The two farmers continued to disagree over whether Trujillo had heard the accusation against Juan Pérez from Yáñez or from Yáñez's mother-in-law. The two men stood their ground. At least they agreed on one thing: neither man doubted the suspicions about Juan and Francisco Pérez and Juana Muñoz. The inquisitors ordered Yáñez back to his cell and dismissed Trujillo.

Juan Pérez entered the Inquisition's prison on the morning that Yáñez and Trujillo confronted each other. Two days later, on 9 November, Pérez appeared at his first interrogation and immediately addressed the accusations against him:

> *Inquisitors*: Do you know, or presume to know, the reason that you
>   have been imprisoned?
> *Juan Pérez*: . . . Before I arrived here, my captors and I stopped at
>   the San Juan Inn, where there was a man called Naranjo, who
>   said . . . : "I'm happy to see [Juan Pérez] in the city because it was
>   said that he had a part in the sambenitos that were put against
>   me in Tecamachalco." I suspect that this was the reason for my
>   imprisonment.[10]

Through the striking coincidence of seeing Hernando Rubio Naranjo at an inn near Mexico City, Pérez learned the reason for his capture. That knowledge inevitably colored the rest of Pérez's long testimony. He would try to demonstrate that, despite even more extraordinary coincidences, he had nothing to do with the crime of Tecamachalco.

> *Inquisitors*: Tell everything you know about this matter.
> *Juan Pérez*: I resided for a few years in Tecamachalco, practicing my
>   trade as a horseshoe maker. About five years ago, I went to live in
>   Oaxaca because of a fight I had with the farmer Diego de Trujillo,
>   who said that I was with his wife. We came to blows and there
>   were wounds.

Pérez's admission of his brawl with Trujillo confirmed what Yáñez
    had declared to the inquisitors two days earlier. Pérez continued
    with his testimony:

I have lived in Oaxaca ever since. Then about three years ago, more or less around the time the sambenitos were put up, I went from Oaxaca to Tepeaca and Cholula [near Puebla] to deliver two hundred pounds of cacao . . . on orders from Andrés Monjaraz, a cleric from Oaxaca. I delivered one hundred pounds in Tepeaca and one hundred in Cholula, which took me six days.[11] On my return to Oaxaca, about one league [about three miles] from Puebla, I found Andrés Morales, from Tecamachalco. He told me that some sambenitos against Rubio Naranjo had been hung there. Andrés Morales didn't know who did it. All this happened in the presence of Francisco Pérez, my brother, now deceased, and a Spanish servant of my brother named Rodríguez. I bade farewell to Andrés Morales. We went on our way to Oaxaca but without entering Tecamachalco.

The timing of Juan Pérez's travel was suspicious. His declaration gave credence to the stories that at the time the scandal took place, Juan Pérez had been with his half-brother, Francisco—if not in Tecamachalco, at least near the town. Likewise, Juan traveled with his shipment of cacao from Tepeaca to Cholula, which meant that he probably stopped halfway in Puebla, at the house of his stepmother, Juana Muñoz. Many details remained unclear, but the evidence was consistent with the statements of several witnesses.

> *Inquisitors*: The Holy Office is not in the habit of arresting persons without sufficient information about their guilt in . . . [acts] against the free exercise of the Holy Office . . . such as taking away or putting up sambenitos. . . .
> *Juan Pérez*: I had no part in it. I didn't put up any, or know about this.
> *Inquisitors*: Who had part in it? Who put them up?
> *Pérez*: I swear before God that I don't know more than what Andrés Morales told me!
> *Inquisitors*: When did he tell you? How much time had passed since the sambenitos had been put up?
> *Pérez*: Three or four days.
> *Inquisitor*: What goods do you own . . . ?
> *Pérez*: I have nothing more than a horse I left with Juan de la Torre, a goldsmith from this city.

Warned to search his memory, the inquisitors sent him back to his prison cell. After their session, the inquisitors drafted a letter for the commissioner Dr. Alzorriz to confirm that in July 1578, the cleric Andrés Monjaraz, from Oaxaca, ordered Juan Pérez to deliver cacao to Tepeaca and Cholula. The inquisitors wanted to know from the cleric the amounts of cacao and the persons who received them. They asked Dr. Alzorriz to send this information as soon as possible.[12]

On 13 December, it was Yáñez's turn to testify again. It had been a week since his last audience, when he confronted Trujillo. Yáñez must have spent a good deal of time in his cell sorting out their exchange, which he now wanted to explain to the inquisitors: "Trujillo may have said that I heard who put up the sambenitos from someone other than my mother-in-law. He may have thought it was Juana de Montoya, whom Trujillo hates because she had been the procuress [*tercera*] between Juan Pérez and Isabel Rodríguez, Trujillo's wife. Regarding this enmity, a trial was under way at the Audiencia."

The name Juana de Montoya, the woman Rubio Naranjo claimed had a "big nature," had come up several times since the first investigation in 1578. Rubio Naranjo suspected her; and a number of witnesses assumed that she had "ruffians" whom she could command to carry out the insult against him. The identity of the man, or men, she could have ordered remained unknown. Some suspected that they could have been her husband's scribe Alonso García and her alleged lover Francisco Yáñez. Now Yáñez provided a new possibility. Perhaps Juan Pérez had put up the sambenitos and the effigy to repay Montoya for procuring him a lover, who was none other than Trujillo's wife.

Yáñez explained why Trujillo could have come to this conclusion: he reported an unrelated incident that proved the close "friendship" between Juan Pérez and Juana de Montoya: "Pérez confessed to Trujillo that a year ago, more or less, he had avenged Montoya for an insult made against her by Juan Blanco, a resident of Tecamachalco. [She told Pérez that Blanco had left her for another woman.] One night, Pérez waited for Blanco near the plaza in Tecamachalco and knocked him down two or three times with a shield [*rodela*], belted him many times, and took off his hat because Montoya had begged Pérez to do so. For doing this, Montoya rewarded Pérez with a coat."[13]

Continuing with their interrogation, the inquisitors wanted to return to the scandal in Tecamachalco:

> *Inquisitors*: Did Pérez put up the effigy and the sambenitos, and did Montoya know it?
> *Francisco Yáñez*: I know nothing more than what I heard from my mother-in-law and from her sister.
> *Inquisitors*: . . . Out of respect for God, we warn you to tell the whole truth so that your case may be dispatched with the usual timeliness and mercy of the Holy Office.

Yáñez: I know nothing more than what I heard from my mother-in-law and from her sister.[14]

Once again frustrated, the inquisitors ordered that Yáñez be returned to his prison cell.

Yáñez's testimony lent further credence to the suspicions that Montoya may have instigated the Tecamachalco scandal in revenge for Rubio Naranjo's insults against her. Juan Pérez may have been one of the "ruffians" willing to do her bidding in return for the favors she had done for him with Trujillo's wife. However, instead of repaying Yáñez for his valuable testimony by letting him go home, the inquisitors reached a new conclusion about him. The farmer's changing statements suggested that he was hiding something—or that he was a coconspirator in the crime, if not its author.

On 14 December, the inquisitors called in Yáñez to tell him that Dr. Lobo Guerrero, the Inquisition's prosecuting attorney, would accuse him of putting up the effigy and the sambenitos against Rubio Naranjo in collaboration with others, whose names the attorney did not reveal. Yáñez perpetrated the crime because of his "capital enmity" toward Rubio Naranjo. Dr. Lobo Guerrero described Yáñez as a "rabble-rouser" (*facineroso*) accustomed to committing crimes and avenging insults in exchange for "rewards." For example, the prosecuting attorney stated that Yáñez had punched a man on the back and mistreated him in return for a cloak from a woman. Dr. Lobo Guerrero recommended a severe punishment to set an example. In case there was insufficient evidence to prove the charges, the attorney recommended putting Yáñez to *quistión de tormento*, or torture.[15] Asked to respond to the charges, Yáñez denied everything, protesting, "Here I stand for anything you ask, but may God not have willed that I had committed the crime or know who did it."[16] Yáñez returned to his prison cell.

On the afternoon of 16 December, two days after accusing Yáñez of putting up the effigy and the sambenitos, the inquisitors called Juan Pérez to his second audience:

Inquisitors: If you remember anything about this matter, tell the truth under the oath you have taken.
Juan Pérez: No, I don't remember anything other than what I've already said.
Inquisitors: The Inquisition's prosecuting attorney wishes to present

the accusation against you; and it would do you much good to
tell the truth.

Pérez: I don't know more than what I've said.[17]

Dr. Lobo Guerrero appeared and read the charges against Pérez, which
were the same as those for Yáñez except on two counts.[18] The attorney did not
claim a "capital enmity" between Pérez and Rubio Naranjo or that Pérez was
a rabble-rouser like Yáñez. Otherwise, the accusations effectively made Pérez
and Yáñez accomplices in the 1578 scandal.

Just as Yáñez had done, Pérez denied all charges against him, insisting
that he knew nothing about the matter and that his trial should end. Dr. Lobo
Guerrero recommended instead that the trial proceed to the next phase. The
inquisitors ended the audience and sent Pérez back to his prison cell.

On the afternoon of 19 December, Yáñez returned before the inquisitors
with his court-appointed defense lawyer, Licenciado Melchor de Ávalos, to
respond to the accusations against him.[19] With nothing new to add, Yáñez
again rejected the accusation. He returned to his prison cell. That same afternoon, Juan Pérez also came before the inquisitors, along with Licenciado
Ávalos as his lawyer. Likewise, Pérez had nothing new to add. He insisted
again that he did not put up the effigy and the sambenitos and that everything
he had declared before was true. In contrast to Yáñez's appearance, Licenciado Ávalos agreed with the accused that the trial against Pérez should end.
The prosecuting attorney insisted that Pérez's trial proceed. The session concluded, and Pérez returned to his jail cell.

On 22 December, the inquisitors called Juan Pérez to appear at their
afternoon session to announce that they were letting him go. Pérez would
have to remain in Mexico City and could not leave without the inquisitors'
permission.[20]

The surviving documentation does not indicate the reasons for the
inquisitors' change of mind regarding Juan Pérez. They ordered Dr. Alzorriz in Oaxaca to corroborate Pérez's story about the shipment of cacao that
brought him near Tecamachalco in July 1578. The commissioner interrogated
the cleric Andrés Monjaraz and a second witness, both of whom confirmed
under oath what Pérez had told the inquisitors. However, these depositions
in Oaxaca took place on 22 February 1582.[21] In other words, this information
arrived in Mexico City more than two months after the inquisitors had freed
Pérez from the Inquisition's prison.

The additional information explained why Pérez was near Tecamachalco at the time of the scandal but did not entirely exculpate him from the initial accusations made by Yáñez. It was still possible that Pérez could have carried the unassembled sambenitos and the effigy along with the cacao shipment he had agreed to deliver. It was also possible that, during his time in Puebla and Tepeaca, Pérez and his brother Francisco made a detour to Tecamachalco. In essence, the initial accusation remained plausible. Something else had changed.

Since November 1581, Yáñez had altered his testimony each time he was interrogated, becoming more elaborate but never conclusive. After his two interrogations, Canon Santiago told the inquisitors that it was impossible to corroborate the veracity of the assertions made by Yáñez, as denounced to the inquisitors in October by Trujillo. The suspicions of Yáñez's mother-in-law and her sister about Juan and Francisco Pérez and Juana Muñoz had come from declarations made by a source now dead and therefore impossible to interrogate. Besides these stories, no other evidence linked Muñoz to the scandal. For this reason, Canon Santiago had to let her go. Rather than confirm Yáñez's accusations, the inquisitors seemed increasingly convinced that he was protecting someone. By mid-December, the Inquisition's prosecuting attorney was ready to accuse both Yáñez and Juan Pérez of being accomplices in the scandal, even though nothing in the investigation linked the two men. Instead, Yáñez's complicated explanations led the inquisitors to question the veracity of his statements and therefore cast a shadow of doubt over Pérez's guilt.

In early November, Yáñez was the key witness in an investigation that led inquisitors to put Juan Pérez on trial. A month later, Yáñez was a suspect. Solving the 1578 crime in Tecamachalco now hinged on the outcome of Yáñez's trial.

PART III

1582

CHAPTER SIX

New and Old Leads

Puebla, 2–8 January 1582

In early January 1582, six weeks after his last interrogation, the Inquisition's commissioner Canon Santiago resumed his investigation in Puebla. The last three witnesses he interrogated in November led to important discoveries that shifted attention away from Juan Pérez and toward the royal scribe Juan de Molina's role in the scandal in Tecamachalco. The new information, collected just as the commissioner was wrapping up his work in Puebla, was a fortuitous turn of events in an otherwise frustrating investigation. Until the last three days of interrogations, Canon Santiago was unable to find any hard evidence to support the declarations made by Diego de Trujillo and Francisco Yáñez accusing Juan Pérez of the crime. Part of Canon Santiago's difficulty was that many of the witnesses who had come before him had forgotten important details or they repeated rumors without much substance. Key witnesses had died or had moved away to unknown destinations. Unexpectedly, Canon Santiago found evidence that raised suspicions about Juan de Molina. On 18 November, the saddle maker Luis de Cepeda, in what was almost an afterthought to his declaration, recounted a recent incident in which Catalina Rodríguez, speaking in a loud and angry tone to her nephew, the Cuban tailor Tomás Peña, implicated Juan de Molina in placing the sambenitos in Tecamachalco. When Canon Santiago interrogated Catalina Rodríguez a day later about that incident, she denied saying anything about the sambenitos. Nonetheless, she provided new details that bolstered suspicions about Juan de Molina. A month and a half later, the Inquisition's commissioner in Puebla was ready to pick up the thread of this investigation.

On 2 January 1582, Peña came before Canon Santiago. The commissioner sought Peña's recollection of his aunt's words denouncing Molina. The tailor confirmed that, in August 1581, he had gone to Catalina Rodríguez to tell her about a quarrel between himself and Molina over the scribe's unwillingness to pay for clothes that Peña had made for him. (Peña did not say so, but Cepeda explained that when Molina refused to pay Peña, the scribe made insulting remarks against Catalina Rodríguez.) According to Peña, Catalina Rodríguez was upset at Molina for mistreating her nephew and said: "It's impossible that this scoundrel Juan de Molina won't be punished for the sambenitos put up in Tecamachalco, when it's said that he had something to do with them! If I knew where Domingo López de Montalbán was, I would ask him if it had been discovered whether Molina had put them up, and inform this to the señores inquisitors."[1]

Domingo López de Montalbán was Catalina Rodríguez's neighbor in Tecamachalco. Domingo's brother and partner in collecting cochineal, Juan López de Montalbán, was Juan de Molina's friend; in 1578, he was the prime suspect in the Tecamachalco scandal. In Rodríguez's declaration on 19 November, she explained that Domingo repeatedly came to her house asking about Molina's whereabouts the night before the effigy and the sambenitos appeared. One day, Domingo told Rodríguez, referring to the sambenitos: "They're going after your son Juan de Molina, because they say he knows about them." Peña's testimony corroborated the fact that her neighbor's questions fueled Rodríguez's suspicions about her "son" and his role in the Tecamachalco incident.

Canon Santiago read back the statements made by Peña. The tailor now corrected himself, insisting that his aunt had not said "sambenitos" but that she referred only to "what happened in Tecamachalco." Peña explained that he asked his aunt what she meant, and she replied: "It's a matter I couldn't tell you about." Rodríguez told her nephew that Domingo López de Montalbán would sometimes come to her house to visit her husband (no name given). Domingo would stay for dinner, and afterward the two men remained seated around the dinner table chatting about an affair in Tecamachalco, "without saying what this was about."

> *Inquisitors*: Do you know about the sambenitos and other insignia of the Holy Office that were put up in Tecamachalco . . . ?
> *Tomás Peña*: I don't know about it—never heard about it.
> *Inquisitors*: . . . Did you ever see Juan de Molina enter Catalina Rodríguez's house and talk to her or with her husband Antón Martín . . . ?

Peña: I didn't see him be with or talk to Catalina Rodríguez. . . .
Inquisitors: Do you know where Juan de Molina is . . . ?
Peña:. . . . I don't know where he is now. . . .
Inquisitors: You heard about the sambenitos and Molina from Cata-
lina Rodríguez. . . . Tell the truth . . . !
Peña: It's true. To say otherwise would be to condemn myself. . . . I
don't know anything more than what I've said.[2]

This ended the interrogation.

On 19 November 1581, Canon Santiago concluded his interrogation of
Catalina Rodríguez by asking her who else could provide additional evidence
in support of her declarations about the royal scribe Juan de Molina. She
replied with impatience that the commissioner should question her neighbor
Domingo López de Montalbán and her husband, "as I've been saying now
for more than an hour." However, her husband was in Cuba. Instead of interrogating Domingo López de Montalbán, Canon Santiago called Domingo's
brother, Juan.

In 1578, the cochineal collector Juan López de Montalbán had been the
first suspect interrogated by the inquisitors. At the time, he had come under
suspicion for allegedly making remarks to Hernando Rubio Naranjo to the
effect that many in Tecamachalco harbored ill will toward him for defaming
the reputation of women in town. Although López de Montalbán's profession
was that of cochineal collector, several witnesses described him as a "good
scribe" capable of writing the words on the placards accompanying the effigy
and the sambenitos in Tecamachalco. At his audiences before the inquisitors
in August and September 1578, López de Montalbán denied ever threatening Rubio Naranjo. Upon close inspection of his handwriting, the inquisitors
concluded that it was not the same as the writing on the defaming signs. With
no hard evidence against him, the inquisitors set him free.

Three and a half years later, Canon Santiago called López de Montalbán
back to Puebla to confirm the three depositions that he had made in 1578,
which now appeared to contain valuable information not noticed, or not
taken seriously, earlier.[3] In his first deposition, on 30 August 1578, López de
Montalbán was more intent on proving his innocence than on identifying any
culprits. He arrived in Tecamachalco in late 1577, only ten months prior to
the scandal, and did not know all the secrets in town that could provide clues
to resolve the case. The newcomer soon met the farmer Francisco Yáñez and
the royal scribe Juan de Molina, and the three became "comrades and always

went together," as Catalina Rodríguez had told Canon Santiago. Now in January 1582, the inquisitors realized that López de Montalbán had met the right people to yield crucial information.

On 2 September 1578, López de Montalbán gave a second, rambling deposition before the inquisitors, which at the time did not hold much promise. He repeated widely known gossip, with one exception. In early August 1578, after Tepeaca's alcalde mayor had ordered López de Montalbán and several other suspects to remain within city limits for their interrogation, he heard from one Tecamachalco neighbor rumors that neighbors suspected Juan de Molina and Francisco Yáñez of having a part in the crime. López de Montalbán also suspected Yáñez because the farmer "has done many things nobody had discovered." One of them included beating Rubio Naranjo with a stick and cutting him with a knife in Quecholac, even though, officially, the identity of the perpetrators remained unknown. However, Yáñez confided in López de Montalbán his participation in that beating in revenge for Rubio Naranjo's defamation of Yáñez's mother and sisters. The inquisitors asked López de Montalbán if Yáñez knew how to write. "Very well," replied the cochineal collector; but when shown the signs posted in Tecamachalco, he could not recognize the handwriting.

On 9 September 1578, the inquisitors released López de Montalbán. No longer worried about having to disprove his guilt, López de Montalbán began to go over past events and gossip. Two days later, he voluntarily went back to the inquisitors to report a string of disparate facts, observations, and rumors that he remembered:

1. As he thought again about the handwriting on the signs put up in Tecamachalco that was shown to him on 2 September, it now reminded him of the Gothic letters on the accounting books in Tepeaca's meat market and on other documents written by the scribe Alonso García, who worked for Juana de Montoya's tax-farming husband.

2. In August 1578, when Juan López de Montalbán was in Tepeaca with other suspects, a man arrived with a delivery of roasted mutton for two other detainees, one of whom was Francisco Yáñez. The messenger did not reveal who sent this gift, but it was not hard to guess. The messenger was Alonso García, the scribe working for Juana de Montoya's husband.

3. Later that day, while walking in the city's market, Francisco Yáñez said to López de Montalbán, "I swear that many women in

Tecamachalco have wept over my imprisonment." When López de Montalbán asked who these women were, Yáñez replied: "Juana de Montoya has wept much."

4. During that time, a Tecamachalco neighbor told López de Montalbán that several months earlier, Hernando Rubio Naranjo had drawn horns on the door of Juana de Montoya's house.

These four observations led López de Montalbán to the following conclusion: Juana de Montoya could have asked Francisco Yáñez to put up the sambenitos in revenge for Rubio Naranjo's insults. Yáñez seemed to care about Montoya's honor. He told López de Montalbán that Rubio Naranjo had bragged that Montoya "had a big nature." Yáñez could have received help from the scribe Alonso García, who could have written the signs accompanying the effigy and the sambenitos. If Alonso García did not do it, someone else could have: Juan de Molina, "a very good scribe," who also wrote in black letter in the books kept by his "father," the scribe Francisco de Molina. Everyone knew that Juan de Molina and Yáñez were "great friends." Moreover, there were rumors that the two had slept in the same house the night before the scandal of the sambenitos. Shortly after the incident, Molina left town for Río de Alvarado, in Veracruz.

In 1578, the inquisitors did not pursue Juan López de Montalbán's chain of thought and elaborate conspiracy theory. At the time, his observations did not stand out from the rest of the gossip and speculation engulfing Tecamachalco. But in 1582, after the recent statements against Juan de Molina and the contradictions in Francisco Yáñez's multiple declarations, López de Montalbán's accusations appeared far more credible. In November 1581, Canon Santiago confirmed that the scribe Alonso García's handwriting did not match that on the signs that accompanied the effigy and the sambenitos. That left Juan de Molina as the more likely accomplice of his friend Yáñez.

Canon Santiago began his interrogation of Juan López de Montalbán by asking if he recalled having made previous declarations against anyone. López de Montalbán did not recall any; but then he recalled that years earlier, he had gone to Mexico City to make declarations before the inquisitors. He asked that the commissioner read those statements. After reading the 1578 depositions, Canon Santiago asked López de Montalbán to ratify or alter the accusations made in his previous depositions. López de Montalbán stood by what he had said and added a few more statements in support of his suspicions about Juan de Molina and Francisco Yáñez.

One year earlier—around January 1581—López de Montalbán was in Tepeaca's plaza when Juan de Molina and a constable approached him. Molina asked López de Montalbán to pardon him for the hatred (*pasión*) between them. López de Montalbán replied, "You're my friend." Molina asked López de Montalbán to accompany him and the constable to the house of Molina's so-called father, Francisco. There, López de Montalbán and Juan de Molina had the following exchange:

> *Juan de Molina*: You know well, Señor Juan López de Montalbán, that Castro and María de Balbuena, his mother, are my enemies because they say that I and Francisco Yáñez had something to do with the sambenitos that were put up in Tecamachalco. I'm saying this in case anyone asks you about it, so that you can say that they're my enemies.
>
> *Juan López de Montalbán*: I've had many masses said to the Holy Spirit and to the souls of Purgatory for the truth to be known, having suffered when I was imprisoned and shackled for seventy days in Tepeaca [in 1578].[4]

Juan López de Montalbán had not forgotten his ordeal of three years earlier. More important, his statement provided further evidence that, years after the scandal in Tecamachalco, people continued to speculate about it, even as far away as the Veracruz region. Juan de Molina was still trying to ward off suspicions about his role in the scandal.

Canon Santiago asked López de Montalbán about the rumors he had heard while in prison in Tepeaca:

> *Canon Santiago*: Do you remember who told you that Francisco Yáñez and Juan de Molina were guilty of [putting up] the sambenitos?
>
> *Juan López de Montalbán*: I don't remember because there were many who came to console me and to visit me.
>
> *Canon Santiago*: Try to remember.[5]

This request ended the interrogation.

Six days later, on 8 January 1582, López de Montalbán asked to speak with Canon Santiago. The cochineal collector had heeded the commissioner's request and now recalled having heard that Juan de Molina and Francisco Yáñez were guilty of the incident in Tecamachalco, not from one person, but from at least four men he could name. One of them was Hernando Rubio Naranjo, who said: "I swear to God and to the Virgin Mary that even if Juan de Molina goes to hell, I'll get him because he had put up" the effigy and the sambenitos.[6] This was further proof about the widespread suspicions about Molina and Yáñez. López de Montalbán shared these suspicions about Molina, who was a "knavish man" (*hombre travieso*). For example, López de Montalbán recalled another incident in 1581, when he visited an uncle who had stables in Río de Alvarado, where Juan de Molina worked as a scribe for the alcalde mayor. There Molina boasted to López de Montalbán about one of the knavish things he had done to Castro and his mother, María de Balbuena, the ones who had threatened to reveal Molina's role in the Tecamachalco scandal. Molina told López de Montalbán that, one time when Castro had gone to Mexico City to sue an official, Juan de Molina wrote a letter to Castro's mother, saying that the man whom her son had intended to sue had stabbed her son. Molina knew that this story about the stabbing was a lie. López de Montalbán finished his voluntary statement to Canon Santiago by repeating that Juan de Molina had left for Río de Alvarado the very same morning that the effigy and the sambenitos appeared. This concluded López de Montalbán's declaration.

Later that day, Canon Santiago asked the farmer Diego de Trujillo and the servant Francisco Hernández to ratify or amend their declarations of November 1581 about Yáñez's accusations against Juan Pérez. Trujillo and Hernández had nothing new to add. Trujillo insisted that he did not testify against Yáñez out of hatred toward his *compadre*; he had only wanted to "discharge my conscience." Yáñez was obviously unhappy with Trujillo. Following his appearance before the inquisitors in November 1581, Trujillo approached his compadre at the courtyard of the church in Quecholac. An upset Yáñez said to him, "Get out of my way. I know more than all of you!"[7]

Canon Santiago concluded the second round of interrogations, which he forwarded to the inquisitors. Neither the opinions of the commissioner nor those of the inquisitors have survived, making it impossible to ascertain their reactions to the latest depositions. However, the next direction of the investigation indicates that Juan López de Montalbán's 1578 declarations, which the inquisitors largely ignored at the time, now seemed of great importance in resolving the case. López de Montalbán's suspicions about the possible authors of the crime confirmed the basic assumption that it was a conspiracy involving two or more men avenging a woman defamed by Rubio Naranjo. López de Montalbán's statements outlined the following plot:

1. Francisco Yáñez: as plot leader, he carried out the actions to avenge Juana de Montoya for the insults that Rubio Naranjo had made against her. Yáñez already hated Rubio Naranjo for insulting his mother and sister, which led him to beat Rubio Naranjo and slash his face with a knife in Quecholac.
2. Juan de Molina: he aided his close friend Yáñez by writing in his "very good scribe's" hand the three signs accompanying the effigy and the sambenitos. He may also have helped Yáñez put up the defaming objects before moving to the Veracruz region.
3. Juana de Montoya: she urged Yáñez, who may have been her lover, to act against the hated Rubio Naranjo. She may also have helped to make the sambenitos and the effigy, whose fine stitches, witnesses concluded, could only be the work of a woman.

In the coming weeks and months, the inquisitors moved with ruthless determination to crack the case. They intended to prove that this hypothesis offered the solution to the mystery of the "San Benito" of Tecamachalco.

Mexico City, 16 January 1582

Eight days after Canon Santiago concluded his interrogations in Puebla, Francisco Yáñez appeared before the inquisitors to make a statement. This time, the farmer requested an audience in order to make an important admission. The night before the sambenitos and the effigy appeared in Tecamachalco, the farmer said, he had slept in town in the same house as four other people:

1. Juan López, a mestizo who worked as a Nahuatl interpreter (*naguatate*)
2. Bárbara, Juan López's Indian servant[8]

3. Bárbara's husband, Francisco, a ladino, or Spanish-speaking,
    Indian, who was also López's servant[9]
4. Juan de Molina, the royal scribe.[10]

They played cards from four in the afternoon until midnight. Molina won, earning fifteen pesos. All five slept in the house and did not get up until the following morning. Yáñez now asked the inquisitors to call these witnesses to corroborate his statements.

CHAPTER SEVEN

The Scribe

From Veracruz to Mexico City,
27 January–Early February 1582

In early February 1582, the Inquisition's jailer informed Licenciados Bonilla and Santos García of the arrival of a shackled prisoner from Veracruz.[1] He was Juan de Molina, the royal scribe whom the inquisitors wanted to question in relation to the incident in Tecamachalco. Surviving documents do not indicate the date on which the inquisitors ordered Molina's arrest. The inquisitors were especially eager to interrogate Molina after Francisco Yáñez confessed that the two of them were together in Tecamachalco the night before the discovery of the effigy and the sambenitos. This admission by the chief suspect in the scandal turned Molina into a key witness and a potential accomplice of Yáñez.

Yet the case against Molina continued to suffer from the same problems that plagued the investigation from its beginning three and a half years earlier. As the Inquisition's notary Jerónimo de Euguí pointed out, the suspicions about Molina and Yáñez were strong, but the evidence was weak.[2] As a "very good scribe," Molina had the skills to write the Gothic letters used in the various signs accompanying the effigy and the sambenitos. If he had helped by writing the signs, he may also have helped Yáñez put them up, along with the effigy and the sambenitos. In other words, more than a mere accomplice, Molina may have acted as a coconspirator. In Tecamachalco, the two men gained a reputation, in Notary Euguí's words, as the "cocks of the walk" and "fast friends," capable of avenging one or more women insulted by Rubio Naranjo. Thus far, no one had identified the handwriting on the defaming signs as Molina's, and the other suspicions remained mere speculation. The depositions in Puebla and in Mexico City between late 1581 and early 1582 only noted a series of apparent contradictions about Juan de Molina's whereabouts on the day before the effigy and the sambenitos appeared. According to rumor, Yáñez and Molina spent that night together in Tecamachalco, even though they lived in Quecholac and Tepeaca, respectively. Molina's father, Francisco de Molina, disputed that assertion. He testified before Canon Santiago that Juan de Molina had left for his new post in Río de Alvarado fifteen days before the scandal. This was an "evident lie," according to Notary Euguí, given the testimony of Juan's "mother" Catalina Rodríguez, who declared that he had slept the night of 20 July in her house. Francisco Yáñez's most recent confession that he and Juan de Molina had slept that night in the same house further invalidated Francisco de Molina's sworn testimony.

Because he had moved to Río de Alvarado, Juan de Molina had not testified since 26 July 1578, despite the suspicions of various neighbors.[3] The cochineal collector Juan López de Montalbán's 1578 testimony, ratified and expanded in January 1582, supported the suspicion that Molina may have helped his friend Yáñez to make and put up the sambenitos and the effigy to avenge a woman—possibly Juana de Montoya—for Hernando Rubio Naranjo's insults. López de Montalbán's ratification seemed to confirm Notary Euguí's suspicions. Yáñez's recent admissions reaffirmed the suspicions that Molina collaborated in the 1578 scandal.

If proving Juan de Molina's role as an accomplice in the crime was important, even more so was his role as a witness against Yáñez, the suspected mastermind of the scandalous actions. Molina could reveal, for instance, the identity of the woman, or women, whom Yáñez had sought to avenge. Various testimonies suspected that Juana de Montoya might have asked Yáñez to carry out the actions against Rubio Naranjo for saying that she was a whore with a "big nature." Molina could also identify any other participants in the plot against Rubio Naranjo.

The inquisitors must have hoped that Molina's arrival at the Inquisition's prison would usher a speedy resolution to the mystery surrounding the scandal in Tecamachalco. Yet Notary Euguí's warning in November 1581 remained equally true in February 1582: the inquisitors lacked sufficient evidence to torture Yáñez and Molina, let alone to convict them for putting up the effigy and the sambenitos. Without torturing them, he realized, "it will never be possible to shed any light" on the truth. Thus, the greatest challenge for Licenciados Bonilla and Santos García was finding sufficient grounds to order the torture of both men. Short of Molina's admission of guilt, the inquisitors would need to demonstrate Molina's evident lies. That could happen only if Molina and Yáñez contradicted each other: the future of the case hinged on these two fast friends turning against each other. Unless that happened, the Tecamachalco crime would remain unresolved.

* * *

On 10 February 1583, Juan de Molina appeared at his first audience.[4] A short, bearded man with big eyes, he introduced himself as Juan González de Molina, a thirty-two-year-old bachelor. He was born in Aldeanueva de Barbarroya, a village under the jurisdiction of the city of Talavera de la Reina, west of Toledo, in Spain. He had lived in the city of Tepeaca and now resided in Río de Alvarado, where he served as royal scribe to Juan de Medina, the alcalde mayor of Tlacotaplan, just south of Veracruz.[5]

Molina told the inquisitors that he was the son of Roque Martínez and Mari González, husband and wife, both farmers. This may have come as a surprise to the inquisitors, who had heard different statements about Molina's parents from the testimonies collected by Canon Santiago. Neighbors and close friends described "Juan de Molina" as the son of Francisco de Molina. Now Juan introduced himself to the inquisitors using his mother's surname (González). Numerous witnesses previously testified that Juan was Francisco's son, even though Juan had never stated this. Until at least 1573, Juan de Molina had gone by the name Juan González, which is how Juan's actual father, Roque Martínez, referred to his son.[6] When did Juan González become Juan de Molina? Rather than clarify these matters, the interrogation proceeded in the usual manner:

Inquisitors: Do you know. . . . the reason for your arrest?
Juan de Molina: I don't know, although I suspect it has to do with the
     sambenitos in Tecamachalco.
Inquisitors: What about this?
Molina: It was perhaps three and a half years ago, more or less, when
     I was in Tepeaca with the scribe Francisco de Molina on my way
     to Río de Alvarado. I went to Tecamachalco. . . . On a day I don't
     remember, around three in the afternoon, I got off [my horse] in
     Tecamachalco at the house of the horseshoe maker Juan Guillén.
     I was with him for a while, telling him about moving to Río de
     Alvarado. Later, I went out to the plaza and found Juan López,

a mestizo who used to be a horseshoe maker. We talked, and when it got dark, we went to his house, where he invited me to stay for supper. Meanwhile, Francisco Yáñez arrived at the house from Quecholac. The three of us had supper, and then Yáñez and López sat down to play cards until midnight. It being late, I didn't go back to Juan Guillén's house. I begged López to make a bed for me to sleep in and went to sleep around nine or ten, leaving them to play. Around midnight, I felt Yáñez walk past my bed so close that he almost stepped on my feet. Next morning around six, before the sun was up, I asked López about Yáñez. He said that Yáñez had left very late at night and didn't sleep there. After that, I left the house, [and] I heard that some sambenitos against Hernando Rubio Naranjo had been put up and taken down. I didn't see them and don't know what they looked like. Two days later, after buying some things for the road, I left for Río de Alvarado. There I've been until almost now. It may have been a year ago that I went to Mexico City to buy some things. . . . I have nothing more to say, and don't know the reason why I have been imprisoned.[7]

Ten days later, on the afternoon of 22 February, the inquisitors called Juan de Molina back for a second audience. Thus far, on his first day of testimony, Molina had apparently resolved several contradictions created by the statements of previous witnesses, by agreeing with Yáñez's earlier declaration that on the night of 20 July 1578, the two men had played cards into the night and then slept in the same house in Tecamachalco. Molina's testimony differed from Yáñez's on one potentially important point: whereas Yáñez had said that everyone stayed in the house until the morning of 21 July, Molina now told the inquisitors that Yáñez might have left the house alone at midnight. However, Molina declared, he had been asleep and did not see where Yáñez had gone. The inquisitors therefore wanted to go over the details about the night of 20 July 1578:

Inquisitors: At what time did you go to sleep?
Juan de Molina: I think it was around nine.
Inquisitors: Did Francisco Yáñez sleep in the house of Juan López?
Molina: When I went to sleep, I left him playing. It was very late when I felt Yáñez leave.

Inquisitors: Why did Yáñez go out of the house around midnight?
Molina: I don't know, and cannot imagine why, only that Yáñez
   prides himself on being brave. When Yáñez came back, I heard
   sounds of horses behind the house. I don't know whose horses
   they were, other than it seemed someone had arrived.[8]

The insinuations in Molina's declaration must have pleased the inquisitors, since they left open the possibility that Yáñez had gone out of the house
and met someone who may have helped to put up the defaming images. However, the assertions remained speculation on Molina's part, since he did not
see where Yáñez went after leaving the house. Before concluding their interrogation, the inquisitors asked Molina a seemingly unrelated question:

Inquisitors: On your way to Río de Alvarado, did you go by
   Quecholac . . . ?
Molina: I didn't go by Quecholac.[9]

The last question sought to throw Molina off balance. It referred to Molina's first and only interrogation, on 26 July 1578, in which he stated that four
days earlier, he had attended a gathering in Quecholac to celebrate the Feast
of Mary Magdalene. Molina testified that on this occasion, the cochineal collector Juan López de Montalbán said that the sambenitos and the effigy were
"little" compared to what Rubio Naranjo had done.[10] These statements cost
López de Montalbán dearly, as he recently told Canon Santiago. The cochineal collector became the chief suspect and spent seventy days in shackles
and time in the Inquisition's prison, until the inquisitors finally set him free.
Had Molina now forgotten that incident in Quecholac?

A week later, on the morning of 1 March, Molina requested an audience
with the inquisitors. He had been thinking about a question that the inquisitors asked during the last interrogation and wanted to correct his previous
declaration. He now remembered that he had gone to Quecholac on 22 July
to celebrate the Feast of Mary Magdalene, the town's patron saint. He traveled with the horseshoe maker Juan Guillén, the Nahuatl language interpreter
Juan López, the cochineal collector Juan López de Montalbán, and many others "because all the farmers from the region" went there.[11] They arrived in
the morning, when the procession was under way. Molina heard mass and
the sermon. He dined along with other farmers in the house of Francisco
Yáñez, who lived in Quecholac. After dinner, Juan de Molina went to see

the farmers play games in the house of the Indian governor, Don Joaquín de Peralta. Molina explained that he had heard Juan López de Montalbán say some words, which Molina did not remember now, against Hernando Rubio Naranjo in relation to the sambenitos. The scribe also recalled that officials later interrogated López de Montalbán about these words. Molina had nothing more to say.

Once more, Molina had resolved an apparent contradiction between his statements and those of other witnesses. However, if the inquisitors hoped that Molina would establish Yáñez's guilt, these three days of testimonies largely reaffirmed Yáñez's statements. Only one matter held any promise: the question of where Yáñez had gone when he left the house around midnight on the evening of 20 July. Since the scribe insisted that he did not know where Yáñez had gone, the inquisitors would have to find out by turning to a different witness.

CHAPTER EIGHT

The Interpreter

Atlixco and Mexico City, 6–12 March 1582

On 6 March 1582, the guardian priest of the Franciscan monastery in Ca-
rrión del Valle de Atlixco, south of Puebla, informed Juan López that the inquisitors required him to come to Mexico City, along with his ladino Indian
servant Francisco. On the morning of 12 March, López appeared before the
inquisitors to answer questions.

Juan López, a forty-five-year-old mestizo, was obese and had an affa-
ble disposition. He did not tell the inquisitors the names of his parents
but only that he was originally from Mexico City. Eventually, he moved to
Tecamachalco, where he had two cousins, the cochineal collectors Domingo
and Juan López de Montalbán. There he lived with two servants in a humble
little house owned by Francisco Yáñez next to the town's church. A couple
of years later, López moved west to the town of Atlixco. Although he had
been a horseshoe maker, he now worked as a *naguatate*, or Nahuatl language
interpreter.[1] He was also a constable assisting the judge who assigned Indian
servants (*juez repartidor de indios*) to the landowners in the region.

The farmer Francisco Yáñez and the royal scribe Juan de Molina admitted under oath that they had spent the night of 20 July 1578 in Juan López's
house with him and his two servants, Francisco and his wife, Bárbara. Yáñez
and Molina agreed that they had eaten supper and played cards. However,
whereas Yáñez said that afterward they had all gone to sleep and had not
left the house until morning, Molina stated that Yáñez had gone out at midnight. López's testimony could therefore help determine which man was
telling the truth.

Before the interrogation began, Juan López explained that he had been unable to bring along his ladino Indian servant Francisco because he did not know where he was. The inquisitors did not seem concerned about the matter and began their questioning:

> *Inquisitors*: Do you know. . . . the reason you have been called to appear before the Holy Office?
>
> *Juan López*: My heart tells me that it's because of a statue and libels against Hernando Rubio Naranjo that turned up in Tecamachalco three or four years ago.
>
> *Inquisitors*: What do you know about them?
>
> *López*: Neither this nor that.
>
> *Inquisitors*: Do you know what day they were put up? Was it a feast day or a working day?
>
> *López*: I don't remember, because although my flesh is fat, my judgment is slim [*gordo de carnes, pero flaco de juicio*].
>
> *Inquisitors*: Who in town do you suspect may have put them up?
>
> *López*: I don't know anyone else's heart, but I suspect that Juan de Molina, the royal scribe, put them up.
>
> *Inquisitors*: Do you suspect Juan de Molina alone, or are there others who may have helped him to put them up?
>
> *López*: I also suspect Francisco Yáñez, a farmer from Quecholac.
>
> *Inquisitors*: Why do you suspect both of them?
>
> *López*: Because before and after they were put up, I heard them speak ill of Rubio Naranjo, that he was a scoundrelly little merchant, this or that, and other ugly words. In particular, I heard Juan de Molina say that Rubio Naranjo was a Jewish dog—always when Rubio Naranjo wasn't present. . . . I think this was all about some jealousy over women.

Next, the inquisitors wanted to know where Molina and Yáñez were on the night the statue and the libels were put up. López lived in "a little house" belonging to Yáñez, who allowed him to live there "out of charity" and under the condition that each time Yáñez came to Tecamachalco, he could sleep there. One the night of 20 July, Yáñez came, and almost at the same time so did "none other than Juan de Molina." They all slept in the house. López was "astonished that Molina, a royal scribe and held to be the son of the scribe of Tepeaca," would want to stay in such a "miserable crumbling house." He brought a small mattress and made Molina's bed in a small room. However,

Molina told López not to make it there "because there were fleas, and to make it instead out there by the entrance [*zaguán*] next to the door to the street." Molina slept there. Yáñez slept in López's bed, wearing a doublet and loose trousers (*jubón y zaragüelles*), "with his boots off." When López got out of bed the following morning, Molina told him that "he had still felt the fleas." The inquisitors continued their interrogation.

> *Inquisitors*: How many days earlier did Yáñez and Molina come to Tecamachalco, and what for?
>
> *López*: Yáñez came to Tecamachalco nearly every day and stayed there because his house is one league [about three miles] away. Molina hadn't come to Tecamachalco for many days, or at least I hadn't seen him until that day. . . . I don't know why they came.
>
> *Inquisitors*: Who else was in the house that night?
>
> *López*: No one else except a Mexican Indian [*indio çerrado*] from Tlaxcala and Bárbara, his Indian wife from Tecamachalco. They slept with me that night in the courtyard.

Having established the identity of everyone who slept in López's house, the inquisitors asked him, once more, to relate where Yáñez and Molina were that evening until the following morning. López's answers were important not only to determine the role of the two men in the scandal but also his own innocence.

> *Inquisitors*: That night, what did Yáñez and Molina do?
>
> *López*: We retired at seven, and I played cards with Yáñez until eleven. Molina went to sleep around eight.
>
> *Inquisitors*: At what time did you get out of bed the following day?
>
> *López*: Yáñez and I got out of bed around six in the morning. When we went to the entrance hall [*zaguán*],[2] we found Molina up, with the door closed. The door didn't have a key; it doesn't have one and never did.
>
> *Inquisitors*: That night, did anyone leave the house with someone else or on his own?
>
> *López*: I was asleep and don't know. I heard Yáñez get up and leave around one. I don't know whether he went to make water or what. All I know is that when he came back, he told me: "This

Indian and his wife sleep a lot." I don't know if Molina got up, because he was out in the entrance.

Inquisitors: How long did Yáñez take to come back?

López: Very little, maybe fifteen minutes, maybe half an hour.

Inquisitors: Did Yáñez go back to sleep when he came back?

López: Yes.

Inquisitors: When Yáñez went out, did he dress up and take a cape or arms with him?

López: I don't know because it was dark.

In short, nobody left the house that night. Yáñez got up, but even if he went outside, it was not long enough to perpetrate the crime. Molina went to bed, and López did not see him again until the following morning. Molina left the house at seven, when the scandal over the statue had already broken out. Yáñez left an hour later. The two men took their horses, but López did not know where they went.

However, the inquisitors noted an apparent contradiction in López's testimony. Earlier, he had stated that he suspected Yáñez and Molina were guilty because they had repeatedly said "ugly words" about Rubio Naranjo. But if the two men stayed inside his house until the following morning, they could not have committed the crime. The inquisitors wanted an explanation.

Inquisitors: Why do you suspect Yáñez and Molina if they were with you in your house the night before the statue was put up?

López: Molina could have left that night without my hearing it because I was asleep and he was in the entrance next to the door, which didn't have a key. I don't know anything more than what I've said.

Inquisitors: Did they agree beforehand that they would sleep in your house?

López: No. The two were close friends.

Inquisitors: When Yáñez got up that night, in order to make water or for another reason, did he have to go through the hall by the entrance where Molina was?

López: No. There was nowhere to go across the entrance but out to the street. I don't know if he went out—only that he didn't need to go outside.

Inquisitors: Did Yáñez and Molina see each other the morning before
   leaving?

López: Yes. The Indian Francisco came from the plaza and told them
   about the scandal of the statue and the libels; and they said that
   they didn't know who could have put them up.[3]

The inquisitors concluded the interrogation, warning López to search his
memory and to tell the truth, which he was covering up. They ordered the
jailer to imprison López. On the morning of 16 March, López returned before
Licenciados Bonilla and Santos García.

Inquisitors: The jailer informs us that you have requested an audience. Tell us what you want, and tell the truth under the oath you
   have taken.

Juan López: The truth is that the night that Yáñez slept in his
   house, I saw him take out of the pockets of his trousers two or
   three papers. One of them was white, about half a page [*medio
   pliego*], on which he wrote for a while, perhaps several hours.
   When he finished writing, he put it with the others in his trousers. I don't know what he wrote on them because I don't know
   how to read or write. Later, when the alcalde mayor gave orders
   to send Yáñez to Tepeaca, on our way there, I asked Yáñez what
   he had written that night because they said that the statue had
   papers with writing on then. Yáñez told me: "They're nothing. I
   don't know anything about that. I'm innocent." That's all I have
   to say.

Inquisitors: When Yáñez was writing, did you see the shape of the
   letters, whether they were large or small? Did he write slowly or
   quickly?

López: He was writing slowly, but I don't know anything more
   because he was away from me, and I don't know anything more
   than to sign my name.[4]

The inquisitors then showed López the original placards on the effigy and
on the sambenitos. He said that he did not recognize them and that he did
not know anything else.

Next, the inquisitors informed Juan López that he was a witness in the cases against Juan de Molina and Francisco Yáñez. López was free either to certify what he had declared or to correct his statements. After listening to his declaration, López had nothing to change. The inquisitors ordered López's release. However, he had to remain in Mexico City and could leave only with their permission. Two days later, they allowed López to return home to Atlixco.

CHAPTER NINE

The Farmer

6–8 May 1582

Between 17 March and 5 May 1582, Licenciados Bonilla and Santos García took a break from Francisco Yáñez's trial, coinciding with Lent and Holy Week. After nearly four years, the inquisitors must have hoped that they were at last close to resolving the scandal in Tecamachalco. Their strategy continued to focus on a plot first outlined in 1578 by the cochineal collector Juan López de Montalbán, which he reaffirmed in January 1582 before Canon Santiago:

1. Francisco Yáñez acted as plot leader, putting up the effigy and the sambenitos to avenge a woman—possibly Juana de Montoya— for Hernando Rubio Naranjo's insults against her. Yáñez already hated Rubio Naranjo for insulting Yáñez's mother and sister(s), which led to the attack on Rubio Naranjo in Quecholac.
2. Juan de Molina aided his close friend Yáñez by writing in his "very good scribe's" hand the three placards accompanying the effigy and the sambenitos. He may also have helped Yáñez put up the defaming objects.
3. Juana de Montoya, or another woman who may have been Yáñez's lover in 1578, may have instigated the humiliating crime against Rubio Naranjo. She may also have helped make the sambenitos and the effigy, whose fine stitches witnesses thought were the work of a woman.

Given the absence of any hard evidence or witnesses, proving such a plot depended on Yáñez and Molina confessing their role in the scandal, which they stubbornly refused to do. The inquisitors seemed determined to resort to what Notary Euguí called "harsher means" to force these recalcitrant men to admit their guilt. Such means seemed necessary to uncover the names of any other accomplices in carrying out the elaborate insult against Rubio Naranjo.

Between January and March 1582, the inquisitors established several contradictions in the declarations of Yáñez and Molina. At last, the testimony of the interpreter Juan López appeared to provide the strongest evidence yet that the two men had been lying about their role in the scandal. In early May, Licenciados Bonilla and Santos García were ready to apply the harsher methods that would finally establish the truth.

* * *

On 6 May, the inquisitors ordered the jailer to bring before them Francisco Yáñez, who had not appeared at an audience since January. The questioning began:

> *Inquisitors*: Have you remembered anything new? Tell the truth under the oath you've made!
> *Francisco Yáñez*: I don't remember anything new.
> *Inquisitors*: The prosecuting attorney for the Holy Office wishes to declare the evidence collected against you. You would do well to declare the whole truth. Tell the truth!
> *Yáñez*: I have nothing more to say.

What made Yáñez so stubborn? A thirty-year-old farmer, he was a castizo and the legitimate son of a mestiza and a Portuguese man, both of whom were dead. Around 1541, Francisco Yáñez, senior, had come to the region of Puebla along with four other Portuguese farmers to cultivate woad (*pastel*), used as a blue dye. German brokers and business associates of the Weslers, German bankers of Emperor Charles V, received a privilege from the emperor to undertake its cultivation.[1] The venture failed, but Yáñez stayed in Mexico, married a mestiza, and settled in Tecamachalco, where Francisco Yáñez, junior, was born around 1551. The younger Francisco Yáñez moved to Quecholac, where he lived with his mestiza wife. He conducted business (*trata e contrata*) in his hometown, as well as in the surrounding towns and cities.[2] He knew how to read and write. He counted among his many acquaintances the Tecamachalco horseshoe maker Juan Guillén, as well as three scribes: Pedro de Beristain from Tecamachalco; Francisco de Molina from Tepeaca; and his close friend Juan de Molina. Yáñez may have had personal or family connections with more powerful figures, such as the *regidor*, or councilman, from Puebla, who paid his bail in November 1581, after Canon Santiago arrested Yáñez. The inquisitors did not ask about his personal wealth, but Yáñez was certainly not poor. He owned a horse. He had a house in Tecamachalco, which Juan López described as "miserable and falling," in addition to his house in Quecholac; he also had fields near Tecamachalco. When Yáñez's mother died in 1581, she left him an inheritance in Tlaxcala. Yáñez did not act like a humble farmer. His friend Juan de Molina said that Yáñez prided himself in being a "brave man." The two friends had the reputation of being "cocks of the walk," and even troublemakers and ruffians. Standing before the inquisitors, Yáñez did not waver. The inquisitors would now try their best to break his steadfastness.

In December 1581, the Inquisition's prosecuting attorney, Dr. Lobo Guerrero, first presented charges against Francisco Yáñez as coconspirator with the horseshoe maker Juan Pérez. Following the dismissal of Pérez's trial, it was now necessary to lay new charges. Dr. Lobo Guerrero entered the room and read the new charges against Yáñez, citing accusations made by witnesses whose names the prosecuting attorney withheld, as it was the tribunal's practice to protect their identity. Of the long list of statements (almost two *fojas*, or about four long pages), the accusation rested on three principal claims:

1. Yáñez was Hernando Rubio Naranjo's declared enemy for insulting his sister and a woman who lived across the street from Rubio Naranjo (Juana de Montoya). For this reason, Yáñez had taken part in an attack on Rubio Naranjo, clubbing the trader and slashing his face with a knife.
2. Yáñez told several persons that he knew the people who put up the effigy and the sambenitos in Tecamachalco.
3. The night before the objects were put up, he slept in a house in Tecamachalco. At midnight, he got out of bed and put up the effigy and the sambenitos on the facade of the town's church.[3]

Asked to respond to these charges under oath, Yáñez admitted slashing Rubio Naranjo's face—but not clubbing him, as stated in the accusation—but only because he did not recognize his victim. Yáñez had simply intended to intervene during a fight between two unnamed men he knew and other men he did not recognize because they were covered up (presumably with hats).

When Yáñez realized that the man he had slashed was Rubio Naranjo, Yáñez let him go. The two remained friends. Regarding the second charge that he knew who put up the effigy, he denied ever saying anything more than what he had already told the inquisitors—namely, the accusations against Juan Pérez that he had heard from his mother-in-law. Finally, Yáñez denied leaving Juan López's house in Tecamachalco on the night of 20 July: "May demons take me away if I ever put up such sambenitos!"[4] The inquisitors concluded the audience by giving a copy of the charges to Yáñez to prepare his formal response with the assistance of his appointed defense lawyer, Licenciado Ávalos.

On the morning of 8 May, Yáñez seemed to have been shaken by the preceding audience. He appealed to the inquisitors, insisting that he was a "good Christian, fearful of God."[5] He had always lived the life of a good man, supporting his family, enjoying a good life and a good reputation. He named five respected men, including Francisco de Molina and Pedro de Beristain, who could vouch for his good character. He had always told the truth about the sambenitos.

Yáñez then attempted to disqualify the witnesses who had testified against him. He pointed out that he had already confessed carrying out the "pranks" (*travesuras*), by which he meant the clubbing and slashing of Rubio Naranjo in Quecholac, with the aid of two friends. However, Yáñez pointed out that none of the witnesses specifically accused him of committing the scandalous actions in Tecamachalco. Their statements conflicted with one another and did not provide concrete evidence of his involvement in the scandal. Yáñez added that he suspected that all the testimonies came from "enemies" who wanted to "harm me." He correctly identified one anonymous witness as the interpreter Juan López. This man, whom Yáñez had allowed to live in his house in Tecamachalco, was a "bad Christian" who for fifteen years had kept the servant Bárbara, wife of López's servant Francisco, as his concubine.[6] Having concluded his defense, the inquisitors ordered the farmer's return to his prison cell.

The Inquisition's prosecuting attorney must have presented charges against Juan de Molina around the time of the accusation against Francisco Yáñez. (Documentation for Juan de Molina's original trial transcript is incomplete.)[7] The charges included accusations that he was Hernando Rubio Naranjo's enemy and that he had called him a "Jewish dog," according to the statements made by the interpreter Juan López. López's statements about the royal scribe's whereabouts on the night of 20 July would also have led to the accusation that Molina had helped put up the statue and the sambenitos.

Charges probably also stemmed from the previous declaration by Juan López de Montalbán, who told Canon Santiago that in 1581, Molina had been worrying that two enemies (María de Balbuena and her son Castro) might accuse him of having put up the effigy and the sambenitos in Tecamachalco. Finally, the Inquisition's prosecuting attorney no doubt pointed out that Molina was capable of writing the signs on the effigy and the sambenitos. Molina denied the charges.[8]

* * *

Despite the popular myth about the Inquisition torturing at will, taking that step was not always easy. Despite their frustrations with the case, Licenciados Bonilla and Santos García had not yet recommended torturing anyone. In November 1581, the Inquisition's notary Joaquín de Euguí had told the inquisitors that, although it would be necessary to have recourse to torture Francisco Yáñez and Juan de Molina (as well as Juana de Montoya) to find out the truth about the Tecamachalco case, there were not sufficient grounds to do so.[9] On the afternoon of 19 May, the inquisitors presented for a vote their case for torturing the two men. Inquisitorial instructions required a majority of three votes, which included the two inquisitors and the bishop of the province where the crime had taken place. In lieu of the absent bishop of Tlaxcala (Puebla) from the Mexican capital, Pedro Moya de Contreras (the archbishop of Mexico City) took part in the deliberation. For Yáñez, the vote was unanimous: the farmer should undergo torture. However, the vote was split over Molina. Although a former inquisitor, Archbishop Moya de Contreras voted not only to spare Molina the torture but also to absolve him of all charges. The documentation does not indicate the archbishop's arguments. Nonetheless, the two inquisitors outvoted the archbishop, so that both the farmer and the scribe would be "put to the question under torment."[10]

Two days after the vote, on 21 May, the first torture session would begin. However, Bonilla and Santos García made a decision that would have important consequences. Rather than first torture Francisco Yáñez as the main suspect in the case, they would begin instead with Juan de Molina. The trial documentation does not include the inquisitors' reasoning, although it does not seem to be pure chance. Yáñez had proved to be a stubborn witness who refused to admit any guilt. It was unclear whether Yáñez would break down under torture. If he held strong and did not confess, Yáñez could claim that this was proof of his innocence.[11] Regarding Molina's confession, the stakes were not as high, since he was only Yáñez's accomplice. The inquisitors may have hoped that Molina would provide additional information to make the most of Yáñez's torture. Whatever the reason, this decision would once again inadvertently delay the conclusion of the Tecamachalco case.

CHAPTER TEN

Under Torment

21 May 1582

The jailer brought Juan de Molina to the torture chamber, where Licenciados Bonilla and Santos García awaited him.[1] Before the actual torture began, the inquisitors asked Molina if he had anything to declare. He refused to admit any guilt. Guards stripped Molina of his clothes and tied cords (*cordeles*) around his arms for the first torture. After the first two painful turns of the cords, he remained strong, refusing to confess. On the third turn, his stamina failed. The terrified Molina broke down. He pleaded for the torture to stop, and the guards released the ropes. Molina now swore "before God" that he would tell the truth:

> *Juan de Molina*: Señor, I put up the statue and Francisco Yáñez the sambenitos. It happened this way: Yáñez left the sambenitos in the darkness of a corner of the church of Tecamachalco. . . . He had the statue wrapped up in blankets [*mantillas*] together with the sambenitos. After midnight, at Juan López's house, Yáñez told me to come along for some matter, and so we left. We took the sambenitos and the statue. He gave me the statue. . . . He put up the sambenitos, and I put up the statue. Afterward, we went back to López's house. I don't know anything more about this matter.
>
> *Inquisitors*: How long beforehand did you and Yáñez discuss and agree to do this?
>
> *Molina*: He hadn't told me until we were there in the house of Juan López, where we met that night. There he told me before

midnight that we were going to take care of a matter, without explaining it until we had reached the corner of the church. He put the statue in my hands and told me to put it up, and I put it up against a wall, on the ground, near the plaza, next to the fence of the church adjacent to the plaza. He said he would put up the sambenitos in two corners. Since it was dark, I didn't see if he nailed them or the way in which he put them up. He told me only that he was putting up the sambenitos against Rubio.

Inquisitors: Where were the sambenitos made, and who made them?

Molina: I don't know.

Inquisitors: What reason did Yáñez give for this insult against Rubio Naranjo?

Molina: Because Rubio Naranjo used his evil tongue against the women of Tecamachalco—in particular, Juana de Montoya, who lives there. Yáñez told me that Rubio Naranjo was a great scoundrel who had boasted in Oaxaca of having [carnal] knowledge of Montoya. Yáñez would complain to me a lot about Rubio Naranjo because Yáñez was involved with her.

Inquisitors: Did Yáñez tell you that Juana de Montoya had asked him to do it?

Molina: He didn't tell me that. But that night on our way to put up the sambenitos, Yáñez kept telling me: "I swear to God that I must insult that scoundrel Rubio Naranjo, who has unleashed his tongue [*que ha puesto lengua*] against women and boasted that he slept with Juana de Montoya."

Inquisitors: What was the statue made of, and what was its size?

Molina: It wasn't big, about three feet [*una vara*] high, made of rags. It had two tongues, one with a needle [*lezna*], and the feet made of sticks. The rags were Indian blankets. It had a placard.

Inquisitors: What did the placard say?

Molina: I don't know.

Inquisitors: Who wrote the placard?

Molina: I'll tell you the truth: I wrote it.

Inquisitors: Where?

Molina: In Tepeaca, alone, because Yáñez begged me to do it.

Inquisitors: What did it say?

Molina: It's been such a long time that I don't remember.

The inquisitors ordered the guards to put the ropes back on Molina's arms, until he cried out:

Juan de Molina: I'll say everything! The sign had many things against Rubio Naranjo—that he was a Jew and an evil man. It's been such a long time, I don't remember.
Inquisitors: How many placards were there?
Molina: I don't remember whether one or two. Show me the signs, and I'll tell you.
Inquisitors: How many signs were there, and where were they placed?
Molina: There were two sambenitos, and each one had its own sign. The statue had two sambenitos, which I put up myself.[2] . . . The statue was made out of two dolls from the market.

Molina described other details about the sambenitos and the statue:

Inquisitors: How long beforehand did you write these signs in Tepeaca?
Juan de Molina: It may have been twenty days earlier.
Inquisitors: Then how can you say that you didn't know about this matter until that night?
Molina: The truth is that twenty days before putting them up, Yáñez came to Tepeaca and told me that he intended to insult Rubio Naranjo for defaming Juana de Montoya by putting up some sambenitos and a statue. There we agreed that I would write the signs, which I did. We met in Tecamachalco three days beforehand and agreed to put them up that night.
Inquisitors: What's the handwriting on the sambenitos?
Molina: Black letter [*gorda escolástica*], slanted, not straight.
Inquisitors: Did you write in your usual handwriting?
Molina: No, I made it look worse.

The inquisitors continued to question the royal scribe about other details of the signs, which Molina explained:

Inquisitors: Did you and Yáñez put them up on your own, or did anyone else come with you?
Juan de Molina: We were alone—Yáñez and me.

Inquisitors: In your opinion, do you think that the statue and the sambenitos were the work of men or women?

Molina: Women.

Inquisitors: Who did Yáñez say had made and sewn them?

Molina: He told me that a woman in Tecamachalco, who is from Oaxaca, married to a certain Enríquez, a trader who's not from here [*medio estrangero*].[3] She was Yáñez's concubine. I don't remember her name.

Inquisitors: Before you put them up, how long did Yáñez have the statue and the sambenitos?

Molina: Twelve or fifteen days before.[4] He would tell me about them and showed me the sambenitos, which he carried in his trousers. I didn't see the statue until the night we put them up.

Inquisitors: What insult did Rubio Naranjo make against the wife of Enríquez?

Molina: None.

Inquisitors: Then why would she have made them?

Molina: Because Yáñez told her to do so. I don't know if she knew why she was making them.

Inquisitors: Why hasn't any of this been known before?

Molina: Because it hasn't been discovered.

Inquisitors: Who else knows about this matter?

Molina: The mestizo Juan López, in whose house we slept. He was told that night. López was our lookout, watching if anyone was out in the street while we put up [the statue and the sambenitos].

Inquisitors: How can you say that he was the lookout if you said that Yáñez and you put them up on your own?

Molina: Yáñez and I went out on our own through a secret door in López's house. López went out alone through the front door to look out. He waited for us under a pepper tree [*árbol del Perú*] on the street across from where we put them up. He told us that no one was there. López waited alone under the tree, watching in case anyone came while Yáñez and I put them up.

Inquisitors: How much time beforehand did López know about this?

Molina: Three days before, when Yáñez and I agreed to meet that night. We discussed it with López, showed him the sambenitos, and explained the reason that they were being put up. López was in on it [*estuvo en ello*] and said to put them up.

Inquisitors: After you did it, did the three of you discuss this matter?
Molina: That same night before we went out, we said that nobody
    would discover it, even if we had to die for it. Each of us said: "I
    swear it won't be discovered because of me."

The inquisitors wanted him to tell if anyone else had known about their
plot, and after the fourth turn of the cords, Molina cried out:

I'll say it! Days before in Quecholac, Yáñez told me about his anger
toward Rubio Naranjo and his intention to put up some sambenitos
in the presence of Antonio de la Parada—Yáñez's close friend, a former farmer in San Pablo who now lives in Puebla with his wife, the
daughter of a cartwright [*carretero*]. Parada replied that he thought
that it was all very good and that, if needed, he would help. But it
wasn't necessary for him to do anything. Parada and Yáñez had beaten
up Rubio with sticks and attacked him with a knife [in Quecholac]. I
only know about it because Yáñez confessed it to me. Yáñez also told
me about his plan to put up the sambenitos in the presence of Bartolomé Lozano, a farmer from Puebla, because he was also a very close
friend of Yáñez; and both would go together to the house of the wife of
Enríquez. Lozano said that [the sambenitos] should be put up because
he thought it was all very good. The night they were put up, Lozano
was in Tecamachalco in case he was needed, which wasn't the case.[5]

Molina interrupted his declaration: "For the love of God, leave me now!"
He felt great pain from his injuries and promised that he would search his
memory and declare everything that was necessary. The inquisitors warned
Molina that, if necessary, they would resume the torture in due course. They
ordered the ropes on the royal scribe untied and the lesions from the torture
treated in the chamber before sending him back to his prison cell. The interrogation ended at eleven in the morning.

Given a day to rest, the inquisitors called Molina back at 2 P.M. on 22 May,
so that he could declare anything that he had not declared under torture. The
royal scribe did so. First, he named four other men who knew about the plot
against Hernando Rubio Naranjo:

1. Francisco Solano, a farmer from Puebla
2. Cristóbal García de Morales, a farmer from Tecamachalco

3. Juan Guillén, a horseshoe maker from Tecamachalco
4. Domingo López de Montalbán, who collected cochineal with his brother Juan López de Montalbán.

Molina explained that the first two—together with Bartolomé Lozano, mentioned during his torture session—were "close friends" of Yáñez. Many evenings, these four friends would go to the house of Rubio Naranjo and, from the street, shout taunts in "African" (*guineo*) so that he would not recognize them.[6] Molina was less certain about whether Juan Guillén and Domingo López de Montalbán knew about the plans to put up the effigy and the sambenitos. Around seven in the evening, when the effigy and the sambenitos were put up, López de Montalbán had come to the house of his cousin, the interpreter Juan López, when the conspirators were laughing and talking about their plan for later that night. Molina suspected that López de Montalbán might have overheard their conversation. In the case of Guillén, Molina suspected him only because he was Yáñez's friend.

The inquisitors were ready to move on to other matters. They asked Molina, "Would you be able to recognize the statue, the sambenitos, and their signs?" Molina said yes. When shown the effigy and the sambenitos, Molina admitted that they were the ones that he and Yáñez had put up and that the signs were the ones that he had written after Yáñez begged him to do so. Regarding the meaning of the needle and the gag on the tongues of the statues, as well as of the spindle and distaff, Molina stated: "I don't know their meaning. Ask Francisco Yáñez, who will explain it."

Next, the inquisitors asked Molina to confirm that yesterday's confession was true, or if he wished to retract or amend anything in it. After reading the declaration and taking his oath to tell the truth, Molina made an important retraction:

> *Juan de Molina*: What I declared about Francisco Yáñez and Juana de
> Montoya being "entangled" [*revueltos*], I don't know for certain,
> nor do I suspect it. On this matter, I didn't tell the truth. The
> same goes for what I said about Yáñez telling me that the wife
> of Enríquez had made and sewn the statue and the sambenitos.
> That's not the case. The rest I said in the torture chamber, and
> today I ratify and declare it; because it's the truth. If necessary, I
> will say it again.

Inquisitors: In addition to what you have stated, what part did Francisco Solano and Cristóbal García de Morales have in the crime?

Molina: They knew that we were going to put up the sambenitos. They were Yáñez's friends; Yáñez would tell them and discuss how he would put them up and insult Rubio Naranjo, and they all laughed as friends. They were in Tecamachalco the night that [the sambenitos] were put up, although I don't know if they knew that it would happen that night. They communicated with Yáñez every day.

Inquisitors: Who do you think made and sewed the statue and the sambenitos?

Molina: I don't know, and Yáñez didn't tell me. He'll tell you.[7]

Then Molina knelt down and begged the inquisitors to be merciful in their punishment. The inquisitors ordered his return to his prison cell.

Three days after his last audience, on the morning of 25 May, Molina returned before the inquisitors to make a startling declaration.

Inquisitors: The jailer has informed us that you wish to make a statement. Say what you want to declare. Tell the truth under the oath you have sworn.

Juan de Molina: I asked an audience to declare that I alone am guilty of this affair. What I said under torture—that Bartolomé Lozano, Francisco Solano, Cristóbal García de Morales, Antonio de la Parada, Domingo López de Montalbán, the mestizo Juan López, and Francisco Yáñez were all in on the crime—is not so. Rather, I alone did it, and not them. Please have mercy on me! Even though Yáñez, the mestizo Juan López, and I slept together that night as I've confessed, I did it alone. I have nothing more to say. Give me my sentence! Give me lashes, and send me to a "hot land," because I'm dying from the pain of the lesions I have![8]

Molina seemed desperate, as if about to face death. He told the inquisitors about money that he had left with the scribe Francisco de Molina (two hundred pesos) and debts owed to him in Río de Alvarado (one hundred pesos). Then in a seemingly contradictory statement, Juan de Molina concluded with another plea: "For the love of God, bring those men I've declared. I suspect them, but I don't condemn them." He had nothing more to say. The inquisitors had no questions for him. The jailer returned the prisoner to his cell.

Molina said that he had lied under torture because he had wanted to answer the inquisitors' questions to stop the torture. But why did he not make these retractions on 22 May, the day after his torture session? If Molina wanted to protect the men he had accused, it was too late. The inquisitors had already ordered the arrest of the alleged accomplices for questioning. Until that happened, Francisco Yáñez's torture would wait.

CHAPTER ELEVEN

Conspiracy

Mexico City, 22–23 May, and Puebla, Early June 1582

Licenciados Bonilla and Santos García were quick to interrogate the five men whom Juan de Molina had accused during his torture session of participating in the crime to humiliate Hernando Rubio Naranjo. All along, the inquisitors had suspected that the elaborate plot required the participation of several individuals. Juan de Molina's testimony revealed that the conspiracy might have involved, in addition to Francisco Yáñez, at least five other men:

1. Juan López, the interpreter in whose house Molina and Yáñez slept on the night of 20 July 1578, accused of acting as a lookout while the statue and the sambenitos were being put up

[In addition, the following friends of Yáñez allegedly knew about the plot and offered their assistance:]

2. Antonio de la Parada, a cartwright from Puebla
3. Francisco Solano, a farmer from Puebla who allegedly was in Tecamachalco on the night of 20 July
4. Bartolomé Lozano, who was in Tecamachalco on the night of 20 July
5. Cristóbal García de Morales, a farmer from Tecamachalco, who was in Tecamachalco on the night of 20 July.

Molina seemed less certain about two additional accomplices: the horseshoe maker Juan Guillén and the cochineal collector Domingo López de Montalbán (Juan López de Montalbán's brother).

Still missing from this conspiracy was a key person—the woman everyone assumed had abetted the authors of the crime and helped make the effigy and the sambenitos. Under torture, Molina had accused Juana de Montoya of possibly knowing about the crime, as well as the so-called wife of Enríquez of helping make the defaming objects. On his next two audiences with the inquisitors, the royal scribe changed his mind about these accusations. The inquisitors would pay special attention to identifying Yáñez's one or more female accomplices.

* * *

On 22 May 1582, the same day that Molina confirmed his confession under torture, the inquisitors wrote a letter to the guardian priest of the Franciscans in Atlixco with orders to arrest, for a second time, the interpreter Juan López and have him brought in shackles to the Inquisition.[1] A day later, the inquisitors wrote to the Inquisition's commissioner in Puebla, Canon Santiago, with instructions to arrest Antonio de la Parada and Bartolomé Lozano, both of whom lived in Puebla. Canon Santiago was also instructed to summon Francisco Solano and Cristóbal Morales de García and inform them to appear before the inquisitors within four days. The inquisitors asked Canon Santiago to ensure that the four men did not know one another's whereabouts.[2]

In early June, Canon Santiago began to round up the suspected accomplices in Puebla. On 4 June, the commissioner captured Antonio de la Parada and released him on bail on condition that within four days, he appear before the Inquisition's secretary, Pedro de los Ríos, or face a stiff fine and the loss of his bail.[3] On 6 June, Canon Santiago issued similar orders to Bartolomé Lozano.[4] On 9 June, it was Francisco Solano's turn to hear these orders from Canon Santiago.[5] The only suspect missing was Cristóbal García de Morales, from Tecamachalco. The Inquisition's commissioner learned that, after the scandal in July 1578, the farmer had moved to Zacatecas to serve as a soldier in the wars between Spanish authorities and rebel Chichimec Indians, leaving behind his wife in great poverty. His present whereabouts were unknown.[6] One by one, the other three suspects made their way to Mexico City to face their interrogators.

Antonio de la Parada

On 8 June, after three days on the road from Puebla to Mexico City, the Inquisition's jailer escorted Antonio de la Parada to his cell, where he spent the night.

On the morning of Saturday, 9 June, Parada appeared at his first audience before Licenciados Bonilla and Santos García. Born in San Sebastián, in the Basque province of Guipúzcoa, Parada was a thirty-four-year-old cartwright who lived in Puebla with his wife, the daughter of a cartwright whose name the documents do not provide. In 1578, he had a farm in the valley of San Pablo, two and a half leagues (less than eight miles) from Tecamachalco. Not surprisingly, he knew the other farmers in the region and had become a close friend of Francisco Yáñez. That friendship was now largely responsible for his summons at the Inquisition. According to Juan de Molina, Yáñez and Parada had taken part in clubbing Rubio Naranjo and attacking him with a knife in Quecholac in revenge for insulting Yáñez's mother and sisters. Later, when Yáñez began to plan his humiliation of Rubio Naranjo in Tecamachalco, Parada had allegedly known and supported the plan, offering to help if necessary.

The inquisitors began by asking Parada if he knew the reason he had been imprisoned. Parada had an idea from a chance encounter with an old acquaintance from Tecamachalco. Thirty-five days earlier, he had seen the cochineal collector Juan López de Montalbán in Mexico City. Pleased to see each other, the two men struck up a conversation:

> *Antonio de la Parada*: Weren't you imprisoned by the Inquisition?
> *Juan López de Montalbán*: They have already let me out. The Holy
>   Office has given me license to go to Peru or anywhere I want to
>   go. Do you know where Francisco Yáñez is?
> *Parada*: I don't know, but I've heard that he was imprisoned by the
>   Holy Office. Thank God, Yáñez never said anything to me, so that
>   he couldn't bear false testimony against me.

Parada was now sorry that he had said those words, and asked for mercy: "I said this with my tongue, not with my heart!" He meant no evil.

> *Inquisitors*: Over what matter would Francisco Yáñez bear false testi-
>   mony against you?[7]
> *Antonio de la Parada*: I don't know. All I know is that the Holy Office
>   imprisoned him.
> *Inquisitors*: What was the reason for Yáñez's imprisonment . . . ?
> *Parada*: After Yáñez was arrested, I saw in Puebla [the farmer] Diego
>   de Trujillo, who had spoken to the Inquisition's commissioner
>   [Canon Santiago], but he didn't tell me about what.[8]

Yet Trujillo told Parada about Yáñez's claim that he knew who put up the sambenitos in Tecamachalco. Parada admitted that this was the reason he feared that Yáñez might bear false witness. The inquisitors warned Parada to tell the truth. Parada insisted that he did not know anything more than what he had just declared. The inquisitors warned him again before sending him back to his prison cell. On the morning of 12 June, Parada appeared again before the inquisitors:

> *Antonio de la Parada*: I requested an audience to tell you that I don't
>   remember anything more than what I've said.
> *Inquisitors*: What were the sambenitos you spoke about before?
> *Parada*: I never saw them. I heard that they were put up against
>   Rubio Naranjo.
> *Inquisitors*: Who put them up? Where? How long ago? How many
>   sambenitos were there? Was there anything else besides the sam-
>   benitos? What was the reason they were put up?
> *Parada*: I don't know who put them up, or anything more than what
>   people in Tecamachalco used to say, which is that there were
>   three sambenitos and a statue. They were put up about five [*sic*]
>   years ago. I don't know the reason. . . .
> *Inquisitors*: From whom in particular did you hear this?
> *Parada*: I don't remember. They used to say that [Rubio Naranjo]
>   was a Jewish dog, but I don't know the reason. All I know is that
>   one Saturday in Tecamachalco, Rubio Naranjo sold me a horse
>   and china in his house. He asked me to stay that night in his
>   house because we were friends, but I didn't want to; and the fol-
>   lowing Monday the sambenitos appeared. We had a quarrel over
>   a woman Rubio Naranjo used to visit in her house, but we had
>   already made peace. One night, Francisco Yáñez, Pedro Hernán-
>   dez,[9] and I gave Rubio Naranjo a thrashing [*cintarazos*]. Yáñez
>   did it while Hernández and I covered his back. Rubio Naranjo
>   came out of it wounded from the beating. This happened months
>   before the sambenitos were put up.

The inquisitors wanted to know who had called Rubio Naranjo a "Jew-ish dog" and why. Parada confirmed what many witnesses had already made plain: the anti-Semitic insult responded not to any suspicions that Rubio Naranjo had Jewish blood but to his notoriety as a "defamer of women." At the time of Rubio Naranjo's thrashing in Quecholac, Parada heard Yáñez say, "I swear to God that if this Jewish dog complains about me, I will have to throw him against a wall!" Parada also knew that Rubio Naranjo had defamed three women, boasting about "having known" them carnally: Juana de Montoya, the widow of Benavides, and the widow of Héctor Carrero. The latter complained to Parada, who had been her husband's friend, that Rubio Naranjo had beaten her up "because she refused to give him her body." The inquisitors continued their interrogation.

> *Inquisitors*: What relationship did Yáñez have with these women?
> *Parada*: Yáñez told me he had relations [*tenía qüentos*][10] with Carrero's widow, and I don't know if with Juana de Montoya. I don't know if this was true.
> *Inquisitors*: Who do you suspect put up the sambenitos and the statue against Rubio Naranjo?
> *Parada*: People would say it wasn't possible for a *criollo* [creole][11] to have made the sambenitos and that it had to be a man from Castile. And so, I suspect Juan de Molina, a royal scribe; and in my heart, I suspect Francisco Yáñez, who is my close friend. Both men were idlers of bad habits who always went together everywhere.
> *Inquisitors*: Did any woman, or women, complain to Yáñez and Molina about Rubio Naranjo's insults asking them for revenge?
> *Parada*: I don't know.

The interrogation turned to other matters, about which Parada had no direct knowledge. He did not know the color and size of the sambenitos and the statue, although he heard that "it was delicate labor and with placards by a good scribe" and that "they looked like something made by a man and a woman." He also heard that Molina and Yáñez were in Tecamachalco the night the sambenitos were put up, but he did not know for certain, since that night he slept at a farm eight miles away. He learned about the scandal only the following day at the assignment of Indian servants in San Pablo. Nonetheless, Parada reaffirmed his suspicions about Yáñez and Molina.

> *Inquisitors*: What kind of people would have planned this business of putting up sambenitos?

Parada: They would have been scoundrels and idlers, and I only
   know three: Juan de Molina, Francisco Yáñez, and Cristóbal García de Morales, who whiled away the time with them.
Inquisitors: How long before they were put up did you hear about the
   sambenitos?
Parada: They didn't tell me anything about sambenitos before they
   were put up. Rather, before and after they were put up, I heard
   Yáñez say that Rubio Naranjo was a Jewish dog and a defaming
   scoundrel.[12]

The inquisitors warned Parada to search his memory. He confirmed his
declaration and added a few details but did not provide any new valuable
information. The inquisitors sent him back to his prison cell.

On 20 June, Parada returned for his third audience before the inquisitors.
They asked him to ratify his two previous depositions as testimony against
Juan de Molina and Francisco Yáñez. Parada confirmed his statements and
said that he would repeat them again because they were the truth.[13]

Francisco Solano

On the morning of 13 June, Francisco Solano appeared before the inquisitors for his first interrogation. Solano was a thirty-one-year-old native of
Puebla, where he still lived. He was a farmer in San Pablo, knew all the
farmers from Tecamachalco, and was a close friend of Francisco Yáñez. As
in the case of Parada, Molina accused Solano of consenting to help Yáñez
humiliate Rubio Naranjo with the sambenitos and the effigy. Canon Santiago did not arrest Solano but required him to go to the Inquisition in
Mexico City within four days. When he arrived, the inquisitors did not
imprison him.

It did not take long for the inquisitors to confirm that Solano's testimony
did not differ much from the one that Parada had given the previous week.
As Parada had declared, Solano, too, heard from the farmer Diego de Trujillo
about Yáñez's claim to know who had put up the sambenitos and the effigy.
Contrary to what Molina had declared, neither Parada nor Solano slept in
Tecamachalco on the night of 20 July: Solano was at his brother-in-law's farm
about six miles from Tecamachalco—a couple of miles closer to town than
Parada, who was on his own farm. As in Parada's case, Solano learned about
the scandal the next day when he went to the assignment of Indian servants

in San Pablo. However, an incident that same day revealed that Solano and Rubio Naranjo had once been enemies.

The same Monday that the scandal broke, 21 July 1578, while the farmers in the region were talking about the events in Tecamachalco, Rubio Naranjo approached Francisco Solano. The defamed man suspected that behind the insult were Yáñez and his two friends Bartolomé Lozano and Cristóbal García de Morales. Since Solano was their close friend, Rubio Naranjo asked him to look into his suspicions. Solano did not want anything to do with the matter; he admitted to the inquisitors that he had once hated Rubio Naranjo. Six or seven months before the scandal, Rubio Naranjo had sent officials to collect a payment from Solano for defaulting on a debt. Resentful, Solano had joined Yáñez and García de Morales in saying "ruinous words" about Rubio Naranjo, including that he was a "bad Christian" of mean business practices (*malos tratos y contratación*).[14] Eventually, however, Solano paid his debt and reconciled with Rubio Naranjo. Solano knew about the beating that Yáñez and Parada had given Rubio Naranjo one night for boasting about having carnally known Yáñez's sister. Solano insisted that he had no part in this affair. He claimed not to know about the sambenitos and the effigy until after they appeared. Before concluding the questioning, the inquisitors warned Solano to search his memory and tell the truth. They ordered his imprisonment in the Inquisition's jail.

On 20 June, Solano appeared for his second audience before the inquisitors. Rather than continue with their interrogation, the inquisitors asked him to ratify or amend his previous testimonies, which would serve as evidence in the trial against Francisco Yáñez. Solano made no changes to his deposition. He only had an inconsequential addition: Yáñez had told him that when he beat up Rubio Naranjo in Quecholac months before the incident in Tecamachalco, Rubio Naranjo had soiled his pants.[15] The inquisitors sent Solano back to his prison cell.

Bartolomé Lozano

Bartolomé Lozano was the third friend of Francisco Yáñez accused by Juan de Molina of knowing and supporting Yáñez's plans to put up the statue and the sambenitos. At age twenty-eight, Lozano was the youngest of the four friends presently testifying before the inquisitors. Like Solano, Lozano lived in his native city of Puebla and was a farmer in San Pablo. Like Yáñez, Lozano was a castizo (the son of a Spaniard and a mestiza or mestizo). Based on Molina's accusations, the Inquisition's commissioner Canon Santiago arrested Lozano in Puebla and released him on bail, requiring him to present himself within four days to the Inquisition in Mexico City. The following day, Lozano left Puebla on a mule, reaching Mexico City on the afternoon of 13 June. He spent the next two nights in the Inquisition's prison.

By the time of Lozano's first audience, on 15 June, Parada and Solano had already testified before the inquisitors. Perhaps for this reason, the inquisitors seemed to have little hope that Lozano would be a helpful witness. When asked if he knew the reason he had been arrested, Lozano said that someone in Puebla asked whether he had been arrested because of having a part in the sambenitos in Tecamachalco; but Lozano replied to the man that he had had no part in it. He told the inquisitors that he did not know anything else.[16] Rather than continue with the interrogation, the inquisitors issued the usual warnings to search his memory and sent Lozano back to his prison cell.

On 16 June, the inquisitors summoned Lozano and asked if he now remembered anything else. As Parada and Solano had affirmed before him, Lozano said that he had only learned about the scandal in Tecamachalco on that Monday morning, on his way to San Pablo for the assignment of Indian servants. He admitted to having slept in Tecamachalco on the previous night at the house of a relative. That evening of Sunday, 20 July, after everyone in the house had gone to sleep, they all woke at the sound of someone playing a guitar or a *vihuela* (small guitar). He stood by the door in his nightshirt listening to the music, and afterward went back to bed and did not get up until the next morning at seven. On his way to San Pablo, some farmers told him about the "great wickedness" that had taken place. The inquisitors wanted to know what more Lozano knew about the incident:

Inquisitors: Before you left Tecamachalco [for San Pablo] on that Monday morning, did you hear anything about this matter?
Bartolomé Lozano: Not until I was on the road, as I have said.
Inquisitors: Besides the sambenitos, did you hear if anything else had been put up?
Lozano: I don't know and didn't hear more than what I said.
Inquisitors: At that time, did you hear who had put them up?
Lozano: I didn't hear about this from anyone.
Inquisitors: At that time or later on, did you suspect anyone?
Lozano: I never heard about it other than people saying a thousand

things [about the scandal, such as that the suspects] had come
from Oaxaca to put them up. I couldn't tell for certain.

Inquisitors: Whom did you suspect?

Lozano: No one.

Inquisitors: Who was playing the guitar that night?

Lozano: I don't know, but I heard that they were some youngsters
[*mozuelos*] who were later arrested by the alcalde mayor of
Tepeaca.[17]

The inquisitors warned Lozano that they had information to the effect that
he knew more than he cared to tell in order to protect someone. Once more,
they warned Lozano to tell the truth. Lozano said that he did not remember
anything else. The interrogation ended, and the prisoner went back to his cell.

* * *

Had Molina tried to mislead the inquisitors by denouncing three men
who seemed to know little about the July 1578 scandal? Parada, Solano, and
Lozano may have been close friends of Yáñez, but their depositions could
not confirm that they had been accomplices or participants, as Molina had
suggested. Fortunately for the inquisitors, they had much better luck with the
fourth man whom Molina had implicated.

Juan López

Juan López, the forty-five-year-old mestizo interpreter and constable for the
judge in Atlixco who assigned Indian servants (*juez repartidor de indios*), last
testified on 16 March, nearly three months earlier, as a witness against Juan de
Molina and Francisco Yáñez. López provided important information about
Yáñez's and Molina's whereabouts on the night of 20 July 1578 and offered
evidence about the two men's repeated insults against Rubio Naranjo. López
declared that he did not see the two friends put up the sambenitos and the
effigy. Under torture, Molina contradicted López's assertion, accusing him of
knowing about the plan and acting as lookout while Molina and Yáñez carried out the deed. Allegedly, López also swore with the other two men that
they would die before revealing their secret.

Arrested for the second time on 13 June, López arrived shackled at the
Inquisition. On 15 June, he appeared before the inquisitors, who again asked

if he knew the reason for his arrest. It was not difficult for López to assume that it had to do with his previous declarations about the crime in Tecamachalco.

> *Inquisitors*: You're right to suspect the cause of your imprisonment. New information has turned up against you to the effect that you have greater guilt in the crime than you've confessed. We advise you to tell the truth out of reverence for God.
>
> *Juan López*: I don't remember anything, but I'll search my memory.[18]

With that, the inquisitors ordered his return to his prison cell. The following afternoon, the inquisitors asked López if he remembered anything more. López had nothing more to declare. Warned once more, the interpreter stood his ground. Next, the Inquisition's prosecuting attorney, Dr. Lobo Guerrero, read the accusation against Juan López, listing five charges:

1. López committed "crimes against this Holy Tribunal," including the use of its symbols (*signos*) to injure others.
2. In particular, as a "bad Christian," he discussed, approved, and offered help to persons who put up sambenitos and an effigy in Tecamachalco against Rubio Naranjo by providing shelter in his house to those persons.
3. In addition, even though he could have stopped the crime, he acted as a lookout while those persons put up the sambenitos and the statue in public places.
4. When called to declare as a witness at the Holy Office, López did not tell the truth, despite his oath do to so.
5. For this reason, he had perjured himself.

Dr. Lobo Guerrero concluded by declaring that if the inquisitors did not think that he had presented sufficient proof to demonstrate the truth of the accusation against Juan López, the inquisitors might decide to question the accused "under torment."[19] Given the opportunity to respond to the charges, López denied them. He admitted giving supper to and providing beds for Yáñez and Molina, as he had done other times. López denied doing anything more than keeping his promise to allow Yáñez to stay there whenever he liked: "There isn't anything more besides what I've said. I'm a miserable man." The inquisitors appointed Licenciado Ávalos to serve as López's defense lawyer. López protested, "I'm a Catholic Christian, and I'm ready to tell the truth about everything and search my memory."[20] Warned again to tell the truth, he returned to his prison cell.

Monday morning, 18 June, a troubled López was ready to report what he could not remember the previous week: "For the love of God, pardon my ineptitude [*incapacidad*] because out of fear of being burned, I didn't tell the truth, like a weak man! I heard that morning when the sambenitos appeared in Tecamachalco that they would burn whoever had done it. Now I want to tell the truth."[21] According to López, the sequence of events that took place nearly four years previously, between the evening of Sunday, 20 July, and the morning of Monday, 21 July, was the following:

1. Sunday, seven in the evening: López was playing cards alone in his house in Tecamachalco when Yáñez arrived and said: "What are you doing, old man?" López replied: "Nothing." Yáñez looked agitated and troubled [*alterado de mudado conturbado*]; he took out from his trousers "some papers" on which he wrote for a while.

2. Sometime later, Juan de Molina arrived. He was covered with a cloak. They talked for a while. Molina then asked López to look outside to see if there was anyone in the vicinity of the church, which was nearby.

3. Eight in the evening: López left his house through a hidden door and did not find anyone in the street.

4. When he returned to the house, López saw, at the front door of the house, Yáñez and Molina covered with cloaks and carrying bundles that he had not seen inside the house. López stayed inside the house.

5. Not long after, Yáñez returned, looking restless, and told López: "Let's play for a lunch, old man," and took the cards lying on the table.

6. Juan de Molina arrived, panting and out of breath. They all sat down.

7. More at ease, Molina told Yáñez: "That's how one must treat them; to do it any other way is for a man to lose what he has."[22] Yáñez smiled.

8. Molina went to bed in the hall next to the front door. Yáñez and López continued playing cards.

9. Eleven at night: Yáñez and López went to bed.

10. Monday morning: When the scandal broke, Yáñez and Molina
    said: "How well we've slept in Juan López's house without leaving
    it the whole night!"[23]

"And that's what happened and the truth," López said, "which I hadn't dared
tell out of fear." Once more, López insisted that he did not know why Molina had
asked him to look outside, although he suspected that Yáñez and Molina had
carried out the deed. The two left, covered by cloaks and hats, carrying bundles.
Molina's bundle was larger. Yáñez looked as though he had a smaller bundle
under his cloak, but it could also have been a sword or his elbow sticking out.

The two friends were "mortal enemies" of Hernando Rubio Naranjo. The
moment that Rubio Naranjo was not beside them, they called him a "burned
Jewish dog." Molina used to pull his own beard, as if he were threatening
Rubio Naranjo—even though to Rubio Naranjo's face, it was all smiles (*cari-
cias*). At some point, López warned Molina that in town, he was suspected of
putting up the sambenitos. Molina replied: "Quiet, quiet, courage, courage!"
(*Calla, calla, ánimo, ánimo*).

Inquisitors: How many days beforehand did they tell you about this
    business?
Juan López: They didn't tell me anything.
Inquisitors: Through what door did you all leave the house . . . ?
López: I left through a hidden door [*puerta falsa*]. I went around and
    came back through the main door, where I found them coming
    out, and I told them that I didn't see anyone and that I had gone
    to the church, which is nearby.
Inquisitors: Where did you wait for them and continue looking out,
    in case anyone came?
López: I went inside the house, where I waited until they returned.
Inquisitors: Why did you imagine Molina and Yáñez went out carry-
    ing something under their arms, as you have said?
López: Right then, I imagined that they were going to fight because
    they pride themselves on being brave. But when I heard the next
    morning about the sambenitos, I understood that they must
    have gone out to put them up, because of what Molina had said:
    "That's the way to treat them; otherwise, they can go ahead and
    cut off what we have." When I first heard this, I wondered if they
    had cut someone's face or done some bravery.

Inquisitors: Your words aren't convincing because one must deduce from the fact that Molina told you to have courage that all of you knew about it. Tell the truth!

López: I didn't know about it!

Inquisitors: Why were you told to have courage if you didn't know anything?

López: I don't know.

Inquisitors: Before you left the house, did the three of you swear to keep it secret?

López: No, because they weren't close friends with me.

Inquisitors: Was it a dark night?

López: I think it was dark.[24]

Once more, the inquisitors commanded López to tell the plain truth. After approving the transcript of the deposition, they sent him back to his prison cell. Later in the afternoon, the inquisitors brought back Juan López to ratify the accusations that he had made earlier in the day against Molina and Yáñez. A brief interrogation followed:

Inquisitors: That night, how long did Yáñez and López stay outside?

Juan López: It didn't take them long to return—about a quarter of an hour, at most.

Inquisitors: In what direction did they go when they went outside?

López: They went in the direction of the church, which is very near the house. [He pointed to the distance, from where he stood to the wall in the audience chamber where the interrogation was taking place.][25]

The inquisitors ordered the man returned to his prison cell.

The following morning, Juan López was back before the inquisitors to respond to the charges against him by other unnamed witnesses. López did not know that the charges came from a single person: Juan de Molina. During his questioning under torture on 21 May, Molina stated that López knew about the plans for the crime ahead of time, saw the sambenitos, swore to keep the plans secret, and knowingly acted as a lookout. López continued to deny all charges, insisting that he never saw the contents of the bundles, which were never inside the house. The anonymous witness claimed that the perpetrators went out at midnight to put up the effigy and the sambenitos, but López insisted that Yáñez and Molina left the house much earlier and were asleep by eleven. López suggested that when the men left the house earlier in the evening, they may simply have hidden the bundles in some dark corner by the church and returned there at midnight to put them up. López noted that Yáñez left his bed around that time and returned a quarter of an hour later. López challenged other details and stood firm in his earlier assertions, and then returned to his cell.[26]

Juan López returned in the afternoon to present his defense, with the assistance of Licenciado Ávalos, the defense lawyer appointed by the inquisitors. López insisted that what he had declared the previous day was true and asked for mercy for not saying it earlier, out of fear. He asked that the inquisitors dismiss the accusations made that morning because they came from a single witness whom he correctly identified. Juan de Molina, López now claimed, was his enemy because of an incident that involved Molina's purported father, Francisco. As part of López's duties as constable of the judge who assigned Indian servants (*juez repartidor de indios*) required to work for landowners, López arrested Francisco de Molina's clerk, for which Francisco had to pay a fine. An angry Juan de Molina threatened López by warning him that "there are more days than sausages"[27]—meaning that López would have his day of reckoning for what he had done to Juan de Molina's father. This concluded López's defense, and he returned to his prison cell.

Contradictions

Since Juan de Molina's torture session, none of the men interrogated had agreed on the identity of the woman, or women, assumed to have been involved in the crime. After first implicating, under torture, Juana de Montoya and the "wife of Enríquez," Molina later denied that they had had anything to do with the crime. The royal scribe could not deny the hand of a woman in making the defaming effigy and the sambenitos, which Francisco Yáñez could not have done all by himself, just as Molina had had to write the placards that Yáñez requested. Molina and the inquisitors assumed that it might have been the work of one of Yáñez's possible lovers. Over the course of many months, numerous witnesses said that Juana de Montoya was such a woman. Molina alone said that the "wife of Enríquez," Yáñez's alleged concubine, might have been the one who made the sambenitos and the effigy. Molina admitted that he was not certain about this. Were other women involved?

Juan de Molina continued to think about these questions following his declaration on 25 May. Three weeks later, on 16 June, he requested an audience with the inquisitors to make two important declarations. First, Molina wanted to reverse the retractions that he had made in the days after his torture. On his last audience on 25 May, he had gone so far as to declare that he alone was responsible for the crime. Now he affirmed that he had told the truth under torture about Antonio de la Parada, Francisco Solano, Bartolomé Lozano, Cristóbal García de Morales, Juan López, and Francisco Yáñez, "who was the principal one" in the crime. As if this were not enough to startle the inquisitors, Molina wished to make another declaration:

> *Juan de Molina*: I think that the sambenitos and the effigy were the
> work of Juana Ramírez, sister of the horseshoe maker Juan Pérez.
> One day, I entered her house and saw two of her daughters with
> dolls from the market, dressing them up [*componiéndolas*]²⁸
> because they are girls. . . . [Juana Ramírez] would have done it
> because she was the concubine of Cristóbal García de Morales
> and has two sons of his. I don't know if she's still his concubine
> because he's away. I don't have anything more to say.
> *Inquisitors*: What is the reason you have not said this about Juana
> Ramírez until now?
> *Molina*: Because I hadn't remembered.
> *Inquisitors*: Why, specifically, would she have made the statue and the
> sambenitos?
> *Molina*: Because Francisco Yáñez would have begged her. He used
> to enter her house and was a close friend of Cristóbal García de
> Morales, who had [Juana Ramírez] as his concubine.
> *Inquisitors*: What moved you [on 25 May] to say that you alone were
> guilty in this matter and none of the others . . . ?
> *Molina*: I said it because I wanted to be done quickly and because I
> was very ill.²⁹

Molina's confession made under torture, his retractions on 22 and 25 May, as well as his latest declaration were read to him. He confirmed that what he said last was the truth. Once again, he declared his suspicions that the "wife of Enríquez" and Juana de Montoya could have made the effigy and the sambenitos because the two women were "friends and comrades." Molina had nothing more to say, and the inquisitors ordered him to return to his prison cell.

Molina's changing versions of his story could not have convinced the inquisitors that the crime of Tecamachalco involved the large number of conspirators he had accused. After the four weeks of interrogations that had elapsed since his torture, the list of likely culprits had not changed significantly from the list before that confession. Of the six men and now three women whom Molina accused of playing a part in the crime, the inquisitors had interrogated only five men. The sixth man, Cristóbal García de Morales, had gone off to war and had not been seen since. Nonetheless, of the five men interrogated, the inquisitors found no credible evidence to support Molina's accusations, except from the mestizo interpreter Juan López. Yáñez, Molina, and López now agreed that the three were together in López's house on the night of 20 July. Molina alone accused López of knowing, approving, and participating in the crime. The inquisitors found confirmation for Molina's accusation in López's own statement that Molina urged him to have "courage" when neighbors began suspecting Molina's participation. Why would Molina have said this if López knew nothing about those accusations?

On 18 June, the inquisitors brought Molina back for confirmation of his latest declaration. Following the Inquisition's standard questioning style, the inquisitors asked Molina if he remembered making any accusations recently: "I remember having said that Francisco Yáñez and I put up the sambenitos in Tecamachalco; and that the mestizo Juan López had acted as lookout; and that Francisco Solano, Bartolomé Lozano, Antonio de la Parada, and Cristóbal García de Morales knew about it."[30] The inquisitors notified Molina that the Inquisition's prosecuting attorney would present him as a witness against Yáñez and López. The inquisitors had no interest in pressing charges against the other men and women whom Molina had accused.

On the afternoon of 20 June, Francisco Yáñez returned for another audience before the inquisitors. It had been just over a month since his last audience on 19 May, the day that the inquisitors secured the vote to torture Molina and Yáñez. Molina's unexpected revelations under torture involving numerous new persons forced the inquisitors to delay Yáñez's questioning "under torment." Molina's declarations, along with the testimonies of Parada, Solano, and López, provided new accusations, which the inquisitors now presented to Yáñez. He listened to the new accusations, which, taken together, portrayed him as the chief author of the crime perpetrated between the evening of 20 July and the early hours of 21 July 1578. The new accusations reaffirmed Yáñez's hatred of Rubio Naranjo. In addition, the testimony challenged Yáñez's claim that on the night of 20 July, he stayed inside Juan López's house. Moreover, one witness portrayed Yáñez as the person who planned the crime, assembled the sambenitos and the effigy, and secured the help to carry out his revenge against Rubio Naranjo. Given his previous stubborn denials, the inquisitors may not have found it surprising that, despite the new testimonies, Yáñez continued to deny point-blank each of the charges without providing alternative explanations. Regarding the new testimony to the effect that he had indeed left the house that evening, Yáñez simply repeated his previous assertions that on Sunday, 20 July, he arrived at López's house at 3 P.M. and stayed there until the following morning. To the claim that he had planned the crime and made the defaming objects, Yáñez simply declared that it was "a very big falsehood."[31] Whatever the rest of the witnesses may have said, he denied everything. The inquisitors concluded the audience.

On 22 June, during Yáñez's appearance with his defense lawyer, Licenciado Ávalos, the farmer insisted that, just as he claimed when facing the first set of accusations, the second set had no merit and that he should be set free. Yáñez offered no counterarguments or an alternative sequence of events that could have explained the contradictions between his declarations and those of his accusers. Simply put, his only explanation was that they were all liars.[32] For the inquisitors, the only way to resolve these contradictions was to question Yáñez under torture.

CHAPTER TWELVE

More Torment

On the afternoon of 22 June 1582, Licenciados Bonilla and Santos García convened the archbishop of Mexico City and former inquisitor general of New Spain, Pedro Moya de Contreras, and four judges of the Audiencia of Mexico: Drs. Pedro Farfán, Lope de Miranda, Francisco de Sande, and Diego García de Palacio. They reviewed the evidence presented in the cases against the farmer Francisco Yáñez and the interpreter Juan López and approved "putting them to the question under torture."[1]

Early on 23 June, the jailer brought López to the audience chamber to face the inquisitors. They asked him if he had anything new to state about his case. López had nothing to say. The inquisitors reminded him of the charge that he had known about the crime, approved it, acted as a lookout, and kept quiet about the crime instead of denouncing it. Given the "variations and contradictions in his confessions," the inquisitors ordered López to face torture. Taken to the torture chamber, López awaited the inquisitors. At half past eight in the morning, Licenciados Bonilla and Santos García took their places in the torture chamber and again warned López to tell the truth and thus avoid the great hardship awaiting him. "If I knew more, I would lie down and tell the truth," López stated.

Perhaps hoping that a disability might spare him the torture, López announced that he had a broken arm as a result of a fall from a horse. Unmoved, the inquisitors ordered that López be stripped of his clothes and left with a pair of linen underpants. Warned again to tell the truth and avoid all harm, López replied as before. The executioner loosely tied cords around López's arms. The questioning continued:

Inquisitors: Tell the truth!
Juan López: I would say more if I knew anything, but I didn't see or
    consent to the crime.
Inquisitors: Tell the truth!

They ordered the first turn of the cords. López "gave many cries, calling out the Holy Trinity, and saying that he had no part in it." The same happened after the second turn. On the third turn, López swore that "if I have to suffer this much, I will say whatever you want me to, but I had no part in it, or anything more than what I said!" He asked for water, and again cried out, "Tell me what you want me to say. . . . If you want me to say I was part of it, I'll say it if I have to!" After the fourth turn, López cried out to God:

> *Juan López*: There's nothing more to it than Juan de Molina told me to look out, as I have said, and I went to look. If this was so that they could put up the sambenitos, I don't know it, only that they went out at eight at night, as I've declared. I didn't go with them. I stayed home; later, they came back to sleep.
> *Inquisitors*: Why did you think they sent you to look out?
> *López*: They told me to go out to the street to see if there was anyone; and I thought that they were going to attack someone with a knife because they were held in the region as brave men.
> *Inquisitors*: Did you know beforehand that the sambenitos would be put up and who would do it?
> *López*: I didn't know anything beforehand, as I've said. Afterward, I imagined that Yáñez and Molina had done it.

López repeated his earlier assertions about what Molina had stated that night and afterward. The inquisitors ordered the executioner to tie López down on the rack for the *garrote*, consisting of tourniquets applied to the biceps and the thighs.

> *Inquisitors*: Did you suspect that the knifing you just mentioned would be done to Rubio Naranjo?
> *Juan López*: Yes, because, as I've said, they were angry with him.

The inquisitors ordered the first tourniquet applied to his right arm. López "gave out great cries." As the tourniquet was applied to his right thigh, López cried out, "If I say anything it's because my bones are broken. I'm a miserable mestizo, no good to be a man!" After warning him to tell the truth, the inquisitors ordered López's face covered with a linen cloth and the first jug of water poured for the water torture that followed. Following the second jug of water poured over López's face, he said, "How can this be done to a poor wretched mestizo!"

Inquisitors: Will you tell the truth if we take you away from here?
Juan López: I'll say it by the Holy Gospel!

Released, López got down onto his knees, kissed the floor, and said, "The truth is as I've declared it. There's nothing more because they never told me anything, and I didn't see anything that night or three nights earlier."[2] This concluded the interrogation. After treating his injuries, the inquisitors sent López back to his cell. It was around half past nine in the morning.

The inquisitors returned to their audience chamber, where the jailer brought Francisco Yáñez. Asked to clarify the many contradictions between his testimony and that of different witnesses in order to avoid torture, the prisoner repeatedly insisted that he had nothing to admit. They moved to the torture chamber, where, at 9:45 A.M., they asked the same question. Yáñez remained silent. When the bells struck 10:00, Yáñez cried out, "May Christ let me die here, because I suffer what I shouldn't!" (lit., "he suffered because he was being charged for something he didn't owe"; *lo que no debe*).[3] This became his repeated insistence: that an injustice was taking place in which he was unfairly paying for the sins of others. The inquisitors did not ask him what he meant, expecting that he would stubbornly protest his innocence despite the overwhelming evidence against him.

With his clothes removed and cords tied loosely around his arms, ready for the first application of the torture, the inquisitors asked Yáñez again to confess: silence. The first turn of the cords was followed by the same question: still silence. After the second turn, Yáñez cried out, "I've told the truth! Kill me, because from now until the end of the world, I won't say another thing! Everyone is lying! Oh, my Lord and Creator! God's Christians, you're killing a Christian who hasn't done anything to you!" Earlier that morning, Juan López suffered four turns of the cords. A month earlier, Juan de Molina confessed after only the third turn. After six turns of the cords, Yáñez continued to cry out that he would not pay for what he had not done: "I wish I had done it not to suffer this!" (*¡Oxalá lo devyera para no pasar esto!*)[4]

Next, Yáñez was tied to the rack, at which point his determination began to crack. He now said that he was "dying for what he shouldn't" and was commending himself to Jesus Christ as a fair judge. He added that he had a suspicion:

Go after the person that I'll tell you, who might certify my suspicion about Juan de Molina, because the night that I was in the house of the mestizo Juan López in Tecamachalco, Molina brought some bags with something in them. Whenever Rubio Naranjo walked by, Molina would tell me that Rubio Naranjo had unleashed his tongue against a certain wife of Ferro, and Molina promised that it would cost Rubio Naranjo dearly. The next day, the sambenitos were discovered. For the love of God, go after the wife of Ferro. She might know about this matter. That heretical dog Molina! I didn't do anything! I don't remember anything![5]

Clearly, this was not what the inquisitors wanted to hear. Rather than stopping, the executioner applied three more tourniquets to Yáñez's right arm and thighs. Again, Yáñez cried out to "bring that woman, and the dog Molina will say if she did it." The woman was in Mexico City. After the fourth tourniquet, Yáñez said: "Do the same to that sodomite [*puto*] Molina, who will say if he did it. . . . Capture that scoundrel, and he'll say why he was carrying his bags full that night!" The executioner applied the sixth and seventh tourniquets, one to each shin. Yáñez repeated his earlier statements, this time with a surprising revelation: "Bring that woman or torture that traitor Molina, whom I suspect. I'll torture him and take out his guts, because if Molina did it, he'll say it! By God's immense goodness, I suspect him because he told me that Rubio Naranjo had defamed the wife of Ferro, who went out with Molina; and that he would make Rubio Naranjo pay; . . . and that [Rubio Naranjo] was a Jewish dog."[6]

The session moved on to the next procedure: water torture. After the second jug of water, Yáñez could no longer bear it. He asked for a drink of water in order to speak: "I did it, señores! Take me away from here; I did it, I put them up, I did it. . . . Molina wrote the signs, and I helped him put them up; and the wife of Ferro made them." Finally, the admission that the inquisitors had sought! The statement was read back to Yáñez, who confirmed it: the wife of Ferro made the sambenitos, and Molina—not Yáñez—wrote the signs because Rubio Naranjo had boasted that he had "mounted" her. The interrogation continued:

> *Inquisitors*: Whom did Rubio Naranjo boast to about what you have said?
> *Francisco Yáñez*: I don't know more than what Molina told me.
> *Inquisitors*: Was it for the same reason that Rubio Naranjo had insulted other women?
> *Yáñez*: I don't know.

Inquisitors: Why did they insult him with the sambenitos and the
  statue?
Yáñez: Because he was a Jew, and he was called this. Molina told me
  so.
Inquisitors: Where and when did you plan to carry out this insult?
Yáñez: That [Sunday] afternoon, when Molina was carrying the bags.
  He told me . . . to help him put them up. He said it like that,
  when we were alone, in Tecamachalco, at two [in the afternoon].
  Later, we played cards at Juan López's house. . . .
Inquisitors: At what time?
Yáñez: Between about midnight and one.
Inquisitors: Who woke up whom to put them up?
Yáñez: I woke him up. Untie me, and I'll tell you the whole truth.[7]

Sitting on the rack, Yáñez continued to explain how he and Molina had
committed the crime. The two went out alone. Juan López did not look out;
he was sleeping inside his house with his two Indian servants. No one except
Yáñez and Molina knew that they had committed the crime.

Inquisitors: Would the "wife of Ferro" have known about it?
Francisco Yáñez: Molina told me that she knew and that she had
  helped him make the statue and the sambenitos because she was
  his mistress [*mançeba*]. I never saw her in my life and don't know
  her name.
Inquisitors: Who else did Molina tell you he had informed?
Yáñez: He didn't tell me anyone else.
Inquisitors: Did the two of you promise to swear secrecy?
Yáñez: Yes.[8]

Yáñez tried to persuade Molina to drop the plan and instead give Rubio
Naranjo "a round of clubs," which the farmer offered to do that same day.
Asked about the statue, Yáñez said that he didn't see it because it was dark,
but he remembered that it had two tongues because Rubio Naranjo was
"loose-tongued" (*deslenguado*).[9] Likewise, he had a limited knowledge about
the sambenitos and the text on the signs. Asked about the meaning of the
signs, Yáñez did not know, except that Molina wanted to put them up because
Rubio Naranjo had insulted that "lady," who at the time lived in Tepeaca,
where Rubio Naranjo said he wanted to move.

The inquisitors then asked Yáñez about his earlier statements accusing others who came from Oaxaca to put up the sambenitos. Yáñez explained that it was all true that his mother-in-law and her sister said this. In other words, he had told the truth about that. Perhaps still uncertain about Yáñez's declaration, the inquisitors pressed him:

> *Inquisitors*: Why haven't you said this until now?
> *Francisco Yáñez*: To avoid paying for it. Haven't you found the wife of Ferro?
> *Inquisitors*: What else do you know about this matter?
> *Yáñez*: God let me not live if I know anything more!"[10]

On this note, the session ended at a 11:45 A.M., two hours after it had begun.

On 25 June, Yáñez requested an audience before the inquisitors. He pleaded with them not to tell Molina that Rubio Naranjo "used to sleep" (*se echava*) with the wife of Ferro because if they did, Molina would surely know who had said it.[11] They could tell everything else to Molina. However, Yáñez went on to deny everything he had declared inside the torture chamber. Simply put, he never talked to Molina about any sambenitos and never put up anything with him. Molina may have put them up on the night that he stayed in Tecamachalco because he was sleeping near the entrance to López's house. After all, Molina hated Rubio Naranjo out of jealousy over the wife of Ferro and promised that Rubio Naranjo would pay for his insult against her.

The inquisitors were not ready to allow Yáñez to return to his prison cell. After hearing the long testimony that he had made during the torture session, the stubborn Yáñez agreed that he had made those statements under torture but denied that they were true. He had confessed only because he had been afraid of drowning during the water torture. When shown the effigy and the sambenitos that were put up in Tecamachalco, Yáñez did not recognize them. He had never seen them in his life and did not help put them up. This was all he had to say, and this ended the audience.

The inquisitors would not take Yáñez's revocation seriously; perhaps it did not surprise them, given his long denials, even during torture. Yet his declaration must have startled the inquisitors. As had long been assumed, the crime in Tecamachalco was the result of a plot involving a woman and several men. If Yáñez was not lying—and, after his denial, who knew?—the inquisitors had it all wrong. Under torture, Molina had lied in an attempt to make his friend carry the brunt of the guilt for the 1578 scandal; the "very good scribe" who knew black letter was the mastermind of the crime, not Yáñez. Not surprisingly, the motive was revenge against Rubio Naranjo's insults. Who was the "wife of Ferro," whom Molina had sought to avenge? Yáñez was the first witness to mention her and insisted that he did not know her name and had never seen her because she lived in Tepeaca. It was not difficult to establish Yáñez's reasons for acting as Molina's accomplice: the two men were "fast friends." In addition, Yáñez had long harbored ill will toward the infamous Rubio Naranjo, who had insulted Yáñez's mother and sisters.

Three years and eleven months after the crime, the investigation had taken another unexpected turn. The inquisitors still needed to confirm the existence of the wife of Ferro and establish for certain Juan de Molina's role as mastermind of the plot that included Francisco Yáñez, Juan López, and Molina's mysterious mistress. Until then, the full meaning of the effigy would remain uncertain.

CHAPTER THIRTEEN

The Wife

Licenciados Bonilla and Santos García quickly summoned the newly discovered "wife of Ferro" to appear before them. Yáñez first mentioned her on the morning of 22 June during his torture session. He did not know her name but only that she had lived in Tepeaca and now lived in Mexico City. On the morning of 25 June, she appeared before the inquisitors. Her name was Ana de Figueroa, born in León, Spain. She was the thirty-year-old wife of Pedro González Ferro, who, in 1578, had been the lieutenant alcalde mayor of Tepeaca. They now lived in Mexico City in the house of Doña Mayor de Nava.

> *Inquisitors*: Do you know, or presume to know, the reason that you have been called?
> *Ana de Figueroa*: No, and no one from my lineage [*linaje*] has been in this [situation].
> *Inquisitors*: Do you know any person who has done something against the Catholic faith or the Holy Office . . . ?
> *Figueroa*: No.
> *Inquisitors*: Do you know any person who has put up sambenitos to insult anyone?
> *Figueroa*: No.
> *Inquisitors*: Have you heard if this has been done in a town where you have resided or nearby?
> *Figueroa*: No.[1]

The inquisitors then warned her that she had been called because they had information indicating that she knew more than what she was saying. They warned her that it was a sin to raise false testimony as well as to protect someone with false testimony.

Ana de Figueroa: I don't know anything. I'm not such a bad Christian
　　that I wouldn't say it.
Inquisitors: When did you live in Tepeaca?
Figueroa: I don't know. I resided there when my husband served as
　　lieutenant of the alcalde mayor Antón Cavallero and later Jorge
　　Cerón [Carvajal].
Inquisitors: During that time, did you hear anything about what you
　　have just been asked?
Figueroa: No.[2]

The inquisitors warned Figueroa to search her memory and ordered the
jailer to imprison her. It did not take long for her to search her memory; that
same afternoon, she appeared again before the inquisitors.

Inquisitors: The jailer informs us that you have requested an audi-
　　ence. Tell the truth as you have sworn to do.
Ana de Figueroa: It's true that I asked for an audience to say that,
　　having searched my memory, I remembered that when I lived
　　with my husband in Tepeaca I heard that someone in Tecama-
　　chalco had put up sambenitos with words I don't know against
　　a certain Rubio Naranjo. It was suspected that Juan de Molina, a
　　royal scribe, and Francisco Yáñez, a mestizo [*sic*], had put them
　　up. Fifteen days later, when we were alone discussing this affair,
　　Molina told me that he had put them up because Rubio Naranjo
　　was a scoundrel. They were on bad terms because Molina was
　　jealous about a certain Doña María, a mestiza who was the wife
　　of a certain Rúa from Tecamachalco. Molina said that it had been
　　a good thing to put up the sambenitos. I asked him, "Why bother
　　with such a scoundrelly act? It would be better to kill Rubio
　　Naranjo if he had insulted you."[3]

The inquisitors did not ask her more questions. After warning her again
to tell the truth, they sent her back to her prison cell.

On the morning of 26 June, the inquisitors had Figueroa brought back
and asked her if she wished to declare anything more. She had nothing to add
to her statements from the previous day. This time, however, the inquisitors
had questions for her:

Inquisitors: When Juan de Molina boasted about putting up the sambenitos, how long had you known him?

Ana de Figueroa: Four years, more or less.

Inquisitors: From where did you know him?

Figueroa: Molina would frequent my house.

Inquisitors: Who else said that he had put them up?

Figueroa: He didn't tell me that, aside from boasting that he had put them up.

Inquisitors: Then why was it publicly suspected that Molina and Yáñez had put them up?

Figueroa: People said it and suspected them. They said that the writing was Molina's and that he was a great scoundrel, very disliked, and a troublemaker with an evil tongue and a defamer of married women. He said that all the men were cuckolds and boasted about this.

Molina told her he had put up the sambenitos only after the fact and did not share with her any other details. For this reason, she did not know where he had stayed when he carried out the action; what the effigy, the sambenitos, and the signs were made of; or whether anyone had helped him to make them and put them up. However, Molina confessed to her his reasons for insulting Rubio Naranjo, whom he called "a Jew": "He was angry with Rubio Naranjo because of that woman [the wife of Rúa, the mestiza Doña María]. . . . When he boasted to me that he had put them up, he said: 'I put them up, and it was done well.'"

Inquisitors: Why did Molina boast to you about putting them up?

Figueroa: Because that scoundrel Molina was smitten [*picado*] and in love with me. That's why he told me, and that's the truth. Who knows why he was jealous about me! He will confess it to the Señor Inquisitor.

Inquisitors: Why would he flatter you by insulting Rubio Naranjo?

Figueroa: Because Rubio was also smitten with me. But Rubio Naranjo was "all air." I valued Juan de Molina's affections [*tenía prendas en los amores*].

Inquisitors: Did you complain to Molina that Rubio Naranjo had insulted you because of his love for you?

Figueroa: No.

Inquisitors: How long before the sambenitos were put up did you tell
  him about killing Rubio Naranjo instead of putting them up if
  Rubio had insulted him?
Figueroa: I didn't tell him anything before he had put them up, only
  afterward. . . .
Inquisitors: What insult did Rubio Naranjo do to you so that you
  would think that it was better to kill him than put up those
  sambenitos?
Figueroa: None.[4]

At this point, the inquisitors warned Figueroa that they had information
regarding a greater guilt than she wished to confess. Urged to tell the truth
and discharge her conscience, she confessed:

Ana de Figueroa: I ask for mercy! The truth is that I knew that young
  man Juan de Molina had the sambenitos, but he didn't tell me
  whom they were for because I saw it clearly. I haven't said this
  out of fear. It's true that he showed me the smaller sambenitos
  and told me that he would put them up against a great scoundrel.
  He showed them to me inside a box in his father's house, where I
  went often. Since it was so long ago, I don't remember what they
  were made of. . . . Then his father came in, and we closed the box.
  Three days later, the sambenitos appeared in Tecamachalco.
Inquisitors: Why did he show them to you?
Figueroa: Because he was in love with me. Because of that love and
  inclination, he showed them to me and told me that he would
  put them up against a great scoundrel, without telling me who he
  was—and I never guessed.[5]

After approving the transcript of her statements, Figueroa once again
asked for mercy. She went back to her prison cell. The next morning (27
June), the inquisitors summoned her to listen to the prosecuting attorney's
accusation against her. Before doing so, they asked her once again to tell the
truth. She asked to wait until the afternoon to have time to think about this
and to search her memory. The inquisitors sent her back to her prison cell.
That afternoon, she told the inquisitors that she was feeling ill and asked
that they postpone the audience until the following morning. Instead, the
inquisitors ordered Dr. Lobo Guerrero, the Inquisition's prosecuting attor-

ney, to present the formal accusation against Figueroa. It consisted of four charges:

1.   She committed the crime of interfering with the Inquisition's work by misusing its symbols and the sambenitos to insult a third party.
2.   In particular, out of hatred for Hernando Rubio Naranjo, she made the sambenitos and the statue in order to insult him.
3.   As a bad Christian, who was Juan de Molina's concubine and committed adultery against her husband, she sewed the sambenitos and the statue, and she ordered Molina to put them up to insult Rubio Naranjo, thus usurping the jurisdiction of the Holy Office and misusing its symbols.
4.   She had perjured herself and deserved great punishments, and if necessary, should be interrogated under torture.

After taking an oath to tell the truth in response to the charges, she again asked that "by the love of God" they give her until the following morning to respond because she was ill.[6] The inquisitors sent her back to her cell.

On the morning of 28 June, Figueroa appeared again before Licenciados Bonilla and Santos García. After the inquisitors asked her to tell the truth, she knelt, clasping her hands, and admitted that out of "the greatest fear," she had not dared tell the truth. She asked for pardon as a woman who had been duped. Now she would come clean about her involvement in the crime:

It was true that I had been entangled with Juan de Molina, who was at odds with Rubio Naranjo and wanted to win me over. This is why Molina told me one day that he would take revenge on Rubio Naranjo and brought two sambenitos to my house. We sewed them up alone inside a room. He brought one that was like a doll from the market [coquinete o muñeca del tianguis].[7] We stuffed it with hay. I kept it for more than eight days, until Molina took it to his house and finished it. Eight days later, they appeared in Tecamachalco. As far as I can remember, [the scandal] happened on a Monday. During those previous eight days, Molina went around those towns, saying that he wanted to go away. I also saw a piece of paper that Molina had brought with some writing on it. It said: "These are the arms—or lineage [hidalguía]—of Rubio Naranjo of Mount somewhere of Moses, or the Mount of the Jews—I don't remember the name. The sign was written on about a quarter of a sheet. [She pointed to half of a folded sheet of paper.] I didn't see any more papers. I don't know if he put up any others because, as I've declared, Molina had them in his house for eight days. The letters were rather large. I helped him sew the sambenitos. He stuffed the hay inside the doll, saying, "This is to label Rubio Naranjo a Jew, and the hay signifies that he should be burned."[8]

Without stopping, Figueroa put her hand over a cross—probably the iron cross in the audience chamber used for taking oaths. She swore that she remembered that when they were making the sambenitos, Molina told her: "I don't know why I trust women who tomorrow will be angry with me." Later, when Molina was taking home the sambenitos, he told her that he did not know if he would go ahead with his plot because "I don't want to put my trust in women." He carried out the plot and came back to tell her: "He came to my house very happy, dressed in green, saying that he had put up the sambenitos and the statue. I told him that I regretted it very much and felt a pain in my heart, wishing that it hadn't been done."[9]

After this long declaration, Figueroa had little to say about the specific charges against her, which she did not refute. The inquisitors then presented her the effigy and the sambenitos with their signs. She seemed confused as she tried to recall events that she must have hoped never to discuss publicly. At first, she said that all she had seen were the two sambenitos that she helped sew, but not the one on the effigy, which she assumed that Molina must have made on his own during the eight days that he kept it before putting it up. She also recalled the feet made of reeds on the effigy, but not the two tongues or the black chicken feathers on the head. Perhaps Molina had done all that work on his own to "perfect" the effigy, but she was not certain.

But taking a second look, Figueroa recalled sewing together the Indian blankets with Juan de Molina, "and this is the plain truth, as a Christian woman." Again, she insisted that she did not make the sambenito on the effigy or put the mane of feathers and the distaff and spindle on the effigy. Then she remembered Molina painting the two faces on the effigy and her sewing the two tongues to the mouths, following his instructions. As they worked on the effigy, Molina, pointing to the statue, said to Figueroa: "This is Rubio Naranjo, and thus it represents him" (*aquélla hera Naranjo y así lo representava*).[10] They worked quickly, in case someone might come into the room, and they did it all in a single afternoon, while her husband was in Mexico City.

When asked about the sign on the effigy, Figueroa said that the handwriting on the paper that Molina had shown her was smaller (*más menuda*, which could also mean that the letters were more slender). Perhaps he had copied what he had shown her onto the sign on the effigy. When the message on the sign was read to her, Figueroa recognized the "Mount Calvary" that she had forgotten earlier. The inquisitors read back to Figueroa the statement she had made that morning, to which Figueroa added only one detail: Molina painted the two faces on the effigy with pen and ink.

> *Inquisitors*: Did Molina tell you if anyone had helped him put up the sambenitos and the effigy, or if someone looked out while he was doing it?
> *Ana de Figueroa*: He didn't mention anyone. He was so happy about having put them up, and that's why he wore his green clothes.[11]

The session ended after the inquisitors appointed Licenciado Ávalos as Figueroa's defense lawyer. She went back to her cell. She returned that afternoon to confirm her testimony implicating Juan de Molina in the crime. She said that it was the truth, not because of any hatred toward him. The inquisitors sent her back to her prison cell.

On Saturday morning, 30 June, the inquisitors summoned Juan de Molina for what would be the culmination of the four-year investigation. The Inquisition's prosecuting attorney, Dr. Lobo Guerrero, presented new testimony against him from an unnamed witness. Now, for the first time, two witnesses mentioned the "wife of Ferro" as having assisted Molina in making the sambenitos and the effigy. One of those witnesses, the seventh, was Ana de Figueroa. Molina recognized that one of his accusers could be none other than his former lover. The detailed declaration read to him left a profound impression on Molina, who, after months of keeping his secret, finally confessed: "It's true that Ana de Figueroa and I did this at her house in Tepeaca."[12] The inquisitors sent Molina back to his prison cell and summoned Figueroa for further questioning:

> *Inquisitors*: Do you know anyone who was arrested for this crime?
> *Ana de Figueroa*: In Tepeaca, I heard it said at that time that an investigation was under way.
> *Inquisitors*: Do you know anyone presently imprisoned by the Holy Office for this investigation?

Figueroa: No.
Inquisitors: What does Juan de Molina look like? If you see him, would you recognize him?
Figueroa: Yes, because he's short, bearded, and has large eyes.
Inquisitors: What you have declared against him—would you say it in his presence?
Figueroa: Yes.
Inquisitors: Why?
Figueroa: Because it's true.[13]

The inquisitors ordered Juan de Molina brought back to the chamber. Figueroa then recognized him as the one who sewed the sambenitos with her. Molina recognized her as his former lover.

Juan de Molina: [addressing Figueroa] Say what you've said and confessed.
Ana de Figueroa: [looking at the inquisitors] Juan de Molina should say it, since he knows it better than me.
Molina: [to Figueroa] Say it.
Figueroa: Here's Molina, who one day brought to my house in Tepeaca two sambenitos. Together we sewed them. We also sewed up a doll. He told me that it represented Rubio Naranjo and that Molina would put it up against Rubio Naranjo. And he read to me the paper that said "Mount Calvary."[14]

Figueroa turned to face Molina: "Why deny it, since it's the truth? Don't deny it, since we did it together; after you put them up, you told me in Tepeaca with great joy that you put them up." A stunned Molina remained silent until he finally asked her:

Juan de Molina: Did I go back to Tepeaca after I put them up?
Ana de Figueroa: [crying and facing Molina] Why do you deny it? It's true.

Figueroa said this to Molina several times. He remained silent. The inquisitors ordered Figueroa to leave the chamber. However, before she left, Molina knelt and addressed the inquisitors: "What Ana de Figueroa has said is true. For the love of God, have mercy! I didn't say it before because it all happened

when I was alone with Ana de Figueroa. It's true."[15] The time had come for
Molina to come clean and present his account of the crime and the role of
the various participants besides Figueroa. Molina addressed the inquisitors:

> Francisco Yáñez isn't the principal in this affair. Neither did I inform
> him days earlier. [On the afternoon of 20 July,] I told him what I
> wanted to do because Rubio Naranjo had boasted about the wife of
> Ferro. Yáñez said to put them up because he favored it. That after-
> noon, I brought to Tecamachalco the effigy and the sambenitos inside
> my trousers. Together, Yáñez and I went after midnight to put them
> up. I put up the effigy and he the sambenitos. At midnight, more or
> less, the mestizo Juan López went out to see if anyone was coming.
> As to whether Yáñez discussed this with anyone else, I don't know.
> But Juan López was present that evening when we discussed how we
> would put them up. I don't know what else to say.[16]

Again, Molina knelt and said: "Have mercy on me, for the love of God!"
The audience ended.

That afternoon, Figueroa returned to present her defense, with the assistance of Licenciado Ávalos. Asked to respond, she stated tearfully: "Juan de
Molina duped me as an ignorant and simple woman. I didn't know the gravity
of the crime. I beg you to consider that I'm married . . . and if I'm punished,
let it take place in secret on account of my husband."[17]

Following this session, the inquisitors could finally end the case. That
same day, 30 June, in the afternoon, Molina confirmed his testimony implicating Figueroa in the crime. On the afternoon of 3 July, Figueroa confirmed
the testimonies made against her by two unidentified witnesses. The first witness was Francisco Yáñez, whose revelations during his torture session and
afterward first alerted the inquisitors about the existence of the wife of Ferro.
Figueroa knew the identity of the second witness because three days earlier,
she had heard Juan de Molina admitting their joint guilt during their face-to-
face encounter.

The previous week, the inquisitors had released Antonio de la Parada,
Bartolomé Lozano, and Francisco Solano. Molina had falsely accused them
of having heard about the planned crime from Francisco Yáñez.[18] By 5 July,
the three were on their way home. Only four persons remained under arrest,
awaiting a final deliberation about their sentences: Juan de Molina, Francisco
Yáñez, Juan López, and Ana de Figueroa.

CHAPTER FOURTEEN

Reconciliation

On Sunday, 22 July 1582, four years and one day to the day after the scandalous San Benito appeared in Tecamachalco, the inquisitors and the four conspirators attended a solemn ceremony in Mexico City's cathedral. Also present during these services were the Inquisition's prosecuting attorney, Dr. Lobo Guerrero; the *corregidor* (equivalent to the governor) of Mexico City, "and many other ecclesiastics and lay persons."[1] In the main chapel, Licenciados Bonilla and Santos García read the names, charges, and sentences of the guilty parties. The two leaders, Juan de Molina and Francisco Yáñez, would each receive two hundred lashes and would row for five years in the royal galleys, without pay. Ana de Figueroa and Juan López each received the sentence of a hundred lashes and banishment for five years from the bishopric of Tlaxcala, as well as from Mexico City. If they failed to comply fully with the sentence, the banishment would double to ten years.

A mass and a sermon followed. Predictably, the central theme of the sermon consisted of a warning to the faithful to adhere to the teachings of the Catholic Church and reject all heresy as the work of the devil. Another important theme was the reconciliation of sinners with the Church. As with the coat of arms of the Inquisition, the olive branch of mercy would temper the harsh sword of justice. Sinners could look to the Inquisition's green cross and allay the fear of punishment with the hope of reconciliation.[2] For the repentant, salvation, with the grace of God, still lay within reach.

On the morning of 23 July, the four conspirators appeared for the last time before Licenciados Bonilla and Santos García at the Inquisition's audience chamber. Each of them swore that, during their time in the Inquisition's prison, they had not said or heard anything against the Inquisition and its officials and that the jailer had treated them well. The inquisitors warned the convicts that, if they failed to keep secret what was said at their trials, or anything else heard while imprisoned, they would receive an additional two hundred lashes. The prisoners promised to keep their secrets.

The prisoners were then escorted outside the Inquisition, naked to the waist, riding on "beasts of burden" (workhorses) in a procession across the main streets of Mexico City. A town crier accompanying the procession announced the crimes committed, as the prisoners received their allotted lashes, overseen by the Inquisition's constable. Later that afternoon, the Inquisition's jailer handed over Juan de Molina and Francisco Yáñez to the jailer of Mexico's royal prison.[3] The royal scribe and the farmer would eventually be shipped across the Atlantic to serve their sentences rowing in galleys of the king of Spain in the Mediterranean.[4] Throughout the procession, each of the four conspirators carried a candle, had a rope around his or her neck, and was dressed as a penitent: in other words, each wore a sambenito.

EPILOGUE

In 1583, the Mexican Inquisition sent a report (*relación de causa*) to the Council of the Supreme and General Inquisition—the Suprema—in Madrid, summarizing the cases recently dispatched. In a paragraph, the document described the Tecamachalco scandal and the sentences meted out to the three men and one woman found guilty of the crimes. The difficulty of resolving the case, the summary explained, merited the harsh sentences: "In these years, there have been frequent defamatory signs [*libelos*] in this land, especially in that town, which could not be resolved; and so the actions and punishment in this [case] seemed right."[1] The degrading punishments were appropriate because all four accused were *gente baxa*,[2] or "people of little esteem" (*poca calidad*). This assertion referred more to the reputation of the condemned established in the course of the trials than to their actual social standing.[3] After all, the Spaniard Juan de Molina was a royal scribe, who had to demonstrate that he descended from Old Christians without any Jewish or Moorish "stain."[4] The farmer Francisco Yáñez owned land and was related to a councilman from Puebla. The inquisitors even called the victim of the defamatory "libels," Hernando Rubio Naranjo, "a bachelor of little esteem," when, in fact, he was relatively wealthy and had family ties to a former judge of the Mexican Audiencia. Even the interpreter Juan López, a mestizo who apparently owned no property, had Spanish cousins and was related to Diego López de Montalbán, who had business dealings with Audiencia judges and even with Viceroy Martín Enríquez de Almansa.[5] However, the widespread rumors reported by numerous witnesses led the Inquisition to assert as fact the low esteem of the culprits and of their victim. The disgraced Rubio Naranjo had had several lovers, and those who conspired to humiliate him supposedly participated in adulterous relationships: Juan de Molina with the married Ana de Figueroa, the interpreter Juan López with the wife of his servant Francisco, and Francisco Yáñez with the married Juana de Montoya. Therefore, although Ana de Figueroa was the wife of the "very magnificent lord lieutenant alcalde mayor"[6] of Tepeaca, the Mexican Inquisition described her to the Suprema as a woman of "vile lifestyle" (*de ruin bivienda*). The low esteem of the accused, as well as the absence of death sentences, explained why the Inquisition dispatched these sentences in a relatively small ceremony rather than convoke another expensive auto de fe, which the tribunal had held annually between 1574 and 1579.

In its brief report to the Suprema, the Mexican Inquisition left out an important detail: except in the case of Ana de Figueroa, major differences of opinion arose over the sentences given to the culprits.[7] On 13 July 1582, the two inquisitors met with three judges of the Audiencia of Mexico and Archbishop Pedro Moya de Contreras, sitting in for the bishop of Tlaxcala, in order to vote on the sentencing of the four culprits.[8] As he had argued when he voted against the torture of Juan de Molina, Archbishop Moya de Contreras, a former inquisitor, recommended the royal scribe's absolution.[9] The archbishop also voted against Francisco Yáñez's sentence of five years in the galleys and two hundred lashes, arguing instead for a milder punishment of one hundred lashes and four years of banishment from Mexico City and the diocese of Tlaxcala (Puebla). The Audiencia's judge Dr. Pedro Farfán and the archbishop were bitter rivals; but on this occasion, Farfán joined the archbishop in opposing Yáñez's harsh sentence, recommending ten years' banishment from the New World.[10] Even more striking, the two inquisitors split over the sentence against the interpreter Juan López. The junior inquisitor, Licenciado Santos García, voted to absolve the interpreter. The judge Dr. Farfán voted to punish López only with banishment.[11] Perhaps the inquisitor and the judge took into account the fact that López's conviction relied solely on the testimony of Juan de Molina, who accused the interpreter of acting as an accessory to the crime. In contrast, there was unanimity on the sentencing of Ana de Figueroa.[12] Unfortunately, there are no additional details about the arguments made during the votes. In the end, supporters of the harsher sentences prevailed in each case. Inquisitorial instructions required the Suprema's review of split votes in Spanish tribunals.[13] However, because of the potential inconveniences caused by the enormous distances between Madrid and the Americas, automatic reviews in the New World tribunals were required only in the case of divided votes on death sentences, which did not apply in the Tecamachalco case.[14]

Although the Tecamachalco case is, in many ways, unique in the history of the Inquisition, the punishments meted out seem unusually harsh when compared with the sentences in other trials from the same period. Rather than involve the heresies and sexual crimes that made up the majority of inquisitorial cases, Tecamachalco's case fell into the miscellaneous category of "acts against the Holy Office," which ranged from injuring officials of the tribunal to making false representations as inquisitorial officials and falsifying inquisitorial documents.[15] From the beginning of their investigation, the Mexican inquisitors insisted that the incident in Tecamachalco had been "in great contempt and disrespect of this Tribunal."[16] The bull *Si de protegendis*, issued by Pope Pius V in 1569, allowed punishments worthy of heretics and traitors for anyone who "killed, wounded, used violence, and offended, either with menace, threats, or fear," or in any other way interfered with the work of inquisitors and its officials.[17] In 1577, the Mexican Inquisition condemned the mestizo soldier Pedro Hernández to two hundred lashes and three years in the galleys for inflicting a wound to the head of the Inquisition's porter.[18] However, most of those condemned for acts against the Holy Office in Mexico received milder punishments, such as fines, banishment, and one hundred lashes, or two hundred for aggravated circumstances.[19] Since galley servitude was the second most severe punishment imposed by the Inquisition, surpassed only by "relaxation," or death at the stake, inquisitors sent to the galleys men (not women) who had committed offenses considered serious, such as bigamy, especially egregious acts of blasphemy and heresy, and truly heinous crimes.[20] For instance, the English pirates from John Hawkins's expedition sentenced at the first auto de fe in 1574 received, according to the degree of their heresies, either two hundred lashes and eight years of galley servitude or three hundred lashes and ten years in the galleys.[21] At the auto de fe of 1575 in Mexico City, the Inquisition sentenced the shoemaker Gonzalo Sánchez, "of the generation of Jews," to two hundred lashes and six years in the galleys for lying about needing to come to the New World to raise funds to ransom his wife and children from their Moorish captors.[22] The two principal culprits in the Tecamachalco case received similar sentences for crimes that involved no acts of violence or heresy. The sexual crimes committed by the principals in the Tecamachalco scandal were incidental to the case and, in the cases of Francisco Yáñez and Juan López, not fully demonstrated.

In the eyes of the inquisitors, the actions of Molina, Yáñez, Figueroa, and López warranted such severe punishment because over the course of four years they had willfully obstructed the work of the Holy Tribunal. The long case had two clearly demarcated stages: the initial failed investigation between July and September 1578; and the renewed investigation starting in October 1581 and concluding with the final sentencing a year later. As we have seen, the first investigation failed primarily because the large number of suspects made it impossible to follow a single line of inquiry. What was not evident at that time was the role of Juan de Molina and Francisco Yáñez in obstructing the Inquisition's investigation through the calculated spreading of rumors and lies.

Throughout the Tecamachalco case, rumor was at once central to its resolution and the cause of its many delays. As part of evaluating the evidence to determine truth from lie, medieval and early modern courts paid attention to the reputation of suspects and witnesses. *Mala fama*, or infamy, could provide sufficient cause to initiate an inquest, to determine the need for torture, or to disqualify a witness.[23] Judges sought to distinguish between, on the one hand, unsubstantiated gossip and rumor, and, on the other hand, reputation based on public opinion and therefore held by the community to be true.[24] The Mexican Inquisition took rumor seriously, as did suspects and witnesses. The Tecamachalco case provides ample evidence that in sixteenth-century Mexico, gossip was not mere women's talk.[25] Whether at gatherings for religious festivities, when collecting their assignment of native labor, visiting neighbors, or simply at spontaneously formed street *corrillos* (groups of people talking), men in sixteenth-century Mexico relied on rumor to establish the reputation of neighbors, to follow scandals in their region, and to find out news about the world beyond. Men and women fully understood that such information was not always reliable. Witnesses were just as likely to support, deny, or take a neutral stance when they reported "vulgar opinion" and rumors (*murmuración*)[26] about the fame and esteem (*fama* and *calidad*) of individuals. However, the difficulty of distinguishing truth from lie in such rumors made judges susceptible to deceit. In fact, Molina and Yáñez repeatedly took advantage of royal and inquisitorial officials' need for information about the reputation of suspects and witnesses to mislead their investigations. In this sense, the two men's modus operandi was common across the early modern Atlantic world, where it was common to have recourse to rumor to disseminate misinformation and advance political goals.[27] Molina and Yáñez, too, proved highly skilled at using false rumor to advance their own cause.

From this perspective, it is possible to see that, from the moment the scandal broke, Juan de Molina and Francisco Yáñez followed a strategy of disinformation to deflect attention from themselves. On Tuesday, 22 July 1578, the day after the discovery of the effigy and the sambenitos, Molina, Yáñez, and Juan López de Montalbán went to the house of the Indian governor Don Joaquín de Peralta, in Quecholac, where men from the region

gathered to celebrate the Feast of Mary Magdalene and to talk about the scandal. On 29 July, the alcalde mayor of Tepeaca arrested López de Montalbán
because of what he had supposedly said at the gathering in Quecholac. In a
letter presented to royal officials, Hernando Rubio Naranjo denounced López
de Montalbán for saying bad things about him, such as that the sambenitos
were "little" compared to the things Rubio Naranjo had done. Rubio Naranjo
had not been present, but he cited as witnesses Molina, Yáñez, Yáñez's close
friend Cristóbal García de Morales, and the shoemaker Francisco López. The
last was present at the gathering but only heard about the alleged statements
against Rubio Naranjo from Yáñez, who also told the shoemaker that he allegedly reprimanded López de Montalbán for his bad words.[28] Rubio Naranjo
found out about López de Montalbán's alleged statements from the alcalde
mayor's scribe, Francisco de Molina—Juan's so-called father—who also heard
the story from none other than Yáñez.[29] By the time the alcalde mayor seques-
tered Yáñez and others in Tepeaca for questioning, Juan de Molina had left to
take on his new position as scribe in Río de Alvarado. The suspicions about
López de Montalbán seemed so convincing that the alcalde mayor of Tepeaca
released everyone else. López de Montalbán's Inquisition trial did not last
long, and he was soon a free man. But by then, the investigation had lost its
momentum. It stalled for the next three years.

Did Francisco de Molina also obstruct the investigation in order to
protect his "son," Juan de Molina? As noted, although many witnesses
described the two men as father and son, Francisco was less than ten years
older than his supposed son.[30] Juan—originally Juan González—had been
Francisco de Molina's apprentice as scribe, and their close relationship may
have prompted Juan to assume Francisco's last name. As the scribe of the
alcalde mayor of Tepeaca, Francisco was in the right place at the right time
from the very start of the investigation to direct attention away from Juan.
Francisco took down many of the first testimonies of suspects and witnesses
in the case and therefore could follow the investigation's progress. Far more
important, Francisco de Molina's authority helped inculpate López de Montalbán by spreading rumors started by Juan de Molina and Francisco Yáñez.
Francisco de Molina continued to repeat those rumors when the Inquisition's notary, Esteban Ordóñez, arrived in Tepeaca in early August 1578
to take the papers of the alcalde mayor's investigation. Notary Ordóñez
passed on to the inquisitors Francisco de Molina's authoritative observations—without noting any suspicions about Juan de Molina.[31] The inquisitors' initial investigation followed the path set out by the alcalde mayor of

Tepeaca, focusing on López de Montalbán, without paying attention to Juan de Molina and Yáñez, even though Rubio Naranjo continued to mention them as suspects in his letters to the inquisitors. Three years later, during the investigation by Commissioner Canon Santiago, Francisco de Molina again tried to protect Juan by lying about his whereabouts at the time of the crime and by dismissing rumors about Juan's and Yáñez's possible involvement in the case. The evidence does not make it clear, but Francisco must have suspected that Juan had something to do with the scandal. Perhaps Francisco did not want to know, out of a sense of loyalty or trust. Either way, the Inquisition did not take action against Francisco de Molina despite his obstructing the investigation.

The breakthrough in the case that set the inquisitors on the right path was in October 1581, when the farmer Diego de Trujillo went to the Inquisition to state that Francisco Yáñez knew the identity of the authors of the Tecamachalco scandal. That breakthrough depended on a strange, ultimately fatal, miscalculation on the part of Yáñez. While collecting their allotment of Indian labor in San Pablo, a conversation about defaming signs discovered in Tepeaca led to their comparison with the sambenitos that had been put up three years earlier in Tecamachalco. This prompted Yáñez to spread the rumor that the authors of the Tecamachalco scandal had been Juan Pérez and his recently deceased brother, with the connivance of their mother. Yáñez decided to spread this false rumor not because he wanted to enjoy the thought of getting away with the crime in 1578 but because he was worried that the truth about the Tecamachalco scandal might not remain a secret forever. Three years after Hernando Rubio Naranjo's mock execution in effigy, persistent rumors threatened the sweet victory against their hated enemy. As Yáñez later told Canon Santiago, the Tecamachalco scandal remained a frequent topic of conversation years after it had taken place. In his own house, Yáñez declared, his family and guests would talk about it "a thousand times, every time they had the opportunity to do so."[32] He insisted that Trujillo also heard the gossip about Juan Pérez from Yáñez's mother-in-law at a dinner in Yáñez's house; she heard it from the late María de Vargas during a casual conversation—claims that Yáñez reaffirmed at his torture session.[33] Yáñez may have hoped that the rumor about Pérez would draw attention away from himself as a suspect in the Tecamachalco scandal. Ironically, even though Yáñez told the truth about the source of that rumor, the inquisitors never believed him and suspected that he had something to hide. Still, the lie about Pérez's involvement in the case delayed the resolution of the investigation for at least two months.

By late December 1581, the inquisitors had dismissed Juan Pérez as a culprit and turned their attention on Yáñez and Molina. Yet Molina's lies and Yáñez's stubborn refusal to answer the inquisitors' questions led to more unnecessary arrests and trials, which again impeded the Holy Office's work and delayed the outcome of the case six more months. A year before his arrest in Veracruz in January 1582, Juan de Molina worried that the constant gossip about the Tecamachalco scandal would cause him trouble. López de Montalbán told Canon Santiago about a chance encounter in 1581, during which Molina told López de Montalbán: "If you're asked, say that Castro and his mother, María de Balbuena, are my enemies because they say that I and Francisco Yáñez had something to do with the sambenitos."[34] Molina lied to María de Balbuena earlier about her son being murdered in Mexico City, which prompted her and her son to threaten Molina with revealing his secret about the Tecamachalco scandal. Just as Yáñez tried to spread the false story about Pérez to deflect his own culpability, Molina now tried to protect himself by asking López de Montalbán to spread information to counter any rumors about Molina. In 1578, Molina's strategy worked. He would try it again before and during his trial.

Juan de Molina's first important lie during his trial betrayed his friend Yáñez by accusing him of masterminding the execution in effigy of Rubio Naranjo in order to avenge Yáñez's supposed lover, Juana de Montoya. In doing so, Molina resorted to the widespread gossip about the affair between Yáñez and Montoya. The strategy worked for Molina for two reasons. First, since Yáñez refused to answer most questions and did not assign blame to anyone else (except Juan Pérez), he failed to counter the charges. Second, the inquisitors seemed all too willing to accept Molina's version of the crime and followed a strategy designed to make Yáñez crack under the weight of the evidence against him, much of which turned out to be false. Therefore, when Molina accused men close to Yáñez—Juan López and Yáñez's friends Antonio de la Parada, Francisco Solano, Bartolomé Lozano, and Cristóbal Pérez de Morales—the inquisitors were ready to believe in the great conspiracy, which at one moment also included several women. In 1578, the growing list of suspects fomented by rumor and gossip helped to derail the investigation; but in 1582, it only slowed it down. By 1582, Molina had become an inexhaustible rumor mill, drawing his information from stories he had probably heard mostly from Yáñez, about Yáñez and his friends, their love interests, and their dislike of Rubio Naranjo. That shared hatred of Rubio Naranjo strengthened the confidence that Molina and Yáñez had in each other. The greatest expression of that trust was that, when Molina proposed to cause the ultimate humiliation to Rubio Naranjo with the elaborate execution in effigy, a reluctant Yáñez agreed. Molina repaid his friend's loyalty with betrayal.

Perhaps out of loyalty to his friend, or because he realized that turning in Molina would also mean his own demise, Yáñez held firm until he could no longer withstand the excruciating torture. When he finally revealed Molina's most guarded secret, Yáñez called his former friend not just a "traitor" but also a "heretical dog,"[35] not unlike how Molina referred to their enemy Rubio Naranjo. Perhaps Yáñez finally realized that his friend had betrayed him and the futility of resisting any longer. By revealing the existence of the "wife of Ferro," Yáñez made it possible for the inquisitors to resolve the case. Molina's resistance collapsed before the presence of Ana de Figueroa. Finally, Molina ceased to invent new rumors to thwart the investigation; dejectedly, he admitted his guilt and asked for mercy.

Although he repeatedly lied, the inquisitors seemed ready to believe Molina's claim that Yáñez was the mastermind of the scandal. The inquisitors were not alone in their willingness to accept Molina's lies. Even after the conclusion of Molina's trial, Archbishop Moya de Contreras continued to vote for Molina's absolution. Perhaps the archbishop had greater trust in Molina because he was a royal scribe and a Spanish official. In the early modern Spanish world, race could affect a person's credibility in court. Spaniards in Mexico would readily impugn the word of an Indian witness when it did not favor them; mestizos and other *castas* (racial castes) did so "less handily because they were not as decisively above them in rank."[36] Yáñez was not an Indian but a castizo, the son of a mestiza and a Portuguese man—even if the Inquisition's prosecuting attorney, Dr. Lobo Guerrero, mistakenly described Yáñez as a mestizo (although he was also confused with a Spaniard).[37] María Elena Martínez notes that although in Spain, "castizo" was a positive term used to describe "a person of good lineage and caste," when officials from the Mexican Inquisition first explained the term to their superiors at the Suprema in 1576, "they did not associate the category with any redeeming qualities."[38] Still, castizos were considered 75 percent Spanish and enjoyed privileges denied to other castas, such as joining the priesthood, exemption from paying tribute, and the acquisition of native labor—which Yáñez gladly used.[39] Potentially worse than being a castizo, Yáñez's father was Portuguese. In 1643, Guillén Lombard stated before the Mexican Inquisition what by then had become common knowledge, namely, that all the Portuguese had gained a reputation as Jews "even if they were not so."[40] A migration of Portuguese

crypto-Jews to Castile and the Spanish colonies began in the 1570s and continued after Philip II's conquest of Portugal in 1580, reaching a high point in
the early seventeenth century and stoking new campaigns against "Judaizers."[41] In Mexico in 1590, Judaizers of Portuguese origin or descent appeared
for the first time at an auto de fe. At the great auto of 1596, twenty-three of
them were reconciled, nine "relaxed" in person, and eight in effigy.[42] Their
persecution would culminate in 1642–49, during the *Gran Complicidad*, a fic-
titious plot by Portuguese crypto-Jews to destroy the Spanish empire with the
aid of foreign powers.[43] Whatever the inquisitors made of Yáñez's Portuguese
origins remains unknown, but they never openly suspected him of having
converso origins or of Judaizing practices.

Besides helping determine the guilt of each of the four culprits, rumor
and gossip proved essential to decipher a fuller meaning of the execution in
effigy in which the Inquisition saw its symbols abused. From the start, neighbors and inquisitors recognized that the aim of the effigy, the sambenitos, and
their signs was to shame Hernando Rubio Naranjo by calling him a Jew. When
at the culmination of the investigation, Ana de Figueroa confessed that Juan
de Molina had made the effigy because that "Jew" Rubio Naranjo deserved to
burn, the true revelation was not the meaning of the insult but the identity of
its author.[44] However, without an intimate knowledge of Rubio Naranjo's bad
reputation, the inquisitors would not have understood the message on one
of the signs claiming that the "great deeds" of the "Comendador of Mount
Calvary" earned him the shameful coat of arms of San Benito. The forked
tongue on the effigy made sense only after learning that the "loose-tongued"
(*deslenguado*) Rubio Naranjo was in the habit of insulting his neighbors and
using his "evil tongue" (*mala lengua*)[45] to spread poisonous rumors. To con-
vey the poisonous nature of *murmuración*, or rumor, one Spanish dictionary
cited Saint Bernard's assertion that "the evil and rumor-making tongue [*lengua maldiciente y murmuradora*] is the devil's paintbrush and like a viper."[46]
The gag tied around the effigy's second tongue turned Juana de Montoya, a
victim of Rubio Naranjo's rumors, into a suspect because she had supposedly
said that she would make someone "tie a gag to the tip of his tongue."[47] The
enigmatic two-faced effigy acquired a distinct meaning in light of the story
that one of Rubio Naranjo's great deeds included besmirching the reputation
of the women of Tecamachalco in Oaxaca. Like the stuffed dummy, Rubio
Naranjo had a "two-sided face" (*cara con dos haces*), which meant that he was
someone "who in one's presence says one thing and another thing in one's
absence."[48] Similarly, rumors confirmed that the black chicken feathers were

a reminder that, despite his sharp tongue, Rubio Naranjo was a coward.[49] One Tecamachalco resident flatly told Commissioner Canon Santiago that Rubio Naranjo was an "evil-tongued *baladronazo*": a great "braggart, prattler, loud babbler, ruffian, coward, he who has words but not hands."[50] For this same reason, the statue carried a distaff and spindle, for although it is "the glory and honor" of a woman to spin, "it is a shameful thing to see a man spin with a distaff next to him where there should be a sword."[51] When describing Rubio Naranjo's amorous interest in her, Ana de Figueroa told the inquisitors that he was "all air," which is to say that for him everything was a hoax.[52]

Taken together, this intimate knowledge of Rubio Naranjo required a broader definition of him as a Jew. Because he was a wealthy trader, some accused him of being a usurer. Yet none of the conspirators seems to have thought that he was one of "those who did not believe in the coming of the Messiah and Savior, Jesus Christ, our Lord, and continue to profess the Law of Moses"—as Sebastián de Covarrubias Orozco's early seventeenth-century dictionary defines *judío*.[53] Rather, Rubio Naranjo was a Jew according to a different, and patently anti-Semitic, definition: someone who was "irreligious, impious . . . soulless, greedy . . . damned, a dog."[54] Yet the trial also revealed that these definitions applied as well to Juan de Molina. Still hoping that she could distance herself from Molina's crimes, Figueroa described Molina to the inquisitors in terms widely applied to Rubio Naranjo. Molina, she said, was "a great scoundrel, very disliked, and a troublemaker with an evil tongue and a defamer of married women. He said that all the men were cuckolds and boasted about this."[55] Molina and Yáñez punished Rubio Naranjo for his sharp tongue, but all three were birds of the same feather. They thought themselves wily and brave, "cocks of the walk," as Molina and Yáñez were once described. Perhaps they had once been friends, playing cards together, boasting about their women, and laughing at gossip, until Rubio Naranjo, the most reckless of the three, dared to go after Molina's woman.

Satisfied that they knew the meaning of the execution in effigy, the inquisitors did not feel the need to find out where Molina had drawn inspiration for the elaborate insult. Perhaps he witnessed an execution in effigy at an auto de fe in Spain, where he had lived until he moved to Mexico in 1569.[56] He grew up in the diocese of Toledo, a city that saw general autos de fe in 1554, 1555, 1565, and 1566.[57] However, Molina could not have seen an execution in effigy in Mexico because the first took place in 1579, when the Inquisition condemned in absentia the French Huguenot pirate Guillermo Potier.[58] The first execution in effigy of a Judaizer in Mexico took place in 1590.[59]

Molina was already in Mexico for the first auto de fe organized by the recently established tribunal in February 1574.[60] He lived in Mexico City at least until August 1573.[61] After he moved from the city, he returned on occasion; he probably saw the sambenitos that hung inside the cathedral, which, by 1578, numbered more than thirty.[62] What is clear is that the very solemnity with which the new tribunal conducted the autos de fe and the authority that it invested in the sambenitos provided a powerful arsenal of images, symbols, and actions from which various individuals—including the royal scribe Juan de Molina—drew ammunition to attack their hated enemies.

The power of religious symbols therefore made them susceptible to theft and misuse. The Inquisition acknowledged as much when it summed up the crime committed by the principal conspirators in the Tecamachalco case: "By apostolic authority, the use of signs and penitential habits [that is, sambenitos]—as a sign of union and reconciliation with Our Holy Mother Church, rather than to offend or insult penitents—belongs to the Holy Office of the Inquisition. Instead of respecting and venerating this Holy tribunal, the said Juan de Molina and Francisco Yáñez usurped its jurisdiction and used the said habits and signs . . . in great infamy and dishonor of a neighbor . . . because he was their enemy and they wished him ill, causing a great scandal in this town and in the entire region."[63]

Molina was not alone in recognizing the power of appropriating the Inquisition's symbols and authority to shame and threaten enemies. The Mexican Inquisition's summary of the Tecamachalco case sent in 1583 to the Suprema explained: "In these years, there have been frequent defamatory signs in this land, especially in that town." The word for "defamatory sign," *libelo*, referred to insulting words, but also to symbols such as horns (calling someone a cuckold) or sambenitos. Symbols and signs could be combined, as in the Tecamachalco scandal. Thus one witness described the sambenitos of Tecamachalco as "signs in the fashion of libels" (*carteles a modo de libelos*).[64] The report sent to the Suprema did not say what those other "libels" were, although some of them must have been the various insults made against Hernando Rubio Naranjo that were mentioned during the long investigation.

Two other incidents stand out for their similarities to the Tecamachalco scandal. First, in September 1578, Rubio Naranjo reported to the Inquisition that a certain Dr. Espinosa had been the victim of a "libel" (*nivelo*) labeling him a *quemado*, meaning that he should burn at the stake. The libel consisted of a bundle of wood hung from the door of Espinosa's house in Tecamachalco.

Rubio Naranjo thought that the similarities of that "libel" to the insult against him merited examination.[65]

Second, in August 1581, several signs appeared in Tepeaca against an unnamed person.[66] (These signs prompted the fateful conversation in San Pablo, when Francisco Yáñez accused Juan Pérez of putting up the sambenitos in Tecamachalco.) The farmer Diego de Trujillo told the inquisitors that the Audiencia judge Diego García de Palacio had begun an investigation of the Tepeaca signs.[67] Unfortunately, the trial documents say nothing more about these two "libels," which appear to have been significantly less elaborate than the execution in effigy conceived by Juan de Molina.

Molina placed several symbols unrelated to the Inquisition on the effigy, which could indicate why the first investigations failed to identify the authors of the scandal. The effigies in the solemn autos de fe, which the Inquisition intended to instill fear in viewers, would not have carried distaffs and spindles. Those symbols of women's work, as well as the chicken feathers, belonged to the revelry of popular traditions across Europe, such as the French charivaris and the British "rough music."[68] The Spaniard Juan de Molina may have drawn inspiration from similar Iberian popular traditions, such as the *cencerradas*, which, like the charivaris, also combined loud music—*cencerro* meaning both an ill-tuned guitar and the bell worn by farm animals—as well as shaming symbols, such as antlers and dummies stuffed with hay, with painted faces, and signs.[69] The name "San Benito" on the Tecamachalco effigy against Hernando Rubio Naranjo also recalls the "satirical saints" of medieval and early modern Iberian Carnival celebrations, some of which were burned.[70] One Spanish tradition going back to at least the early eighteenth century was the *Judas*, a "figure or representation of the traitor Judas, which is hung or burned in the streets on Maundy Thursday or another day during Lent"—a tradition that may have found inspiration in the autos de fe.[71]

Besides indicating different possible sources for Molina's actions, these traditions help us understand the initial focus of the alcalde mayor of Tepeaca's investigation. He first suspected the group of young men who, on the evening of 20 July 1578, serenaded Tecamachalco with guitar music and entertained neighbors with the "black-speaking" Francisco Miguel. The execution in effigy could well have been a particularly nasty prank by those unmarried young men against the ill-reputed Rubio Naranjo. In 1564, King Philip II sought to stop persons who "go about at night around public plazas, saying and singing dishonest words and songs" by issuing a law that punished such insults with one hundred lashes and two years of banishment from the territory.[72] Concerns about the large number of unmarried young men in the province of Tepeaca causing trouble in Indian towns like Tecamachalco had led to calls to limit their migration to the region.[73]

The spontaneous, youthful revelry targeting Rubio Naranjo on the eve of the scandal was one of several extraordinary coincidences. The investigations made clear that the revelers in Tecamachalco had no knowledge of Juan de Molina's plan, which he had prepared days in advance. Although Molina and Yáñez did not mention the revelers, they must have heard the seven men when they approached Rubio Naranjo's house between nine and ten in the evening to serenade and taunt him. Rubio Naranjo lived across from the church, which was near Juan López's house, where Molina and Yáñez awaited the right moment to carry out their plan; at midnight, the coast was finally clear for them to nail the two sambenitos to the walls of the church and to hang the effigy from the church's doors. Those plans might have changed, had the serenading revelers kept their earlier promise to stay up all night. Ironically, they would pay for going early to bed by becoming the first suspects of the scandal.

That coincidence had its logical explanation in the response of the young Lope Jaramillo when his newfound friend Francisco Miguel asked who Hernando Rubio Naranjo was: "He's a man with an evil tongue. No man in this town is on good terms with him."[74] The timing of the serenade may have been fortuitous, but not the likelihood that the loose-tongued Rubio Naranjo would face trouble in Tecamachalco. In yet another strange coincidence, the "black-speaking" Miguel would turn out to have known about the infamous Rubio Naranjo in faraway Zacatecas, where the trader apparently also ran into trouble.[75]

It is obvious that Hernando Rubio Naranjo was predisposed to get into trouble wherever he went. At the time of the scandal in July 1578, it had been only a week since his return to Tecamachalco, after several months in Oaxaca, where he had fled following the beating that Yáñez and his friends had given him in Quecholac, which left him with a slashed face and soiled pants. Most of his neighbors in Tecamachalco must have hoped that he would stay in Oaxaca for good. Rubio Naranjo may have thought so as well, which might explain why he did not hesitate to insult publicly the women of Tecamachalco from far away. It did not take long for Rubio Naranjo to get into trouble in Oaxaca. In Guaxotitlan, he was beaten up for having an affair with a married

woman. Perhaps that left him no choice but to flee the region. To the surprise
of Tecamachalco's residents, Rubio Naranjo returned with the vain hope of
a fresh start. From this perspective, the Tecamachalco scandal reads like the
chronicle of a revenge foretold.

Like everyone else, Juan de Molina knew that Rubio Naranjo was
almost universally disliked in town, which he must have hoped would let
him get away with his revenge without suffering the consequences. One
detail mentioned by a few witnesses, but about which the inquisitors
did not express much curiosity, was the strange moniker given to Rubio
Naranjo on the sign placed on the double-faced effigy: the "Comendador of Mount Calvary." The title of comendador originally referred to the
Spanish religious-military orders of Santiago, Calatrava, and others who
received *encomiendas*, or grants of lands and service, in return for fighting the Muslim infidels. Spaniards transplanted the encomienda system
to the Americas, but not the title of comendador. This may explain why,
when trying to recall those words, one witness thought that it said "conquistador." Yáñez thought the sign read "Señor of Tecamachalco." Ana de
Figueroa remembered only that it said something about "Mount of Moses,"
or "Mount of the Jews."[76] (A disingenuous Molina claimed that he did not
remember at all what the signs said.) Even when they did not remember
the exact words, nearly all witnesses knew that this enigmatic title meant
that Rubio Naranjo was a great Jew.

The unusual title "comendador" suggests another association that perhaps made sense only to the Castilian Juan de Molina. A century earlier, a
mythical comendador was the victim of the wrath of his abused subjects
for threatening the honor of women. In 1476, the Comendador of Fuente
Ovejuna, a village in Andalusia not far from the border of Molina's Castile, died at the hands of angry villagers.[77] Explaining the origins of the
expression *Fuente Ovejuna lo hizo*, or "Fuente Ovejuna did it," Covarrubias
recounts the following story in his dictionary (first published in 1611): "In
the year 1476 . . . when all of Castile was wrecked by feuds, one evening
in the month of April the people of Fuente Ovejuna agreed to kill Hernán
Pérez de Guzmán, *Comendador Mayor* of the Order of Calatrava, for the
many grievances they alleged he had done to them. Entering his house,
they stoned him to death; and although judges were sent and many men
and women were tortured, they could not get them to say any other words
than 'Fuente Ovejuna did it.' From here came the expression that, when
in a notorious crime no one in particular is found to have done it, despite

many suspects, it is said: 'Fuente Ovejuna did it.'"[78] Likewise, during the first
investigation in 1578, as the number of potential suspects grew and eventually forced the Inquisition to suspend it, the inquisitors could have said in
frustration: "Tecamachalco did it!"

It is impossible to know whether Juan de Molina was inspired by the story
of Fuente Ovejuna. However, that story provides an interesting perspective
from which to rethink the purpose of resorting to the execution in effigy
to take revenge on Hernando Rubio Naranjo. The symbolic death of Rubio
Naranjo sought to bring to an end the Comendador of Mount Calvary's
tyrannical lordship in the name of "all the neighbors" of Tecamachalco. In
Renaissance Italy, *immagini infamanti*, or defaming images, including effigies, provided a symbolic means for the entire community to punish a person
for offenses against communal morality.[79]

Still, why did Molina choose to destroy his hated enemy with what
was essentially a symbolic death? After all, an execution in effigy was
not the same as death at the hands of an angry mob—as happened to the
Comendador Mayor of Fuente Ovejuna. After the scandal, the humiliated
Rubio Naranjo fell ill.[80] But in a few days, he recovered and demanded the
punishment of those who had injured his honor. The cochineal collector
Juan López de Montalbán allegedly said that the sambenitos were "little"
compared to what Rubio Naranjo had done.[81] Instead of taking comfort in
the thought that he was lucky to be alive, Rubio Naranjo took these words
as evidence that López de Montalbán was his enemy. Nonetheless, Rubio
Naranjo must have realized that he could not remain in Tecamachalco.
In 1581, he was living in Tlaxcala, where his lover, the widow Catalina
Rodríguez de San José, granted him powers to act as her and her children's
administrator.[82]

Juan de Molina's two principal accomplices questioned his decision to
punish Rubio Naranjo in such a strange way. Still pretending that she was
innocent, Ana de Figueroa declared that when Molina told her about the sambenitos he had put up, she asked him: "Why bother with such a scoundrelly
act? It would be better to kill Rubio Naranjo if he insulted you."[83] During his
torture session, Yáñez said that even after agreeing to carry out the elaborate
insult, he tried to persuade Molina to give Rubio Naranjo "a round of clubs
and forget that."[84] After all, Yáñez and his friends beat up Rubio Naranjo and
slashed his face, and no one ever caught them. However, Molina refused to
change his plan. Back in Juan López's house after carrying out the crime, an
out-of-breath Molina tried to reassure Yáñez by proclaiming: "That's how one

must treat them; to do it any other way is for a man to lose what he has."[85] Perhaps it required someone with legal expertise like the royal scribe Juan de Molina to appreciate the words of the *Siete Partidas* that for a defamed man, "death would be better for him than life."[86] This was something that Molina, his three accomplices, and their humiliated enemy must have pondered for the rest of their lives.

NOTES

Preface

1. Seymour B. Liebman dates Douglas's purchase of the manuscripts to 1907; see his "The *Abecedario* and a Check-List of the Mexican Inquisition Documents at the Henry E. Huntington Library," *Hispanic American Historical Review* 44, no. 4 (November 1964): 554–67, esp. 554. However, an article in the *Mexican Herald* of 2 May 1909 (sec. 2, p. 12) indicates that the purchase took place in April 1909. In addition, the antiquarian bookseller Willson Wilberforce Blake (1850–1918), based in Mexico, listed the lot of Inquisition manuscripts for sale as late as 1909; see *Blake's Catalogue of Autographs and Manuscripts, Printed Books on the Inquisition . . .* , no. 8 (Mexico City, March 1909), 9. It is not listed in his 1910 catalog; see *Ninth catalogue . . . by W. W. Blake* (Mexico City, June 1910). Both catalogs are available at www.archive.org.

2. The missing trial is not at the AGN or the Huntington. I have been unable to locate the missing trial in other major archives and libraries that contain documents from the Mexican Inquisition: Biblioteca Nacional de México, Biblioteca Nacional de Antropología e Historia (Mexico City), Center for Jewish History (New York), Hispanic Society (New York), Gilcrease Museum (Tulsa), Library of Congress, New York Public Library, and libraries of the University of California at Berkeley, University of Pennsylvania, University of Texas (Austin), and Tulane University.

3. A "Summary Report for the Mexican Inquisition Papers at the Huntington" is drawn from Liebman's description ("*Abecedario* and a Check-List," 565), which is the same as in the "List of Mexican Inquisition Documents at the Huntington Library Bequeathed by Mr. Walter Douglas" (undated), prepared by Haydée Noya, a cataloger in the Department of Manuscripts at Mexico's Archivo General de la Nación. The unpublished "Summary Report" and Noya's list are part of the Huntington's finding aid for its Mexican manuscripts. E. N. Adler relied on E. Nott Anable, who misread Blake's catalogs (see n. 1 above) and made numerous mistakes describing what became the Huntington manuscript, dating the Tecamachalco case to 1673; see E. N. Adler, "American Autos," *Jewish Quarterly Review* 17, no. 1 (October 1904): 67–77, esp. 75–76.

4. Maureen Flynn, "Blasphemy and the Play of Anger in Sixteenth-Century Spain," *Past and Present* no. 149 (November 1995): 29-56, esp. n. 13.

5. Stealing, poaching, and borrowing have all been used to describe the act of appropriation of objects, images, or ideas; see Michel de Certeau, *The Practice of Everyday Life*,

trans. Steven Rendall (Berkeley, Calif., 1984), 166. For a discussion of the applicability of the concept of appropriation to the medieval and early modern periods, see Kathleen Ashley and Véronique Plesch, "The Cultural Processes of 'Appropriation,'" *Journal of Medieval and Early Modern Studies* 32, no. 1 (winter 2002): 1–15.

6. Francisco Bethencourt, *The Inquisition: A Global History, 1478–1834*, trans. Jean Birrell (Cambridge, 2009), 295–99; Nancy Farris, "Introductory Essay: The Power of Images," *Colonial Latin American Review* 19, no. 1 (April 2010): 5–28; Alejandro Cañeque, "Imagining the Spanish Empire: The Visual Construction of Imperial Authority in Habsburg New Spain," in idem, 29–68.

7. On the possibility of the failure of "mechanisms of persuasion," see Roger Chartier, "The Powers and Limits of Representation," in *On the Edge of the Cliff: History, Language, and Practices*, trans. Lydia G. Cochrane (Baltimore, 1997), esp. 96–98.

8. Pierre Ayrault, *L'ordre, formalité, et instruction judiciare dont les Grecs et Romains ont usé és accusations publiques*, 3rd ed. (Lyon, 1642), 437; see also David Freedberg, *The Power of Images: Studies in the History and Theory of Response* (Chicago, 1989), 259.

9. On the ways in which the Spanish legal doctrine of *fama* informed the Inquisition's practice, see Aniceto Masferrer Domingo, *La pena de infamia en el derecho histórico español* (Madrid, 2001), esp. 347–65. More broadly, see Edward Peters, "Wounded Names: The Medieval Doctrine of Infamy," in *Law in Mediaeval Life and Thought*, ed. Edward B. King and Susan J. Ridyard (Sewanee, Tenn., 1990), 43–89; and Thelma Fenster and Daniel Lord Smail, eds., *Fama: The Politics of Talk and Reputation in Medieval Europe* (Ithaca, N.Y., 2003).

10. Quoted in Ramón A. Gutiérrez, *When Jesus Came, the Corn Mothers Went Away* (Stanford, Calif., 1991), 178–79. This stark notion of honor in medieval and early modern law did not always reflect the more flexible social reality, in which honor could be "challenged, threatened, lost, gained, and even regained . . . because it was not an internalized prescription for proper ethical action—it was not primarily synonymous with integrity, or honesty, or virtue"; see Ann Twinam, *Public Lives, Private Secrets: Gender, Honor, Sexuality, and Illegitimacy in Colonial Spanish America* (Stanford, Calif., 1999), 33. For a comparative perspective on Latin American and Spanish forms of honor, see Sonya Lipsett-Rivera, "*De Obra y Palabra*: Patterns of Insults in Mexico, 1750–1856," *The Americas* 54, no. 4 (April 1998): 511–39; and Lyman L. Johnson and Sonya Lipsett-Rivera, *The Faces of Honor: Sex, Shame, and Violence in Colonial Latin America* (Albuquerque, N.Mex., 1998), esp. the editors' introduction. See also Scott K. Taylor, *Honor and Violence in Golden Age Spain* (New Haven, Conn., 2008).

11. Emmanuel Le Roy Ladurie, *Montaillou: The Promised Land of Error*, trans. Barbara Bray (New York, 1978). The original French version appeared in 1975.

12. AHN, Inq. Libro 1064 (Relaciones de causas, México, c. 1572–c. 1614), fol. 88r–88v ("Relaciones de causas despachadas, 1583"); I have consulted a microfilmed copy of the document at HEH MSS MFilm 831, reel 1.

13. HEH HM 35097, fs. 181–189v.

14. Natalie Zemon Davis, *The Return of Martin Guerre* (Cambridge, Mass., 1984), esp. chap. 11.

15. Unfortunately, research at the Archivo de Notarías de Puebla did not yield additional information on any of the protagonists in the Tecamachalco case.

16. See the introduction to Richard L. Kagan and Abigail Dyer, *Inquisitorial Inquiries: Brief Lives of Secret Jews and Other Heretics* (Baltimore, 2004), which provides additional references; Carlo Ginzburg, "The Inquisitor as Anthropologist," in *Clues, Myths, and the Historical Method*, trans. John and Anne Tedeschi (Baltimore, 1989), 156–64; and the introduction to Ginzburg's *The Cheese and the Worms: The Cosmos of a Sixteenth Century Miller*, trans. John and Anne Tedeschi (New York, 1982).

17. See Henry Kamen, *The Spanish Inquisition: A Historical Revision* (New Haven, Conn., 1997), 144–45; and Irene Silverblatt, *Modern Inquisitions: Peru and the Colonial Origins of the Civilized World* (Durham, N.C., 2004), 55–58.

Prologue

1. PFY, f. 39.

2. Ibid., fs. 5 (gag around the tongue) and 175v (needle through the tongue).

3. The sign read in Spanish: "Yo, gran comendador del Monte Calbario, Rubio Naranjo, os mando a todos los beçinos deste pueblo que, como a tal señor, me acudais con todos los bienes de mis antepasados, que son las armas del más que dichoso S. Benito, pues ninguno mejor q[ue] io las puedo tener por mis grandes açañas, como a todo el mundo es notorio"; PFY, f. 5.

4. The two signs read in Spanish: "Nadie me quite mis armas" (PFY, f. 5); and "El que de aquí te quitare, se vea en otro tanto" (PFY, f. 39v).

5. For the anti-Semitic literature in early modern Spain blaming the Jews for Jesus Christ's death, see Julio Caro Baroja, *Los Judíos en la España Moderna y Contemporánea*, 3 vols., 2nd ed. (Madrid, 1978), esp. 2:415–56; Albert A. Sicroff, *Los estatutos de limpieza de sangre: Controversias entre los siglos XV y XVII* (Madrid, 1985); and Patricia E. Grieve, *The Eve of Spain: Myths of Origins in the History of Christian, Muslim, and Jewish Conflict* (Baltimore, 2009).

6. PAMT, f. 25v (wind flapping the sambenitos).

7. Alejandra Gámez Espinosa, *Los popolocas de Tecamachalco-Quecholac: Historia, cultura y sociedad de un señorío prehispánico* (Puebla, 2003), esp. chap. 5.

8. Peter Gerhard, *A Guide to the Historical Geography of New Spain*, rev. ed. (Norman, Okla., 1993), 278; and Leonardo Lomelí Vanegas, *Breve historia de Puebla* (Mexico City, 2001), 20.

9. Hildeberto Martínez, *Codiciaban la tierra: El despojo agrario en los señoríos de Tecamachalco y Quecholac (Puebla 1520–1650)* (Mexico City, 1994), 32–34.

10. On the ethnic makeup of the native population, see ibid., 11; and Gámez Espinosa, *Los popolocas*.

11. On the Spanish conquest of Tecamachalco, see Lomelí Vanegas, *Breve historia de Puebla*, 53.

12. See *Anales de Tecamachalco, 1398–1590*, ed. Eustaquio Celestino Solís and Luis Reyes García (Mexico City, 1992), 24. For the reduction in population, see René Acuña, ed., *Relaciones geográficas de Tlaxcala*, 2 vols. (Mexico City, 1984–85), 2:228.

13. These governors, along with two *alcaldes*, were elected annually; see Hildeberto Martínez, *Tepeaca en el siglo XVI: Tenencia de la tierra y organización de un señorío* (Mexico City, 1984), 128–29.

14. For the description that follows, see Acuña, *Relaciones geográficas*, 2:218–60.

15. Raymond L. Lee, "Cochineal Production and Trade in New Spain to 1600," *The Americas* 4, no. 4 (April 1948): 449–73.

16. For the dates of construction, see Xavier Moyssén, "Tecamachalco y el pintor indígena Juan Gerson," *Anales del Instituto de Investigaciones Estéticas* (Mexico) 33 (1964): 23–39, esp. 23. Moyssén gives 1541 as the start of construction, although others date the resettlement of Tecamachalco to 1543.

17. On Franciscan fortress-churches, see Samuel Y. Edgerton, *Theaters of Conversion: Religious Architecture and Indian Artisans in Colonial Mexico* (Albuquerque, N.Mex., 2001), 41; and George Kubler, *Mexican Architecture*, 2 vols. (1948; reprint, Westport, Conn., 1971), 1:94–96, 2:388.

18. See Rosa Camelo Arrondo, Jorge Gurría Lacroix, and Constantino Reyes Valerio, *Juan Gersón: Tlacuilo de Tecamachalco* (Mexico City, 1964), esp. 24–28.

19. Ibid., 50–51.

20. For the contemporary relevance of Gersón's biblical scenes in light of Franciscan interpretations of the Spanish conquest, see María Elena Landa Ábrego, *Juan Gerson, Tlacuilo* (Puebla, 1992), esp. 21–25; and Sergio [Serge] Gruzinski, *El águila y la sibila: Frescos indios de México* (Barcelona, 1994), 108–11.

21. Acuña, *Relaciones geográficas*, 2:235–37. The term "residents" (*vecinos*), sometimes stood for "heads of a family," which would mean one hundred Spanish families. Another chronicle, from 1585, claims that the Spanish residents in town were "almost one hundred"; *Relación de las cosas que sucedieron al padre fray Alonso Ponce en las provincias de la Nueva España*, Colección de Documentos Inéditos para la Historia de España, vols. 57–58 (Madrid, 1873), 57:141–42. Gerhard indicates a population of two hundred vecinos, mostly in the region of San Pablo, between Acatzingo and Quecholac; *Guide to the Historical Geography*, 280.

22. Acuña, *Relaciones geográficas*, 2:230, 231–32.

23. PFY, f. 30v.

24. Martínez's *Codiciaban la tierra* offers numerous examples of such abuse.

25. On the racially mixed *república de los españoles* in Mexico, see Herman L. Bennett, *Africans in Colonial Mexico: Absolutism, Christianity, and Afro-Creole Consciousness, 1570–1640* (Bloomington, Ind., 2003), esp. 27–28.

26. See Francisco Yáñez's background, described in Chapter 4 of this volume.

27. R. Douglas Cope, *The Limits of Racial Domination: Plebeian Society in Colonial Mexico City, 1660–1720* (Madison, Wisc., 1994), 23.

28. David Nirenberg, *Communities of Violence: Persecution of Minorities in the Middle Ages* (Princeton, N.J., 1996), 93.

29. On the protean image of the Jew, see also Steven F. Kruger, *The Spectral Jew: Conversion and Embodiment in Medieval Europe* (Minneapolis, 2006), esp. xx–xxi.

30. For the long history behind the insult "Jewish dog," see Kenneth Stow, *Jewish Dogs: An Image and Its Interpreters: Continuity in the Catholic-Jewish Encounter* (Stanford, Calif., 2006), esp. 4, 36.

31. On effigies, see Freedberg, *Power of Images*, esp. chap. 10.

32. Ayrault, *L'ordre, formalité, et instruction judiciaire*, 408. His comments apply to all crimes meriting postmortem punishment, including executions in effigy.

33. The effigy's description is from Pius II's *Commentaries*, quoted in Cecilia M. Ady, *Pius II (Aeneas Silvius Piccolomini): The Humanist Pope* (London, 1913), 193–94. Most authors describe two effigies of Malatesta, although there was a third: see David S. Chambers, *Popes, Cardinals and War: The Military Church in Renaissance and Early Modern Europe* (London, 2006), 198 n. 25.

34. See Wolfgang Brückner, *Bildnis und Brauch: Studien zur Bildfunktion der Effigies* (Berlin, 1966), 294–95, 306–7; see also Freedberg, *Power of Images*, 261–62.

35. *Dietari de la Deputació del General de Cathalunya*, vol. 2 (Barcelona, 1977), 116–17.

36. Angus MacKay, "Ritual and Royal Propaganda in Fifteenth-Century Castile," *Past and Present* 107 (May 1985): 3–43, esp. 10. MacKay also describes the 1431 deposition in effigy ordered by John II of the *Infante* Enrique as *Comendador* of the Order of Santiago (16).

37. Shima Ohara, "La propaganda política en torno al conflicto sucesorio de Enrique IV (1457–1474)," Ph.D. diss., Universidad de Valladolid (2004), 195; available at Biblioteca Virtual Miguel de Cervantes (www.cervantesvirtual.com).

38. I have not found any instances of formal executions in effigy in early modern Spain outside of autos de fe. Brückner's authoritative study of effigies, *Bildnis und Brauch*, cites many examples across Europe, but none for Spain. Samuel Y. Edgerton, Jr., argues that Italians "preferred a more subtle form of image punishment," such as *pitture infamanti*, or defaming images, rather than executions in effigy; see his *Pictures and Punishment: Art and Criminal Prosecution during the Florentine Renaissance* (Ithaca, N.Y., 1985), 71.

39. *Historia crítica de la Inquisición en España*, 10 vols. (Madrid, 1822), 9:233; cited in Henry Charles Lea, *A History of the Inquisition of Spain*, 4 vols. (New York, 1906–7), 4:517–18 n. 110 (bk. 9, chap. 2); available at libro.uca.edu.

40. Antonio Domínguez Ortiz, "Las presuntas 'razones' de la Inquisición," in *Historia de la Inquisición en España y América*, ed. Joaquín Pérez Villanueva and Bartolomé Escandell Bonet, 3 vols. (Madrid, 1984), 3:58 n. 1. Domínguez Ortiz provides no numbers.

41. Jaime Contreras and Gustav Henningsen, "Forty-Four Thousand Cases of the Spanish Inquisition (1540–1700): Analysis of a Historical Data Bank," in *The Inquisition in Early Modern Europe*, ed. Gustav Henningsen and John Tedeschi (DeKalb, Ill., 1986), 100–129, esp. table 1 (p. 114). The Inquisition of Portugal, whose first auto de fe dates

to 1540, burned 633 effigies; see Cecil Roth, *The Spanish Inquisition* (New York, 1964), 124 (which does not indicate the sources). For the limitations of the statistical studies of inquisitorial sentences, see Kamen, *The Spanish Inquisition*, 198.

42. Solange Alberro, *Inquisition et société au Mexique, 1571–1700* (Mexico City, 1988), 86, 387 (table II.4). According to Contreras and Henningsen (see n. 41 above), there were only forty-two executions in effigy for Mexico between 1574 and 1696.

43. Contreras and Henningsen, "Forty-Four Thousand Cases," table 1.

44. Lea, *History of the Inquisition*, 3:81 (bk. 6, chap. 8). His source is Fidel Fita, "La Inquisición toledana: Relación contemporánea de los autos y autillos que celebró desde el año 1458 hasta el de 1501," *Boletín de la Real Academia de la Historia* 11 (1887): 289–322, esp. 304 (8 May 1487).

45. Lea, *History of the Inquisition*, 3:216 n. 19 (bk. 7, chap. 5). The examples that Lea cites of these *statuae duplicatae* are from autos de fe in Barcelona in 1488 and 1489.

46. Nicolau Eimeric and Francisco Peña, *Manual de los inquisidores*, trans. Luis Sala-Molins and Francisco Martín (Barcelona, 1983), 231.

47. See instruction no. 19 of the Grand Inquisitor Torquemada (Prior of Santa Cruz), 1484, transcribed in Miguel Jiménez de Monteserín, *Introducción a la Inquisición española: Documentos básicos para el estudio del Santo Oficio* (Madrid, 1980), 98–100.

48. For this apocryphal story, see Adolfo de Castro, *Historia de los judíos en España* (Cádiz, 1847), 188–89; and Antonio Márquez, *Literatura e Inquisición en España (1478–1834)* (Madrid, 1980), 117.

49. Constance H. Rose, "The Marranos of the Seventeenth Century and the Case of the Merchant Writer Antonio Enríquez Gómez," in *The Spanish Inquisition and the Inquisitorial Mind*, ed. Ángel Alcalá (Boulder, Colo., 1987), 53–71, esp. 63.

50. I. S. Révah, "Un pamphlet contre l'Inquisition d'Antonio Enríquez Gómez: La seconde partie de la 'Política Angélica' (Rouen, 1647)," *Revue des Études Juives* (ser. 4, t. 1) 121, nos. 1–2 (January–June 1962): 81–168, esp. 113–14.

51. The first mention of *estatuas* that I have found is Grand Inquisitor Fernando de Valdés's instruction no. 62 from 1561: "La sentencia absolutiva se ha de leer en Auto público"; see Jiménez de Monteserín, *Introducción a la Inquisición española*, 229.

52. Consuelo Maqueda Abreu, *El Auto de Fe* (Madrid, 1992), 130, 139–40; and Bethencourt, *Inquisition*, esp. 252–53, 266–68, 279–81.

53. See a high-resolution image at http://www.museodelprado.es/coleccion/galeria-on-line/galeria-on-line/zoom/1/obra/auto-de-fe-en-la-plaza-mayor-de-madrid. On illustrations of autos de fe, see Francisco Bethencourt, "Auto da Fé: Ritual and Imagery," *Journal of the Warburg and Courtauld Institutes* 55 (1992): 155–68, esp. 164, 167.

54. "Auto de Fe de 1680," transcribed in Jiménez de Monteserín, *Introducción a la Inquisición española*, 690.

55. María Victoria Caballero Gómez, "El Auto de Fé de 1680: Un lienzo para Francisco Rizi," *Revista de la Inquisición* 3 (1994): 69–140, esp. 98–99. Gregorio Fosman made an engraving of this auto de fe for a book published in 1680 by José del Olmo.

56. E.g., the German engraving of the great 1559 auto de fe in Valladolid, an idealized representation based on accounts of the ceremony. Nonetheless, it correctly shows effigies carried on poles, followed by coffins. Likewise, Bernard Picart's rendering of an auto de fe in Madrid—most likely inspired by Fosman's engraving—shows effigies hanging from poles followed by coffins; see J. F. Bernard, *Cérémonies et coutumes religieuses de tous les peuples du monde* (Amsterdam, 1723–43), vol. 2, illustration facing p. 28. A digital version is available at http://digital2.library.ucla.edu/picart/illustrations.html. On Picart's work, see Lynn Hunt, Margaret Jacob, and Wijnand Mijnhardt, *The Book That Changed Europe: Picart and Bernard's Religious Ceremonies of the World* (Cambridge, Mass., 2010), esp. 207.

57. Lea, *History of the Inquisition*, 3:437 (bk. 8, chap. 3).

58. Fernando de Valdés's instruction no. 81 (1561), in Jiménez de Monteserín, *Introducción a la Inquisición española*, 239–40; see also Kamen, *Spanish Inquisition*, 243.

59. See Martin Austin Nesvig, *Ideology and Inquisition: The World of the Censors in Early Mexico* (New Haven, Conn., 2009), esp. 104–13. Looking at the period 1522–1700, Solange Alberro contrasts 2,401 trials in Mexico and Central America with 4,027 *relaciones de causas* in the Granada tribunal alone. The combined extension of the sixteen tribunals in the Iberian Peninsula and the Canary Islands was 580,000 square kilometers, compared with 3 million square kilometers in New Spain; see Alberro, *La actividad del Santo Oficio de la Inquisición en Nueva España, 1571–1700* (Mexico City, 1981), 257.

60. See Richard E. Greenleaf, *Zumárraga and the Mexican Inquisition, 1536–1546* (Washington, D.C., 1962), 8–11.

61. Ibid., 13–14. Greenleaf indicates 152 cases for 1536–43, whereas Nesvig indicates 120 cases for 1536–41; see Nesvig, *Ideology and the Inquisition*, 108.

62. Greenleaf, *Zumárraga*, 68–74; and Patricia Lopes Don, *Bonfires of Culture: Franciscans, Indigenous Readers, and the Inquisition in Early Mexico, 1524–1540* (Norman, Okla., 2010), chap. 5.

63. Montúfar arrived at his post in 1554 but began his inquisitorial activities in 1556; see Greenleaf, *Zumárraga*, 15.

64. For inquisitorial activity not led from Mexico City, see Yolanda Mariel de Ibáñez, *La Inquisición en México durante el siglo XVI* (Mexico City, 1946), 92 (Zumpango, 1547), 95 (Chicahuastepec, 1559), 94 (Yucatán, 1560). Greenleaf notes that in 1560, the alcalde of Toluca assumed quasi-inquisitorial powers; see *Zumárraga*, 18. See also the list of inquisitorial cases prior to 1571 in Alfonso Toro, ed., *Los judíos en la Nueva España*, 2nd ed. (Mexico City, 1982), 85–161.

65. See Inga Clendinnen, *Ambivalent Conquests: Maya and Spaniard in Yucatán, 1517–1570* (Cambridge, 1987), esp. 74–76 (number of tortured, deaths, suicides), 79 (criticism of friars); and chap. 7 (Toral's intervention).

66. Richard Hakluyt later published the accounts of some of the survivors of this incident; see Peter C. Mancall, *Hakluyt's Promise: An Elizabethan's Obsession for an English America* (New Haven, Conn., 2007), 190, 232–33.

67. Jaime Contreras, "Las coyunturas políticas e inquisitoriales de la etapa," in Pérez Villanueva and Escandell Bonet, *Historia de la Inquisición*, 1:701–13.

68. Álvaro Huerga, "La implantación del Santo Oficio en México," in Pérez Villanueva and Escandell Bonet, *Historia de la Inquisición*, 1:724–29.

69. Stafford Poole, *Pedro Moya de Contreras: Catholic Reform and Royal Power in New Spain, 1571–1591* (Berkeley, Calif., 1987), esp. 28–34.

70. José Toribio Medina, *Historia del Tribunal del Santo Oficio de la Inquisición en México* (henceforth, *Inquisición en México*), 2nd ed. (Mexico City, 1952), 38–40, 47.

71. Francisco Santos Zertuche, *Señorío, dinero y arquitectura: El palacio de la Inquisición de México, 1571–1820* (Mexico City, 2000), esp. 39, 44–46.

72. Poole, *Pedro Moya de Contreras*, 31–33.

73. Ibid., 37.

74. On this vast subject, see two classic studies: Edward Muir, *Ritual in Early Modern Europe*, 2nd ed. (Cambridge, 2005); and Norbert Elias, *The Court Society*, trans. Edmund Jephcott (New York, 1983).

75. Medina, *Inquisición en México*, 61–67; and Ibáñez, *La Inquisición en México durante el siglo XVI*, 121–34 (1574 auto). See Ibáñez for autos prior to 1574 (67 [1528], 77 [2 June 1539]), as well as other ceremonies with similarities to autos de fe (79, 83, 84). The execution of Carlos of Texcoco took place at an auto de fe in Mexico City on 30 November 1539; see Greenleaf, *Zumárraga*, 73.

76. The ceremony took place on 13 August 1574, on the Feast of Saint Hippolytus; see Medina, *Inquisición en México*, 67. See the 1574 inventory of sambenitos in AGN, Inq. vol. 77, exp. 35, fs. 232–233r.

77. See Nesvig, *Ideology and Inquisition*, 206. On the professional background of inquisitors, see Alberro, *Inquisition et société*, 39; and Kamen, *Spanish Inquisition*, 195.

78. Medina, *Inquisición en México*, 74, 76–77.

79. The victim was the Licenciado Cristóbal Badillo (or Vadillo), archdeacon of the cathedral of Michoacán; AGN, Inq. vol. 80, exp. 9, f. 277 (16 December 1575).

80. AGN, Indiferente Virreinal (Inquisición), caja 178, exp. 6, fs. 35v, 37–41.

81. AGN, Inq. vol. 79, exp. 305, f. 367. Andrada's sentencing took place *fuera de auto* (lit., "away from an auto de fe"). These so-called *autillos* were closed to the public inside the Inquisition's premises in the case of clerics or for minor offenses that did not warrant a more costly public ceremony; see Maqueda Abreu, *Auto de Fe*, 46–54.

82. AGN, Inq. vol. 71, exp. 8, fs. 384–419v.

83. AGN, Indiferente Virreinal (Inquisición), caja 5018, exp. 61, fs. 22–23.

84. Silverblatt, *Modern Inquisitions*, 90.

85. See the description of the order followed by the Mexican Inquisition between 1571 and 1594 by the Inquisition's secretary Pedro de los Ríos, transcribed in Genaro García, *La inquisición de México*, 2nd ed., vol. 5 of *Documentos inéditos o muy raros para la historia de México* (Mexico City, 1974), 31–41.

86. Medina, *Inquisición en México*, 39. It is unclear whether this banner bore the coat of arms of the Inquisition, which consisted of the cross representing Christ's death

and humankind's redemption, flanked on its right by the olive branch of mercy, and on the left by the sword of punishment; see Bethencourt, *Inquisition*, 107.

Chapter 1. False Start

1. PFY, f. 1. Usually, the Inquisition appointed commissioners to a diocese, but Seguera was the commissioner for the Franciscans.

2. Ibid., f. 39v.

3. Ibid., f. 1v (30 July 1578). The spelling of early modern names varies. Accordingly, the inquisitor's first name is sometimes given as Alfonso Fernández de Bonilla.

4. Ibid., f. 2.

5. Kamen, *Spanish Inquisition*, 283.

6. HEH HM 35097, f. 40v.

7. The *oidor* was the Licenciado Bernabé de Valdés y Cárcamo, who married Doña Catalina Ruiz Mexía. The couple had a daughter who married Francisco Díaz del Castillo, son of the famous Spanish conquistador and chronicler Bernal Díaz del Castillo; see Bernal Díaz del Castillo, *Historia verdadera de la conquista de la Nueva España: Manuscrito "Guatemala,"* ed. José Antonio Barbón Rodríguez (Mexico City, 2005), 1030. Doña Catalina Ruiz Mexía's relationship to Rubio Naranjo is not indicated.

8. PAMT, f. 12.

9. "Inhibitoria . . . de los Inquisidores al alcalde mayor" (31 July 1578), incorporated into PFY, f. 11.

10. Sebastián de Covarrubias Orozco, *Tesoro de la lengua castellana o española*, ed. Felipe C. R. Maldonado, rev. ed. (Madrid, 1995), 881.

Chapter 2. Trial and Failure

1. In 1541 and 1568, Lope Jaramillo, Sr., received at least two grants of land for cattle; see lists of grants of lands in Martínez, *Codiciaban la tierra*, n.p.

2. The documentation does not transcribe the black language spoken by Francisco Miguel. One may guess what he may have sounded like from characters in numerous early modern Portuguese Spanish theatrical and literary works that "speak in black" or in "Guinean" in imitation of the broken Spanish of the "wild" (*bozal*) African. Sometimes, the words do not make sense; see John Beusterien, *An Eye on Race: Perspectives from Theater in Imperial Spain* (Lewisburg, Pa., 2006), 108–9; Jerome C. Branche, *Colonialism and Race in Luso-Hispanic Literature* (Columbia, Mo., 2006), esp. 67; and Baltasar Fra Molinero, *La imagen de los negros en el teatro del Siglo de Oro* (Madrid, 1995), 20–25. I thank José Cartagena Calderón for these references.

3. Lope Jaramillo later denied having said this to Francisco Miguel.

4. Francisco Miguel denied saying these last words.

5. PAMT, f. 30.

6. PJLM, f. 51–51v.

7. Ibid., fs. 44–46v. Rubio Naranjo dated the letter 5 September 1578, but the Inquisition acknowledged its receipt on 4 September.

8. Galiano was an *obligado*, i.e., he collected taxes in return for paying a fixed sum of money in advance to the town. He was a native of the village of Chillón, presently in the province of Ciudad Real (Castilla–La Mancha), near the border of the provinces of Badajoz (Extremadura) and Córdoba (Andalusia); AGN, Inq. vol. 194, exp. 4 (investigation of the "purity of race" of Juan de Reina, 1592), n.p.

9. PJLM, fs. 55v–57.

10. Ibid., fs. 60–61.

11. PAMT, f. 14.

12. The woman was Isabel Suárez, sister of Juana Muñoz and the aunt of the horseshoe maker Juan Pérez; PFY, f. 83v.

13. PJLM, f. 53v.

Chapter 3. Surprise Witness

1. This quotation and the statements that follow are in PFY, fs. 62–63.

2. "Finished them": The original reads *los barnicó*, from the verb *barnizar*, "to varnish"; but it seems unlikely that the effigy and the sambenitos were literally coated with a varnish. Other testimonies will speak about one of the sambenitos being "painted or glued together" (*pintado o pegado*); ibid., f. 69v.

3. Medina, *Inquisición en México*, 76.

4. Ibid., 104–5.

Chapter 4. The Mother, the Son, and the Stepson

1. PFY, f. 67v.

2. Since Francisco Hernández was a common name, it is unclear whether he was the same person as the mestizo from Tecamachalco by the same name tried by the Inquisition in 1610 for bigamy. The Inquisition suspended the trial after determining that Hernández was not a mestizo but an Indian, and therefore not subject to the tribunal's authority; AGN, Inq. vol. 287, exp. 7. See also Richard E. Greenleaf, *Inquisición y sociedad en el México Colonial* (Mexico City, 1985), 134 n. 33, 185.

3. PFY, f. 70v.

4. Ibid., f. 71v.

5. "*O pobre de mí si anda por allí mi hijo*"; ibid., f. 71v.

6. Ibid., f. 72.

7. The quotations that follow from Catalina Gómez's second testimony come from ibid., fs. 72v–74.

8. AGN, Real Audiencia-Tierras contenedor 813, vol. 1874, exp. 11 (1578, Yáñez described as a Spaniard); and PFY, f. 120 (described as a mestizo).

9. The quotations that follow from Francisco Yáñez's first testimony come from PFY, fs. 75–76v.

10. Ibid., f. 77.

11. The word that Yáñez used to describe how the sambenitos were made is *pegado*, which can mean joined together, glued, or pasted. There was considerable confusion about how exactly the sambenitos had been made. Diego de Trujillo had used the word *barnizar* (to finish or varnish); Francisco Hernández was unsure whether the sambenitos had been painted (*pintados*) or glued (*pegados*).

12. PFY, f. 77–77v.

13. Ibid., f. 78–78v.

14. Muñoz's biographical information comes from her *discurso de su vida*, or account of her life, given to Canon Santiago; ibid., f. 79.

15. PJP, p. 51.

16. During her testimony (PFY, fs. 79–80v), Muñoz provided two similar versions of her exchange with Vargas. I follow here the livelier language of the second version (f. 80v) and supplement it with a few details from the first version (f. 79v).

17. PFY, f. 81–81v.

18. Ibid., f. 82–82v.

19. Isabel Suárez did not remember if the sambenitos had appeared on Rubio Naranjo's house; for her statement, see ibid., fs. 83–84.

20. Back in 1578, Rubio Naranjo had suspected Alonso Rodríguez, a mestizo from Puebla, because they had become "enemies" after Rubio Naranjo called on an overdue loan that he had made to Rodríguez, who, as a result, lost his horse. Afterward, Rubio Naranjo said that Rodríguez made numerous disparaging remarks about him; see p. 35 above.

21. For a brief description of the Tecamachalco monastery in 1585, see *Relación de las cosas que sucedieron al padre fray Alonso Ponce*, 57:142.

22. *Guayas de mí si allá cogerán a mi hijo que me lo pararán*; PFY, f. 85.

23. Ibid., f. 85–85v.

24. Ibid., fs. 86–87v.

25. Canon Santiago sought a *carta de edicto* (lit., a "letter of edict"), also known as an "edict of faith," by which the Inquisition required individuals to come forward with information about suspects involved in the offenses outlined in the edict. Unlike an "edict of grace," the edict of faith did not provide a period during which individuals who denounced themselves for committing heresies would not face punishment; see Kamen, *Spanish Inquisition*, 174–75.

26. Canon Santiago to inquisitors, 14 November 1581; PFY, f. 108.

27. Ibid., f. 93v.

28. Alonso García's testimony is in ibid., fs. 91–93.

29. *Si a mi hijo allá hubieran cogido cual me hubieran parado*; ibid., f. 94v.

30. Ibid., f. 96–96v.

31. Ibid., f. 98.

32. As a public scribe (*escribano público*), Francisco de Molina would have recorded licenses for the alcalde mayor in land sales, notarized depositions, and prepared other types of legal papers; see Charles Gibson, *Tlaxcala in the Sixteenth Century*, 2nd ed. (Stanford, Calif., 1967), 77.

33. AGI, Contratación 5537 (Catálogo de Pasajeros), libro 3, fol. 382v (8 June 1569), available at Portal de Archivos Españoles (http://pares.mcu.es).

34. For Francisco de Molina's post at the Audiencia, see AGI, México, 170, no. 58A (investigation of the "purity of race" of Juan González), n.p. (22 August 1571; available at http://pares.mcu.es); for his part in the 1578 investigation by the alcalde mayor of Tepeaca, see PAMT, fs. 18ff.

35. PFY, f. 99v.

36. *Gayón*: "Term from the criminal world (*Germanía*); same as ruffian"; *Diccionario de la lengua castellana*, 6 vols. (Madrid, 1726–39), 4:36; *al pelo*: "To the point, exactly, made to order"; *Diccionario de la lengua española*, 20th ed., at http://buscon.rae.es/drae.

37. Francisco de Molina's deposition is in PFY, fs. 99–100v.

38. Ibid., f. 80v.

39. Ibid., f. 101v.

40. *Baladrón*: "El fanfarrón y hablador que siendo cobarde blasona de valiente"; see Covarrubias Orozco, *Tesoro de la lengua*, 158.

41. The question refers to an accusation made in 1578 by Rubio Naranjo; see p. 36 above.

42. Luis de Cepeda's statement is in PFY, fs. 101–3.

43. Catalina Rodríguez said that the sambenitos appeared on a *castillo*, or castle, as early colonial fortress-churches were sometimes called; ibid., f. 104.

44. Pedro Hernández, one of the first suspects interrogated during the Inquisition's first investigation in 1578, declared under oath to the inquisitors that he did not know what a sambenito was; see p. 35 above. As we will later see, Madalena Rodríguez, the twenty-year-old wife of Luis de Cepeda, did not know, either.

45. PFY, f. 104v.

46. Ibid., fs. 104v–105.

47. Ibid., f. 105v.

48. Ibid., f. 106–106v.

49. The quotations that follow come from ibid., fs. 109–10: Euguí to Inquisitors, 20 November 1581.

50. See Hildeberto Martínez, *Colección de documentos coloniales de Tepeaca* (Mexico City, 1984), doc. 180 (pp. 479–85): "Comisión al doctor Pedro Farfán, oidor de la Real Audiencia, para que vaya a averiguar los pleitos que los naturales de la provincia de Tepeaca siguen contra los labradores españoles, sobre despojo de tierras y otros agravios. México, enero 7 de 1581."

51. PFY, f. 109v: Euguí to Inquisitors, 20 November 1581.

52. PJP, p. 51v: Alzorriz to Inquisitors, 20 November 1581. There is no numeration of the *fojas* in the records of this trial. I follow the pagination according to the AGN's *Guía General* (www.agn.gob.mx/guiageneral).

Chapter 5. Mistrial

1. PJP, p. 50v: arrest of Juan Pérez, 16 November 1581.

2. Ibid., p. 59: Inquisitors to Alzorriz, 9 December 1581.

3. PFY, f. 76v.

4. Ibid., f. 63v.

5. As reported by Isabel Suárez; ibid., f. 83v.

6. The chamber's description comes from Santos Zertuche, *Señorío, dinero y arquitectura*, 40–42, 54–56, 66–67.

7. PFY, f. 114–114v.

8. Ibid., f. 115.

9. Ibid., f. 117.

10. The quotations from Juan Pérez's testimony come from PJP, pp. 53–54.

11. The shipment of cacao was measured in *cargas*: half of the eighty *cargas* went to Cholula and the rest to Tepeaca. One *carga* was equivalent to ten *arrobas*; one *arroba* was twenty-five *libras* (pounds); see Robert Ferry, "Trading Cacao: A View from Veracruz, 1629–1645," *Nuevo Mundo Mundos Nuevos*, Debates, 2006, at http://nuevomundo.revues.org/1430.

12. PJP, p. 59.

13. PFY, f. 118v.

14. Ibid., f. 119.

15. Ibid., f. 120–120v.

16. Ibid., f. 121.

17. PJP, p. 54.

18. Ibid., p. 55–55v.

19. The sources for this case do not indicate the defense lawyer's first name. In August 1572, the first inquisitor, Pedro Moya de Contreras, appointed the Licenciado Melchor de Ávalos (or Dávalos), *abogado de presos*; AGN, Inq. vol. 67, exp. 5, f. 104 (29 April 1579). Ávalos was also a lawyer and *fiscal* of Mexico City's Audiencia, until he left Mexico in March 1584 (according to the new calendar) to serve as judge (*oidor*) in the Audiencia of Manila. He died in 1590. He is well known for two letters that he wrote to Philip II in 1585 on the treatment of Muslims in the Philippines; see Lewis Hanke and Agustín Millares Carlo, eds., *Cuerpo de documentos del siglo XVI sobre los derechos de España en las Indias y las Filipinas* (Mexico City, 1943), xxix–xxx.

20. PJP, p. 57.

21. Ibid., pp. 59v–61.

Chapter 6. New and Old Leads

1. PFY, f. 123.

2. Ibid., fs. 123v–124.

3. For Juan López de Montalbán's declarations before the inquisitors in 1578, see pp. 36–37 above.

4. PFY, fs. 128v–129.

5. Ibid., f. 129.

6. Ibid., f. 129v.

7. Ibid., f. 132.

8. The identity of the Indian woman married to the ladino Indian Francisco is unclear. At times, the sources suggest that her name was Bárbara; but she may have also been an *india bárbara*, i.e., a "savage Indian," which could have meant that she was a Popoloca; see Gámez Espinosa, *Los popolocas*, 125. On the Spanish notions of *indios bárbaros*, or savage Indians, see David J. Weber, *Bárbaros: Spaniards and Their Savages in the Age of Enlightenment* (New Haven, Conn., 2005), esp. 14–15.

9. Yáñez mistakenly called the ladino Indian Alonso.

10. PFY, f. 135.

Chapter 7. The Scribe

1. In late January 1582, the Inquisition's commissioner in Veracruz arrested Molina in Río de Alvarado and sent him the next day to Mexico City with a constable; AGN, Inq. vol. 81, exp. 1: Inquisitors to Commissioner in Veracruz, 27 January 1582; AGN, Indiferente Virreinal (Inquisición), caja 5025, exp. 109: Commissioner in Veracruz to Inquisitors: 27 January 1582. In the latter, the commissioner mistakenly called Juan de Molina "Juan *Gómez* de Molina," perhaps because Molina was also using his mother's surname, González, which he would use before the inquisitors at his first audience (see below).

2. See pp. 74–75 above.

3. PAMT, fs. 30v–31.

4. PJM, fs. 144–145v.

5. By Río de Alvarado, Molina probably meant the town of Alvarado (aka Atlacintla). Whereas Francisco de Molina was a public scribe (*escribano público*), his "son" was a royal scribe (*escribano real* or *escribano del rey*). These different classifications of scribes responded partly to the different documents that they were allowed to prepare, over which there were often disputes; see Patricio Hidalgo Nuchera, "El escribano público entre partes o notarial en la Recopilación de Leyes de Indias de 1680," *Espacio, Tiempo y Forma* (ser. 4, Historia Moderna) 7 (1994): 307–30.

6. AGI, México, 170 n. 58, n.p.: testimony by Roque Martínez on 2 December 1572 as part of the inquiry to confirm the necessary requirements for receiving the title of royal scribe for Juan González; available at http://pares.mcu.es.

7. PJM, f. 144–144v.

8. Ibid., f. 145.

9. Ibid., f. 145v.

10. See p. 34 above.

11. PJM, f. 145v.

Chapter 8. The Interpreter

1. A document from February 1581 indicates that Juan López also acted as Nahuatl translator ("person who understands the Mexican language") for the town crier in Quecholac. The town crier had someone else translate to Popoloca, suggesting that

López, a native of Mexico City, did not know the language of the indigenous population of the Tecamachalco region; see Martínez, *Colección de documentos coloniales de Tepeaca*, 484–85.

2. "In Spanish Colonial architecture, the *zaguán* was a massive wooden gate that was often sheltered and wide enough to permit wagons, coaches, or carts to enter a courtyard. . . . Pedestrians entered the courtyard either through a small door adjacent to the zaguán or through a small door set into the *zaguán* itself"; see Cyril M. Harris, *American Architecture: An Illustrated Encyclopedia* (New York, 1998), 369.

3. PJL, fs. 178–80, transcribed in PFY, fs. 136–138v.

4. PJL, f. 180–180v.

Chapter 9. The Farmer

1. Jean-Pierre Berthe, "El cultivo del 'pastel' en Nueva España," *Historia Mexicana* 9, no. 3 (January–March 1960): 340–67, esp. 348–49, 365 n. 29.

2. PAMT, f. 28v.

3. PFY, fs. 160–161v.

4. Ibid., f. 162.

5. Ibid., f. 162v.

6. Ibid., f. 163.

7. Molina's trial is missing and presumed lost. Fortunately, the key passages were transcribed in other trials related to the Tecamachalco case, especially in Francisco Yáñez's trial.

8. PFY, f. 146.

9. Ibid., f. 109–109v: Euguí to Inquisitors, 20 November 1581.

10. *Libro primero de votos de la Inquisición de México, 1573–1600* (México, 1949), 111.

11. Aside from clear violations of the instructions, inquisitors got around the rule limiting torture to a single session by "suspending" a torture session and "resuming" it at a later time; see Kamen, *Spanish Inquisition*, 187–91. For irregularities in the application of torture in the Mexican Inquisition during the seventeenth century, see Medina, *Inquisición en México*, 218.

Chapter 10. Under Torment

1. Inquisitorial instructions required the presence during torture of a representative of the bishop of the diocese where the crime had taken place. In this case, the bishop of Tlaxcala appointed Licenciado Bonilla in his place.

2. The effigy actually had one sambenito on the statue and the sign held by the effigy. Rather than a mistake, Molina used the word "sambenito" for the actual "penitential garment" as well as for the "defamatory signs"; *Diccionario de la lengua castellana*, 6:35 (*sambenito*). See also the discussion of the Spanish term *libelo* in the Epilogue to this volume.

3. Molina's statement is unclear on several points. I have not been able to establish

the identity of the "wife of Enríquez." Molina stated that she was a *mujer de Tecamachalco que es de Oaxaca*. Since her husband was an *extranjero*—which can mean both a foreigner and an outsider—I am assuming that the couple was originally from Oaxaca.

4. This statement, as well as several others made at different times during his trial, points to unresolved contradictions regarding the date in which plans for the execution in effigy started. According to several testimonies, Hernando Rubio Naranjo returned to Tecamachalco from his stay in Oaxaca one week before the scandal. It therefore makes little sense for the authors of the scandal to have thought about their revenge twenty or more days before Rubio Naranjo's return. Such confusion may be the result of the long time that elapsed between the date of the scandal and these interrogations.

5. For Juan de Molina's confession under torture, see PFY, fs. 146–149v. To facilitate the reading, I have occasionally replaced pronouns with the names of the persons Molina referred to instead of inserting these names in brackets. I have also replaced the "wife of Galiano" with Juana de Montoya.

6. PJM, f. 149v. Molina may be referring to the incidents on the night of 20 July 1578 described on pp. 33–34 above.

7. PJM, fs. 149v–150v.

8. Ibid., f. 151. Death sentences could be commuted to service in the wars against Chichimec rebels, who lived in "hot land." In 1578, Francisco Yáñez's friend Cristóbal García de Morales went to serve there, although it seems that he volunteered.

Chapter 11. Conspiracy

1. PJL, f. 151.

2. PFS, f. 159: Inquisitors to Canon Santiago, 23 May 1582.

3. PAP, fs. 187v–188v.

4. PBL, fs. 205v–206.

5. PFS, f. 159v.

6. PBL, f. 207: Canon Santiago to Inquisitors, 10 June 1582.

7. This passage is confusing. The inquisitors first asked Antonio de la Parada why Juan López would bear false testimony against him, and after Parada said that he did not know, they corrected themselves and asked why Yáñez would do so.

8. PAP, f. 191–191v, mostly transcribed in PFY, f. 153–153v.

9. Parada mistakenly called the man Luis Hernández, instead of Pedro Hernández.

10. A *cuento* is a story. The expression *tener cuentos* often means to have a dispute with someone, although Parada's statement is in response to a question about which women Yáñez "knew," which we have seen that Parada uses in a sexual sense.

11. The precise meaning of *criollo* in Parada's statement is unclear. Peter Boyd-Bowman has documented the use of the term in the 1560s and 1570s for American-born black slaves; see *Léxico hispanoamericano del siglo XVI* (London, 1971), 238; see also Herman L. Bennett, *Africans in Colonial Mexico: Absolutism, Christianity, and Afro-Creole Consciousness, 1570–1640* (Bloomington, Ind., 2003), 3. By surmising that such an elaborate crime could only have been committed by a Castilian, it seems

that Parada may have used *criollo* in the sense of an American-born person not of Spanish origin.

12. PAP, fs. 192–94, mostly transcribed in PFY, fs. 153v–155v.

13. PAP, f. 194v.

14. See Solana's testimony in PFS, fs. 200–202, esp. 201v (*malos tratos y contratación*). Solana's testimony is partly transcribed in PFY, fs. 157–158v.

15. PFS, f. 202v; and PFY, 158v.

16. PBL, f. 208–208v.

17. Ibid., fs. 208v–210.

18. PJL, f. 187.

19. Ibid., fs. 188–89.

20. See Juan López's testimony in ibid., fs. 187–90.

21. Ibid., f. 190.

22. *Así se han de tratar éstos, que de otra manera es perder el hombre lo que tiene*; ibid., f. 191.

23. Ibid., f. 191v.

24. Ibid., f. 192–192v, mostly transcribed in PFY, fs. 140–42.

25. PJL, f. 193–193v.

26. Ibid., fs. 193v–197.

27. "There are more days than sausages" (*más días hay que longanizas*): Covarrubias, *Tesoro de la lengua*, 720 (*longaniza*). Juan López's statements are in PJL, f. 197–197v.

28. In this context, the meaning of the word *componiéndolas* is not entirely clear. Molina may have meant that the girls were adorning or mending the dolls. Molina mistakenly describes Juana Ramírez as the sister of Juan López, rather than of Juan Pérez— the man Francisco Yáñez had accused of being behind the scandal. Pérez and López had the same first name and both were mestizos and horseshoe makers, although López worked as an interpreter and a constable.

29. PFY, 151v.

30. Ibid., f. 152v.

31. Ibid., f. 169.

32. Ibid., f. 169–169v.

Chapter 12. More Torment

1. PJL, f. 198, transcribed in *Libro primero de votos*, 112.

2. See López's confession under torture, in PJL, fs. 199–201v.

3. PFY, f. 172.

4. Ibid., f. 174v.

5. Ibid., f. 173. I have replaced the pronouns with the names.

6. Ibid.

7. Ibid., f. 173v.

8. Ibid., f. 175.

9. Ibid., f. 175v.

10. Ibid., f. 177. Yáñez's confession under torture is partially transcribed in PAF, fs. 161v–164v.

11. Ibid., fs. 177–78.

Chapter 13. The Wife

1. PAF, f. 170–170v.

2. Ibid., f. 170v.

3. Ibid., f. 171.

4. Ibid., fs. 171v–173.

5. Ibid., f. 173v.

6. Ibid., fs. 174–76 (accusation and her response).

7. As we have seen with other testimonies, Figueroa interprets the word *sambenito* as meaning the actual "penitential garment" as well as the "defamatory signs" or objects, such as the two-headed effigy.

8. PAF, fs. 176v–177.

9. Ibid., f. 177.

10. Ibid., f. 178.

11. Ibid., f. 178v.

12. PJM in PAF, f. 167v.

13. PAF, 167v.

14. Ibid., f. 168. I have replaced some of the pronouns with the names of the persons.

15. Ibid., f. 168v.

16. PJM in PAF, fs. 168v–169.

17. PAF, f. 182–182v.

18. PAP, f. 195 (25 June 1582); PFS, f. 214 (25 June 1582); and PBL, f. 201 (27 June 1582).

Chapter 14. Reconciliation

1. PFY, n.p. (f. 188v).

2. On the Inquisition's theme of reconciliation, see Kamen, *Spanish Inquisition*, 210–11.

3. PFY, n.p. (f. 189–189v).

4. Ruth Pike, *Penal Servitude in Early Modern Spain* (Madison, Wisc., 1983), chap. 1 ("The Galleys"), esp. 4, available at libro.uca.edu.

Epilogue

1. AHN, Inq. Libro 1064 (Relaciones de causas, México, c. 1572–c. 1614), fol. 88–88v ("Relaciones de causas despachadas, 1583").

2. See the definition of *gente baxa* in the *Diccionario de la lengua castellana*, 4:44. Regarding the application of defaming punishments on non-nobles, see Enrique Gacto, "Aproximación al Derecho penal de la Inquisición," in José Antonio Escudero, ed., *Perfiles jurídicos de la inquisición española*, 2nd ed. (Madrid, 1992), 175–204, esp. 183–85.

3. On the difference between honor and reputation, see Tamar Herzog, *Upholding Justice: Society, State, and the Penal System in Quito (1650–1750)* (Ann Arbor, Mich., 2004), 211 n. 40.

4. AGI, México 170 n. 58: confirmation for the title of royal scribe for Juan González.

5. Stafford Poole, "Institutionalized Corruption in the Letrado Bureaucracy: The Case of Pedro Farfán (1568–1588)," *The Americas* 38, no. 2 (October 1981): 149–71, esp. 160. The relationship between Juan López and Diego López de Montalbán is unclear. Diego was the uncle of the cochineal collectors Domingo and Juan López de Montalbán—the first suspect in the Tecamachalco case—and they were Juan López's cousins.

6. "Muy magnífico señor Pedro González Ferro, teniente de alcalde mayor por su magestad en esta dicha ciudad y provincia" of Tepeaca; 1576 document by the public scribe Francisco de Molina; in Martínez, *Colección de documentos coloniales de Tepeaca*, 184.

7. Sentencing required the vote of "consultors" (usually judges), of the bishop under whose jurisdiction the crimes had taken place, as well as of the inquisitors. See Kamen, *Spanish Inquisition*, 196–97; and Nesvig, *Ideology and the Inquisition*, 66–67 (bishop's "ordinary jurisdiction").

8. The three judges were Drs. Pedro Farfán, Lope de Miranda, and Francisco de Sande, a former governor of the Philippines. A fourth consultor who had previously voted to approve the tortures of Francisco Yáñez and Juan López, the Audiencia judge Dr. Diego García de Palacio, did not vote in the sentencing.

9. *Libro primero de votos*, 112–13.

10. PFY, f. 180v; reprinted in *Libro primero de votos*, 112–13. On the enmity between Moya de Contreras and Farfán, see Nesvig, *Ideology and the Inquisition*, 211; and Poole, *Pedro Moya de Contreras*, esp. 95–99.

11. PJL, f. 202v; reprinted in *Libro primero de votos*, 112–13. It is impossible to know the reasons for Dr. Farfán's leniency, but it should be noted that he had several illegal business dealings with Diego López de Montalbán, uncle of the cochineal collectors Juan and Domingo López de Montalbán, who were Juan López's cousins. On the other hand, Diego López de Montalbán also had illegal business dealings with another of the Audiencia judges acting as consultors, Dr. Francisco de Sande, which did not stop him from recommending the harsher punishment. Archbishop Moya de Contreras investigated those business dealings, which were prohibited to judges of the Audiencia; he had Diego López de Montalbán tortured and presented charges against Drs. Farfán and Sande. Dr. Farfán was eventually punished with heavy fines and suspension from holding office, but Dr. Sande came out unscathed from the investigation; see Poole, "Institutionalized Corruption," 160; and idem, *Pedro Moya de Contreras*, 97–98, 111.

12. PAF, f. 182v; *Libro primero de votos*, 112–13.

13. Rosa Ávila Hernández, "El Tribunal de la Inquisición y su estructura administrativa," *Nova Hispania* 1 (1995): 45–109, esp. 71–72.

14. Article 24 of the Grand Inquisitor Diego de Espinosa (Cardinal of Sigüenza)'s "Instruction to the Inquisitors of New Spain," transcribed in Julio Jiménez Rueda, *Don*

Pedro Moya de Contreras: Primer Inquisidor de México (Mexico City, 1944), 169–88, esp. 178–79; and Huerga, "La implantación del Santo Oficio en México," 728.

15. Contreras and Henningsen use this category in their statistical survey "Forty-Four Thousand Cases," 114 (table 1). Although vague, it was used by the Inquisition, which renders it more helpful than other categories. Ibáñez lists such cases under the even more vague category "Various," which comprises the largest group (277 cases) tried by the Mexican Inquisition between 1528 and 1599, followed by blasphemy (259 cases), "heretical propositions" (247 cases), and bigamy (246 cases); see her *La Inquisición en México durante el siglo XVI*, table on p. 11. Solange Alberro does not use the category of acts against the Inquisition but instead includes such cases along with blasphemy in a category that she labels "minor religious crimes." According to her statistical survey of trials for 1571–1700, these minor religious crimes represented about a third of all trials (568 trials), followed by heresies (527 trials); see her *Inquisition et société*, 90, 386 (table II.3).

16. PFY, f. 11: Bonilla and Dávalos to Cerón Carvajal, 31 July 1578.

17. From *Edictos generales que se leen en los lugares del distrito . . .* (Lima, seventeenth century); transcribed in Pedro Guibovich Pérez, *Censura, libros e inquisición en el Perú colonial, 1570–1754* (Seville, 2003), 88–89 n. 87.

18. Hernández struck the Inquisition's porter when the latter assisted a man attacked by Hernández and other men; see Antonio M. García Molina-Riquelme, *El régimen de penas y penitencias en el Tribunal de la Inquisición de México* (Mexico City, 1999), 272.

19. Ibid., xxii; see also 63 n. 217 for examples of punishments for acts against the Holy Office. The historian Molina-Riquelme, who has investigated the punishments imposed by the Mexican Inquisition from foundation to abolition, found only one case, from 1646, of a man sentenced to the galleys for falsely claiming to be a commissioner of the Inquisition (273–74).

20. Ibid., chap. 3 ("La pena de galeras").

21. In 1574, authorities also garroted two pirates, an Englishman and a Frenchman, before burning their bodies at the stake. In 1573, Robert Barret, who was Francis Drake's cousin and had also been captured with other members of Hawkins's expedition, died at the stake in 1573 at an auto de fe in Seville; see Ibáñez, *La Inquisición en México durante el siglo XVI*, 129, 130, 133–34.

22. Seymour B. Liebman, *The Jews of New Spain* (Coral Gables, Fla., 1970), 139.

23. Edward Peters, *Torture*, 2nd ed. (Philadelphia, 1996), 56, 81.

24. Herzog, *Upholding Justice*, chap. 6 ("Rumor and Reputation"), esp. 214.

25. Natalie Zemon Davis, *Fiction in the Archives: Pardon Tales and Their Tellers in Sixteenth-Century France* (Stanford, Calif., 1988), 101–2.

26. On *murmuración*, see Natalia Silva Prada, "Cultura política tradicional y opinión crítica: Los rumores y pasquines iberoamericanos de los siglos XVI al XVIII," in Riccardo Forte and Natalia Silva Prada, eds., *Tradición y modernidad en la historia de la cultura política: España e Hispanoamérica, siglos XVI–XX* (Mexico City, 2009), 89–143,

esp. 102–5; and Donald Ramos, "Gossip, Scandal and Popular Culture in Golden Age Brazil," *Journal of Social History* 33, no. 4 (summer 2000): 887–912, esp. 887–92 (*murmuração, voz popular*).

27. See Keith M. Bothelo, *Renaissance Earwitness: Rumor and Early Modern Masculinity* (New York, 2009); and M. T. Jones-Davies, ed., *Rumeurs et nouvelles au temps de la Renaissance* (Paris, 1997). For the eighteenth century, see Rebecca Earle, "Information and Disinformation in Late Colonial New Granada," *The Americas* 54, no. 2 (October 1997): 167–84.

28. PAMT, fs. 30v–32v: testimonies given by Juan de Molina, Cristóbal Morales de García, and Francisco López, 26 July 1578.

29. Ibid., f. 30: Rubio Naranjo to Cerón Carvajal, n.d. (received on 26 July 1578); PJLM, f. 40: Inquisition's notary of secrets Esteban Ordóñez reporting to the inquisitors rumors about Juan López de Montalbán that the scribe Francisco de Molina had heard from Francisco Yáñez (9 August 1578).

30. In November 1581, Francisco de Molina told Canon Santiago that he was forty years old; PFY, f. 99. At his first hearing in February 1582, Juan de Molina stated that he was thirty-two years old; PJM, f. 144. See more on their relationship in Chapter 7 of this volume.

31. PJLM, fs. 39–40v: Ordóñez's declaration to the inquisitors, 9 August 1578.

32. PFY, f. 77.

33. Ibid., f. 176v. For what follows, see Chapter 9 of this volume.

34. PFY, f. 128v.

35. Ibid., f. 173 (*perro herege*), 173v (*traidor*).

36. Richard Boyer, *Lives of Bigamists: Marriage, Family, and Community in Colonial Mexico* (Albuquerque, N.Mex., 1995), 101.

37. PFY, f. 160; for Yáñez's description as a Spaniard, see AGN, Real Audiencia-Tierras contenedor 813, vol. 1874, exp. 11 (1578).

38. María Elena Martínez, *Genealogical Fictions: Limpieza de Sangre, Religion, and Gender in Colonial Mexico* (Stanford, Calif., 2008), 165, 340 n. 90.

39. Ibid., 165, 336 n. 23. When the farmer Diego de Trujillo overheard Yáñez boasting that he knew the authors of the 1578 scandal, the two men were on their way back from collecting their Indian servants at the *repartimiento* of San Pablo; PFY, f. 69v.

40. Quoted in Ricardo Escobar Quevedo, *Inquisición y judaizantes en América española (Siglos XVI–XVII)* (Bogotá, 2008), 37.

41. In addition to Escobar Quevedo's book cited in n. 40 above, see Jonathan I. Israel, *Diasporas Within a Diaspora: Jews, Crypto-Jews and the World Maritime Empires (1540–1740)* (Leiden, 2002), esp. 17–19, 29, and chap. 3 ("Portuguese Crypto-Judaism in New Spain [1569–1649]").

42. Liebman, *Jews of New Spain*, appendix A, esp. 305–9; and Escobar Quevedo, *Inquisición y judaizantes*, appendix 2, 365–402.

43. J. I. Israel, *Race, Class and Politics in Colonial Mexico, 1610–1670* (London, 1975), 124–30.

44. PAF, f. 176v and in summary of the investigation in PFY, n.p. (f. 184v); and Covarrubias, *Tesoro de la lengua*, 844 (*quemar*).

45. For *mala lengua*, see the definition for *mordaz* (biting, as in "biting criticism"): "He who has a prejudicial and evil tongue [*mala lengua y perjudicial*], is like a dog that bites and feeds [lit., 'eats flesh'] off the brother's honor"; Covarrubias, *Tesoro de la lengua*, 763. *Deslenguado*: "He who has the habit of speaking ill of others; *irse de lengua*: "to speak too much with prejudice to a third party" (709).

46. The quotation is from Saint Bernard's sermon "De triplici custodia," quoted in the definition of the word *murmuración* (rumor); see Covarrubias, *Tesoro de la lengua*, 769–70 (added to the dictionary's 1673 edition by Benito Remigio Noydens).

47. PJLM, f. 45v.

48. Covarrubias, *Tesoro de la lengua*, 265 (*cara*).

49. Ibid., 574 (*gallina*).

50. PFY, 102v: testimony of Luis de Cepeda to Canon Santiago, 18 November 1581; and Covarrubias, *Tesoro de la lengua*, 158 (*baladrón*).

51. Covarrubias, *Tesoro de la lengua*, 644 (*huso*), 872 (*rueca*).

52. PAF, f. 172v; and Covarrubias, *Tesoro de la lengua*, 34 (*todo es burla*).

53. Covarrubias, *Tesoro de la lengua*, 688.

54. "Irreligioso, impío, pero más concretamente, desalmado, avariento, de voracidad terrible en materia de dinero; . . . maldito, perro"; see Francisco J. Santamaría, *Diccionario de mejicanismos* (Mexico City, 1959), 647. The anti-Semitic implications are evident in the dictionary's assertion: "This type [of person] is very common among the inhabitants of New York." The anti-Semitic attacks on Rubio Naranjo recall Anthony Bale's assertion that "[t]he Other—the Jew in the text—is neither alien nor outside, neither separate from nor opposite to the Christian selves . . . who discussed this Jewish Other"; see A. Bale, *The Jew in the Medieval Book: English Antisemitisms, 1350–1500* (Cambridge, 2006), 166.

55. PAF, f. 172.

56. In 1587, the Suprema informed the Inquisition of Valencia that it was "unheard of to relax in statue [i.e., execution in effigy] outside an auto" (*es una cosa tan nueva como relajar en estatua fuera de auto*); but the rule was not always respected; see Maqueda Abreu, *Auto de Fe*, 88–90.

57. Jean-Pierre Dedieu, *L'Administration de la foi: L'Inquisition de Tolède (XVIe– XVIIIe siècle)* (Madrid, 1989), 89, 275. Molina probably embarked to New Spain from the port city of Seville, which also held numerous autos de fe. Perhaps he only heard about an execution in effigy—with one of those double-faced effigies known to have been used during the early autos de fe in the late fifteenth century.

58. AGN, Inq. vol. 77, exp. 35, f. 235 (1577–79); see also HEH HM 35096, "Abecedario de relaxados, reconciliados y penitenciados en la Nueva España," f. 156v (91v of original pagination). "Guillermo Potier" is the Spanish rendition of a name that may have been Guillaume Poitiers. In 1571, Spanish authorities captured Potier/Poitiers after he took part in a series of attacks and pillaging in the Yucatán Peninsula led by Captain

Pierre Chuetot; see Adela Pinet Plasencia, *La Península de Yucatán en el Archivo General de la Nación* (San Cristóbal de las Casas, Mexico, 1998), 137. Potier, whose inquisitorial trial has not survived, was condemned as a Lutheran heretic, although he was more likely a Huguenot, like the rest of Chuetot's band of pirates; see Mickaël Augeron, "Pour Dieu et la Fortune: Les huguenots à la conquête des Amériques dans la seconde moitié du XVIe siècle," in *Connaissances et Pouvoirs: Les espaces impériaux (XVIe–XVIIIe siècles), France, Espagne, Portugal,* ed. Charlotte de Castelnau-L'Estoile and François Regourd (Pessac, France, 2005), 39–62, esp. 50–51.

59. The first two men executed in effigy for Judaizing were Baltasar Rodríguez Carvajal, who was absent, and Francisco Rodríguez Matos, who was dead; see AGN, Inq. vol. 77, exp. 35, f. 237 (nos. 40–41 on the list of sambenitos for 1590).

60. For the first auto de fe under the new inquisitorial regime in Mexico, see the Prologue to this volume.

61. AGI, México, 170 n. 58, n.p.

62. AGN, Inq. vol. 77, exp. 35, f. 235 (1577–79).

63. PFY, n.p. (f. 183v).

64. Ibid., f. 99: statement made by Francisco de Molina on 17 November 1581.

65. PJLM, f. 60: Rubio Naranjo to Bonilla and Dávalos, 15 September 1578 (received on 18 September).

66. Catalina Gómez, Francisco Yáñez's mother-in-law, described the same incident, but what Trujillo referred to as "signs," she called "papers" (*papeles*); PFY, f. 71v. Here we may be seeing the confusion caused by the double meaning of "sambenito" as the penitential garment and insult (or libel); see *Diccionario de la lengua castellana,* 6:35 (*sambenito*).

67. PFY, f. 62–62v.

68. On the satirical nature of distaffs and spindles in early modern Spanish literature, see Miguel Zugasti, "Poneos ruecas en la cinta: El trueque *espadas-ruecas* o el itinerario de un motivo burlesco de la tópica del mundo al revés," in *Pulchre, bene, recte: Estudios en homenaje al Prof. Fernando González Ollé,* ed. Carmen Saralegui Platero et al. (Pamplona, 2002), 1443–77, esp. 1448–54. Julio Caro Baroja describes a figure of Carnival (*Carnestolendas*) dressed in feathers and with a chicken—referring to the poultry and other meats not eaten during Lent—in *mojigangas,* or masques celebrated during Carnival, at the royal court in the seventeenth century; see his *El Carnaval (Análisis histórico-cultural)* (Madrid, 1984), 128. On rough music, see the classic study by E. P. Thompson, "Rough Music," in his *Customs in Common: Studies in Traditional Popular Culture* (New York, 1993), 467–538, esp. 498, 509.

69. Julio Caro Baroja, "El Charivari en España," *Historia 16* 47 (1980): 54–70; Jesús María Usnáriz, "El lenguaje de la cencerrada: Burla, violencia y control de la comunidad," in *Aportaciones a la historia social del lenguaje: España, siglos XIV–XVIII,* ed. Rocío García Bourrellier and Jesús María Usunáriz (Madrid, 2006), 235–60; and José Manuel Fraile Gil, "Peleles y coplas del Carnaval madrileño," *Revista de Dialectología y Tradiciones Populares* 62, no. 2 (July–December 2007): 207–28, esp. 215 n. 8. Caro

Baroja and Fraile Gil cite examples from the nineteenth and twentieth centuries, although they argue that these traditions have long histories dating to at least the early modern period. Thompson describes numerous British examples of executions in effigy, although many are also from the modern period; see *Customs in Common*, esp. 480–81.

70. Caro Baroja, *Carnaval*, 110–14. Caro Baroja does not indicate Saint Benedict as one of the names of these Carnival saint-effigies, although the names were often puns, just as "San Benito" was a pun for *sambenito*.

71. *Diccionario de la lengua castellana*, 4:324; and Caro Baroja, *Carnaval*, 126 (on the possible auto de fe inspiration), 140–43. Since the Tecamachalco figure was made of Indian cloth (tochomite), it is relevant to mention Mexican traditions of stuffed effigies, some of which had two faces—which have been documented for *estatuas* in autos de fe only for the fifteenth century; see Cecelia F. Klein, "None of the Above: Gender Ambiguity in Nahua Ideology," in *Gender in Pre-Hispanic America*, ed. idem (Washington, D.C., 2001), 183–253, esp. 211–19 (the two-faced Maximon).

72. *Novísima Recopilación*, libro 12, tít. 25, ley 6; quoted in Usnáriz, "Lenguaje de la cencerrada," 247 n. 83.

73. Martínez, *Codiciaban la tierra*, 134, which refers to a 1591 ordinance by the alcalde mayor of Tepeaca, but which reflected concerns about an ongoing problem mentioned in earlier decades.

74. Lope Jaramillo later denied having said this to Francisco Miguel.

75. PJLM, f. 97v: statement by Francisco Rodríguez Zapatero, in whose house Francisco Miguel lodged during his brief stay in Tecamachalco.

76. Ibid., f. 39v (*conquistador*): reported by the Inquisition's notary Esteban Ordóñez; PFY, f. 176 (*Sr. de Tecamachalco*); PAF, fs. 176v–177 (*Monte de no sé dónde o de Moysén*); and Molina's declaration in PJM transcribed in PFY, 147.

77. The Spanish playwright Lope de Vega (1562–1635) wrote the most famous version of the incident in his play *Fuenteovejuna* (first published in 1619; the title's spelling varies). For the rebellion's myth and its historical sources, see the introduction to Francisco López Estrada's edition of *Fuente Ovejuna*, 7th ed. (Madrid, 1996). Lope de Vega also wrote two plays about another tyrannical comendador who abused women in the village of Ocaña, in the same diocese of Toledo as Molina's hometown. However, the mythical and historical sources do not describe the lynching that Lope added to his plays; *Peribáñez y el Comendador de Ocaña / La mujer de Peribáñez*, ed. Felipe B. Pedraza Jiménez (Barcelona, 1988), 13–23.

78. Covarrubias, *Tesoro de la lengua*, 563.

79. Edgerton, Jr., *Pictures and Punishment*, 62–66; Freedberg, *Power of Images*, esp. 257.

80. PFY, f. 83: testimony by Isabel Suárez, 12 November 1582.

81. PAMT, f. 30 (Rubio Naranjo's letter presented in person to the alcalde mayor of Tepeaca on 26 July 1578).

82. Rosaura Hernández Rodríguez, *Catálogo de documentos del siglo XVI del Archivo General del Estado de Tlaxcala* (Mexico City, 1988), 446, ficha no. 1783: AGET-RIP, libro no. 4, 1581, fs. 177v–179v.

83. PAF, f. 171; copied in PFY, n.p. (f. 182v).

84. PFY, f. 175.

85. PJL, f. 191; transcribed in PFY, f. 141v.

86. On these statements, see the Prologue to this volume.

KEY NAMES

Frequently repeated names are in bold.

Alzorriz, Sancho (Dr. Alzorriz): the Inquisition's commissioner in the Diocese of Oaxaca and dean of Oaxaca's cathedral chapter

Ávalos, Melchor de (**Licenciado Ávalos**): the Inquisition's defense lawyer

Beristain, Pedro de (senior): Spanish scribe and resident of Tecamachalco

Beristain, Pedro de (the younger): son of Pedro de Beristain (senior)

Bonilla, Alonso Fernández (**Licenciado Bonilla**): inquisitor (in 1578 and 1581–83 trials)

Cepeda, Luis de: mulatto saddle maker; married to Madalena Rodríguez

Cerón Carvajal, Jorge: alcalde mayor of the province of Tepeaca; carried out the first investigation of the Tecamachalco scandal in 1578

Dávalos, Alonso Granero (**Licenciado Dávalos**): inquisitor (in 1578 trial)

Euguí, Jerónimo de (**Notary Euguí**): the Inquisition's notary (*notario del juzgado*) in 1581–82

Figueroa, Ana de: Spanish wife of Pedro González Ferro; resident of Tepeaca in 1578 and of Mexico City in 1582; tried in 1582 by the Inquisition

Galiano, Benito: sheep-farmer and tax-collector; husband of Juana de Montoya

García, Alonso: Spanish scribe who worked for Benito Galiano

García de Morales, Cristóbal: farmer and resident of Tecamachalco; friend of Francisco Yáñez; in 1582, he was a soldier in Zacatecas, fighting against the Chichimec rebels

Gómez, Catalina: Spanish resident of Tepeaca; mother-in-law of Francisco Yáñez, mother of Catalina Núñez, and sister of Leonor Gómez

Hernández, Francisco: servant farmer; born in Puebla and resident of San Pablo in 1581

Hernández, Pedro: mestizo goatherd, resident of Tecamachalco; investigated by the Inquisition in 1578

Jaramillo, Lope (the younger): son of Lope Jaramillo (senior); resident of Tecamachalco

Lobo Guerrero, Bartolomé (**Dr. Lobo Guerrero**): the Inquisition's prosecuting attorney (*fiscal*) in 1582

López, Juan: mestizo Indian interpreter (*naguatate*) and constable of the judge who assigned Indian servants (*juez repartidor de indios*) for landowners; resident of Tecamachalco in 1578 and of Atlixco in 1581–82; tried by the Inquisition in 1582

López de Montalbán, Domingo: Spanish cochineal collector; brother of Juan López de
   Montalbán; resident of Tecamachalco in 1578

López de Montalbán, Juan: Spanish cochineal collector; brother of Domingo López
   de Montalbán; resident of Tecamachalco in 1578; tried by the Inquisition in 1578

Lozano, Bartolomé: castizo farmer and resident of Puebla; friend of Francisco Yáñez;
   tried by the Inquisition in 1582

Martín, Antón: husband of Catalina Rodríguez; resident of Tecamachalco in 1578; in
   1581, he was a sailor in Havana, Cuba, under the command of the governor of
   Florida

Miguel, Francisco: mestizo shoemaker and glassmaker visiting Tecamachalco in July
   1578; investigated that year

Molina, Francisco de: Spanish public scribe, said to be the father of Juan de Molina;
   scribe of the alcalde mayor de Tepeaca during the first investigation of the Tecamachalco scandal in 1578

Molina, Juan de: Spanish royal scribe, said to be the son of Francisco de Molina; friend
   of Francisco Yáñez; resident of Tepeaca until 1578, when he moved to Río de
   Alvarado, Veracruz, to serve as scribe of the alcalde mayor of Tlacotaplan; tried by
   the Inquisition in 1582

Montoya, Juana de: native and resident of Tecamachalco; wife of Benito Galiano; suspected of being Francisco Yáñez's lover

Morillo, Juan: Spanish farmworker and resident of Tecamachalco in 1578

Moya de Contreras, Pedro: first inquisitor of New Spain until 1574 and archbishop of
   Mexico City from 1574

Muñoz, Juana: widow of Francisco Pérez (senior), mother of Francisco Pérez (the younger), and stepmother of Juan Pérez; resident of Puebla; investigated by the Inquisition in 1581

Núñez, Catalina: mestiza wife of Francisco Yáñez and daughter of Catalina Gómez; resident of Quecholac

Ordóñez, Esteban: the Inquisition's notary (*notario de secretos*) in 1578; succeeded in his
   post by Jerónimo de Euguí

Parada, Antonio de la: Basque cartwright; resided near Tecamachalco in 1578 and resident of Puebla in 1582; friend of Francisco Yáñez; tried by the Inquisition in 1582

Peña, Tomás: mestizo Cuban tailor; nephew of Catalina Rodríguez

Pérez, Alonso: Spanish attorney (*procurador de causas*) of Hernando Rubio Naranjo;
   son-in-law of Juana Muñoz

Pérez, Francisco (the younger): son of Juana Muñoz and Francisco Pérez (senior) and
   half-brother of Juan Pérez; died in 1580

Pérez, Juan: mestizo horseshoe maker; son of Francisco Pérez (senior), half-brother of
   Francisco Pérez (the younger), and stepson of Juana Muñoz; native of Tecamachalco
   and resident of Oaxaca since 1576; tried by the Inquisition in 1581

Ríos, Pedro de los: the Inquisition's secretary in the 1570s and 1580s

Rodríguez, Catalina: native of Tepeaca, resident of Tecamachalco in 1578, resident of

Tepeaca until 1581, and resident of Puebla in 1581; wife of Antón Martín and aunt of Tomás Peña; said to be the mother of Juan de Molina (not to be confused with Catalina Rodríguez de San José)

Rodríguez, Madalena: wife of Luis de Cepeda and friend of Catalina Rodríguez; resident of Puebla

Rodríguez de San José, Catalina: resident of Tlaxcala; widow; lover of Hernando Rubio Naranjo (not to be confused with Catalina Rodríguez)

Rubio Naranjo, Hernando: trader (*tratante*); victim of the humiliation perpetrated on 21 July 1578, when he resided in Tecamachalco

Santiago, Alonso Hernández de (**Canon Santiago**): the Inquisition's commissioner in the diocese of Puebla in 1581–82 and canon of the cathedral of Puebla

Santos García (**Licenciado Santos García**): inquisitor (in 1581–82 trials)

Solano, Francisco: resident of Puebla; farmer in San Pablo; friend of Francisco Yáñez; tried by the Inquisition in 1582

Trujillo, Diego de: Spanish farmer and resident of San Pablo; friend and "compadre" of Francisco Yáñez

Vargas, María de: former lover of Hernando Rubio Naranjo, with whom she had a daughter; in 1578, she allegedly implicated Juan Pérez and Juana Muñoz in the Tecamachalco scandal, which she later denied; died before November 1581

Yáñez, Francisco: castizo farmer; born in Tecamachalco, resident of Quecholac; husband of Catalina Núñez, son-in-law of Catalina Gómez, and friend of Juan de Molina; tried by the Inquisition in 1581–82

GLOSSARY

Definitions and explanations for the terms below refer to events described in this book. For a broader description of terms related to the Inquisition, readers may wish to consult Henry Kamen, *The Spanish Inquisition: A Historical Revision* (New Haven, Conn., 1997), and Joseph Pérez, *The Spanish Inquisition: A History*, trans. Janet Lloyd (New Haven, Conn., 2005).

Abogado de los presos: often referred to simply as *abogado*; defense lawyer; in the Inquisition, this was the lawyer, usually appointed by the inquisitors, to assist the accused in their defense

Alcalde mayor: the chief royal official in a province, charged with policing and judicial duties, more like a provincial governor than a mayor

Audiencia: the royal appellate court in Mexico City; more generally (and not capitalized), the name given to the sessions, or audiences, of witnesses and suspects before the inquisitors; *audiencia del tormento*: torture session

Auto de fe: the ceremony during which the Inquisition published the sentences of its prisoners and surrendered them to civil authorities, who carried out the punishments and executions

Castizo/Castiza: the child of a European and a mestizo/mestiza

Comendador: the knight commander of a religious-military order

Comisario: the Inquisition's official commissioner—frequently an ecclesiastic—appointed in a diocese (or in a religious order) to carry out the orders of the inquisitors, such as interviewing witnesses and arresting suspects

Compadre: a Spanish term with multiple meanings; in the context of this book, it is used loosely to describe a relative or friend

Cordeles: cords; also the name given to the torture consisting of tying cords around a prisoner's arm and twisting them

Coroza: cone-like miters worn by accused heretics during the autos de fe

Encomienda: grants of lands and service made by Spanish monarchs

Estatua: statue; effigy used in an auto de fe in place of a heretic who was not present or who died before the execution

Fiscal: Prosecuting attorney; the Inquisition's officer charged with making formal accusations in trials

Garrote: a stick or club; also the name given to the torture consisting of tightening cords around the biceps, thighs, or shins while the victim lay on the rack; the garrote was used to tighten the cords in a tourniquet

Libelo: a defamatory sign

Licenciado: licentiate, or university graduate

Mestizo/Mestiza: the child of a European and an Indian

Oidor: a judge in the Audiencia

Proceso: trial

Relación de causa: trial report sent by an inquisitorial tribunal to the Suprema

Sambenito: penitential tunic worn by those found guilty of heresy by the Inquisition; more generically, it stood for a defamatory sign (*libelo*)

Suprema: the Council of the Supreme and General Inquisition, the royal council in Madrid that oversaw the work of the Inquisition across the Spanish empire

Tochomite: Indian wool cloth

INDEX

Page references in italics refer to illustrations

empire, 11–12; Spanish Inquisition's
use of, 12–18; Suprema on, 200n56; for
treason, 16. *See also* effigies

fama: in sixteenth-century society, xiii–ix,
166; in Spanish law, 180n9. *See also*
defamation; rumor

Farfán, Pedro, 75, 190n50; approval of
torture, 145, 197n8; on conspirators'
punishment, 164; and Domingo López
de Montalbán, 197n11; and Moya de
Contreras, 164, 197n10

Ferro, Pedro González, wife of. *See* Figueroa,
Ana de

Figueroa, Ana de: confession of, 156–58;
confrontation with Juan de Molina,
159–60; construction of Tecamachalco
effigy, 156–59; defense attorney of, 158,
160; on effigy, 176; identity of, 129, 142,
148, 149, 150, 170, 194n3; Inquisition's
charges against, 155–56, 157; knowledge
of sambenitos, 155; punishment of,
161–62, 164, 165; report of Inquisition
on, 163–64; residence in Tepeaca,
153; on sambenitos, 196n7; testimony
before inquisitors, 152–60; testimony
concerning Juan de Molina, 153–58,
172, 177; testimony concerning Yáñez,
153, 177

fortress-churches, Franciscan, 6, 182n17
Fosman, Gregorio, 184n55
Fraile Gil, José Manuel, 202n68
Franciscans: inquisitorial activity of, 19;
interpretation of Spanish conquest,
182n20
Francisco (ladino servant), 101, 108, 109, 112,
192n8
"Fuente Ovejuna did it" (saying), 176–77

galleys, sentencing to, 21, 22, 161, 162, 165
García, Alonso, 86; handwriting of, 96;
in investigation of 1578, 37; in
investigation of 1581, 63; Juan López
de Montalbán on, 37, 38; testimony
before Santiago, 64–66; writing sample
from, 65

García de Morales, Cristóbal: Juan de Molina's
testimony concerning, 124, 126, 128,
142; military service of, 194n8; Parada's
testimony concerning, 133; Solano's
testimony concerning, 134; whereabouts
of, 129, 143
García de Palacio, Diego, 145
gente baxa, 196n2; in Tecamachalco affair,
163–64
Geographical Relations (1580), 5
Gersón, Juan, religious paintings of, 7, 8, 9,
182n20
Gómez, Catalina, 201n66; testimony before
Santiago, 51–54, 188n7
Gómez, Juan, Rubio Naranjo's accusation of,
38, 40
Gómez, Leonor, 54, 55, 61
González, Pedro, 56
Greenleaf, Richard E., 185n64
Guerre, Martin, xvi
Guillén, Juan, 104, 105, 106, 115; Juan de
Molina's testimony concerning, 125, 128

Hawkins expedition (John Hawkins):
execution of members, 198n21;
sentencing of, 165; Spanish attack on,
19, 185n66
Henningsen, Gustav, 198n15
Henry IV (king of Castile), deposition in
effigy, 12
heretics: execution in effigy, 12; postmortem
sentences on, 16
Hernández, Francisco, 188n2; testimony
before Santiago, 99; Trujillo's testimony
concerning, 45–47, 52; Yáñez and, 82
Hernández, Pedro (goatherd): in investigation
of 1578, 32, 33, 34, 35; on sambenitos,
190n44
Hernández, Pedro (soldier), Inquisition's
punishment of, 165
Holy Office. *See* Council of the Supreme and
General Inquisition; Inquisition
honor: loss of, xiii–ix, 30; in medieval law,
180n10; versus reputation, 197n3;
in Spanish society, 21, 30. *See also*
defamation; reputation

ACKNOWLEDGMENTS

The initial research and writing of this book took place in 2007–8 at the Huntington Library, San Marino, California, with the support of a yearlong fellowship from the National Endowment for the Humanities and a one-month grant from the General Research Fund of the University of Kansas. I am thankful to Robert Ritchie, former director of the Huntington Library's research center; Bill Frank, curator of Hispanic, cartographic, and Western historical manuscripts; and the rest of the librarians and staff at the Huntington. The staffs of numerous archives and libraries in the United States, Mexico, and Spain provided valuable help, especially at the Archivo General de la Nación, Mexico City; the Archivo General de Notarías del Estado de Puebla; and the Archivo General de Indias, Seville. Linda Arnold, from Virginia Tech University, generously answered my questions about Mexican documents. At the University of Kansas, I have been fortunate to count on the assistance of the staff at Digital Media Services. In particular, Gwen Claassen and Pam LeRow helped me with the preparation of the manuscript; and Tony Barman drew the sketch of the facade of the church of Tecamachalco for the imagined display of the images that provoked the scandal at the center of this book. Darin Grauberger of the Cartographic Lab at the University of Kansas produced the maps. Ryan Gaston, James Quinn, and Stephanie Stillo, current and former graduate students in the Department of History, generously helped me at various stages of this project. Finally, I wish to acknowledge the generous support of the Vice Chancellor for Research and Graduate Studies Book Publication Award of the University of Kansas.

Several colleagues and friends invited me to present my research: Lisa Bitel and Janet Hoskins at the Center for Religion and Civic Culture's interdisciplinary seminar "Visualizing Religion," University of Southern California; Charlene Black-Villaseñor, Cecelia Klein, Teófilo Ruiz, and Kevin Terraciano at a talk for UCLA's departments of Art History and History, and the Center for Medieval and Renaissance Studies; and Patricia Manning at the Early Modern Seminar at the Hall Center for the Humanities, University of Kansas. In addition, I also received valuable suggestions, comments, and help from friends, colleagues, and students, including Jonathan Boyarin, Tamar Herzog, Elizabeth Kuznesof, Kenneth Mills, Isidro Rivera, Natalia Silva Prada, Leslie Tuttle, and Sherry Velasco. I am especially grateful to Peter Mancall for his enthusiastic encouragement and his invaluable comments. Above all, thanks to Marta Vicente for her suggestions and support at all stages of this project.